D0078333

DISORDERLY
DISCOURSE

OXFORD STUDIES IN ANTHROPOLOGICAL LINGUISTICS

William Bright, General Editor

DISORDERLY

DISCOURSE

Narrative, Conflict, & Inequality

EDITED BY

CHARLES L. BRIGGS

New York   Oxford
OXFORD UNIVERSITY PRESS
1996

Oxford University Press

Oxford   New York
Athens   Auckland   Bangkok   Bogota   Bombay
Buenos Aires   Calcutta   Cape Town   Dar es Salaam
Delhi   Florence   Hong Kong   Istanbul   Karachi
Kuala Lumpur   Madras   Madrid   Melbourne
Mexico City   Nairobi   Paris   Singapore
Taipei   Tokyo   Toronto

and associated companies in
Berlin   Ibadan

Copyright © 1996 by Oxford University Press, Inc.

Published by Oxford University Press, Inc.
198 Madison Avenue, New York, New York 10016

Oxford is a registered trademark of Oxford University Press, Inc.

Library of Congress Cataloging-in-Publication Data
Narrative resources for the creation and mediation of conflict / edited by Charles L. Briggs. Includes index.
  p.   cm.—(Oxford studies in anthropological linguistics ; 7) Contents: Introduction / Charles L. Briggs—
Telling troubles: narrative, conflict, and experience / Donald Brenneis—The trickster's scattered self / Ellen
B. Basso—Embarrassment as pride : narrative resourcefulness and strategies of normativity among Cretan
animal-thieves / Michael Herzfeld—Detective stories at dinnertime / Elinor Ochs, Ruth C. Smith, and
Carolyn E. Taylor—Ideological dissonance in the American legal system / William M. O'Barr and John M.
Conley—Consensus and dissent in U.S. legal opinions / Elizabeth Mertz—"We want to borrow your
mouth" : Tzotzil marital squabbles / John B. Haviland—Disorderly dialogues in ritual impositions of order
: the role of metapragmatics in Warao dispute mediation / Charles L. Briggs.
ISBN 0-19-508776-3.—ISBN 0-19-508777-1 (pbk.)
1. Discourse analysis, Narrative.   2. Conversational analysis.
3. Conflict management.   4. Language and culture.   I. Briggs, Charles L., 1953-   .   II. Series.
P302.7.N38   1996
401'.41—dc20   95-46001

All the selections in this volume, except for the introductory chapter and chapter 3, were originally
published, in different form, in the journal Anthropological Linguistics (vol. 30, nos 3–4, 1988), and are
reprinted by permission. Chapter 4, "Detective Stories at Dinnertime: Problem Solving Through Co-
Narration," was originally published in 1989, in different form, in the journal Cultural Dynamics (vol. 2,
no. 2, pp. 238–57) and is likewise reprinted by permission.

9 8 7 6 5 4 3 2 1

Printed in the United States of America
on acid-free paper

Contents

Contributors

ELLEN B. BASSO — Department of Anthropology, University of Arizona

DONALD BRENNEIS — Anthropology Board of Studies, University of California, Santa Cruz

CHARLES L. BRIGGS — Department of Ethnic Studies, University of California, San Diego

JOHN M. CONLEY — Law School, University of North Carolina

JOHN B. HAVILAND — Department of Linguistics, Reed College

MICHAEL HERZFELD — Department of Anthropology, Harvard University

ELIZABETH MERTZ — Northwestern University School of Law, American Bar Foundation, Chicago

WILLIAM M. O'BARR — Department of Cultural Anthropology, Duke University

ELINOR OCHS — Department of TESL/Applied Linguistics, University of California at Los Angeles

RUTH C. SMITH — Department of Communication, Purdue University

CAROLYN E. TAYLOR — Department of Speech Communication, University of Illinois at Urbana-Champaign

DISORDERLY
DISCOURSE

Introduction

Conflict is a common feature of social life, and representations of conflict frequently form central foci of expressive economies. A number of researchers have suggested that verbal disputing constitutes a crucial means by which children and adolescents learn to construct their identities and to position themselves vis-à-vis their peers. Gossip narratives similarly play a prominent role in everyday talk among adults in shaping everyday understandings of social conflict.[1] In recounting wars of "independence," foundational narratives of modern nation-states impose perceptions of the past, notions of community, and identities and modes of conduct.[2] In short, narratives constitute crucial means of generating, sustaining, mediating, and representing conflict at all levels of social organization.

Given the ubiquity of both narratives and conflict, it is hardly surprising that they have formed important foci of research in a wide range of disciplines. With notable exceptions, however, conflict and narrative have been treated in relative isolation. With regard to the literature on conflict, historians and political scientists have frequently examined confrontation and violence with regard to societies and nation-states, while psychologists have pursued intrapsychic and interpersonal conflict. Sociology is internally divided between those pursuing "macro" versus "micro" approaches. Nevertheless, neither the proponents of the bird's-eye view nor those of the worm's-eye view have been terribly interested in the role of discourse in conflict.[3] When written or oral narratives do figure in analyses, they are generally used as sources of information *about* conflicts rather than as central facets of conflict processes and objects of analysis in themselves.

Most narrative specialists have focused on the structures that provide a framework for the content of narratives or on textual dimensions of their production and reception. Although literary critics and linguists have often seen narrative discourse and language as quasi-autonomous, standing at a critical distance from social life,

3

anthropologists have frequently mined the referential content of narratives for symbols of culture, ethnicity, personality, and the like. The status of narrative production and reception as situated social activities that play a crucial role in constituting—not merely reflecting—everyday life has seldom been explored in any depth.

The rationale that lies behind this collection of essays goes beyond simply attempting to fill a gap in the scholarly literature. Rather, the contributors have located themselves in a creative space that has been generated by substantive reorientations in the study of both conflict and narrative. Underlying assumptions that informed past work in these areas presented strong obstacles to exploring the relationship between narrative and social conflict; however, many of these premises have now been challenged. Social models have gravitated toward dynamic, processual, and practice-based approaches that link institutional, national, and transnational cultural forms to the texture of everyday life. Language is similarly now viewed less as an abstract structure that is internalized identically by every speaker (as in the views held by Saussure 1959 [1916] and Chomsky 1965) than as consisting of socially and politically situated practices that are differentially distributed on the basis of gender, class, race, ethnicity, and other phenomena. Most important, while definitions and orientations toward these subjects vary considerably, practitioners in a wide range of disciplines see discourse—particularly narrative discourse—and conflict as central foci of description and analysis; interest in exploring the many ways they intersect has accordingly grown substantially.

This is the first collection of essays to focus primarily on the role of narrative in creating, sustaining, and mediating conflict. The contributors use differing perspectives on conflict and narrative to illuminate a wide range of disputes that emerge in a variety of settings and societies. The essays make theoretical and methodological contributions to our understanding of the intersection between narrative and conflict. The remainder of this introduction places these issues in the context of recent advances in reasearch on conflict and narrative discourse, pointing out the sorts of problems that they address and some of the ways in which they contribute to the available literature.

Conflict

The static models of social systems that prevailed until recent decades considered maintaining social equilibrium and sharing cultural norms as the primary basis for the creation of groups at all levels of social "integration," whereas conflict was often considered to be an abnormal or pathological state that must be resolved in order to ensure the "survival" of the collectivity. Research that centers on discourse has helped prompt scholars to view conflict as a crucial part of the social construction of reality. Studies of disputes among children and adolescents suggest that conflict provides a central facet of the socialization process.[4] Eder (1990:67) notes, for example, that resolution is not even a relevant goal in the case of conflicts between boys. Schiffrin suggests that arguing can serve as an important means of conveying sociability among adults (1984, 1990). "Resolution" may indeed be a relatively rare outcome; among the family disputes examined by Vuchinich (1990:134–35), only 26 percent ended in submissions or compromises, whereas 66 percent resulted in standoffs. Social theorists similarly have come to view social and cultural forms as historically contingent products that emerge through conflict, and the process of *differentiating* an Other from a Self is often deemed to be more crucial to the creation of both identities and communities than the presence of a shared cognitive substratum. Many scholars would thus agree with Simmel's (1955 [1908]) observation that conflict provides a central force for the constitution of social relations.

Some of the most interesting explorations have focused on a critical reexamination of the concepts of strategy, manipulation, and self-interest, on the one hand, and norms and rules on the other. Recent research has demonstrated that these basic categories of political involvement cannot be accepted per se as motives for the actions of individuals or as explanations for observed courses of events. With respect to manipulation and self-interest, Myers and Brenneis (1984) have pointed out that political discourse can still be taken quite seriously even when it has no effect on the immediate outcome of events. Simply gathering people together to talk can signal the creation or re-creation of community and political order. Myers suggests that for the Pintupi, an Australian Aboriginal group, the discourse that emerges in meetings does not stand for or presuppose the existence of the polity: "[T]he meeting . . . *is* the polity for Western Desert Aborigines" (1986:438). Attempting to construct shared interpretations of past, present, and future events— or contesting attempts to impose unanimity—can shape social memory and social organization as well as impose limits of perception. Comaroff and Roberts have similarly argued that "it is in the context of confrontation—when persons negotiate their social universe and enter discourse about it—that the character of that system is revealed" (1981:249). Both sets of authors argue that political discourse goes beyond questions of individual interest; it rather provides a fundamental basis for the creation of social community and the social construction of reality.

Clearly, the work of Michel Foucault and Pierre Bourdieu has contributed in many ways to the increased visibility of issues of power and conflict. In a wide range of studies of the emergence of such modern institutions as the clinic (1973 [1963]), the asylum (1965 [1961]), and the prison (1977 [1975]), Foucault points to the status of truth, knowledge, modes of acquiring information, and forms of subjectivity as historically realized products of struggle and domination rather than as neutral "social facts" that exist part from interests, strategies, and institutionalized mechanisms of control. Bourdieu (1977) stresses the way that social hierarchy structures the limits of perception, as much for anthropologists as for the people they study. He urges researchers to envision culture less as a set of conscious models than as unconscious practices, particularly as rooted in the way people use their bodies and structure the space around them. The emphasis that both authors place on relating large societal and institutional structures to the details of everyday life has provided a substantive challenge to scholars in a wide range of disciplines.

Clearly, a number of problems can emerge from uncritical adoption of these insights by linguistic anthropologists and other researchers. One pitfall revolves around a tendency to identify all cultural forms as instances of power relations and to see power as being everywhere the same; historical and cultural specificities often fall victim to a universalistic and functionalist deus ex machina. Another difficulty concerns the way discourse is situated theoretically with respect to other social and cultural forms. Unlike many social/cultural anthropologists, Bourdieu (1991) sees patterns of language use as being of central importance to social life. He characterizes speech as a mode of production that embodies fundamental social relations and processes, and he pays particular attention to the way that the acquisition of discursive competence both shapes and is shaped by political economy. Gal (1989), Irvine (1989), and Woolard (1985) have nevertheless criticized Bourdieu for according discourse an overly passive role in social life, arguing that language use not only reflects but also constitutes relations of domination. Cicourel (1993) and Woolard (1985) go on to suggest that Bourdieu seems to presuppose the existence of relatively fixed and homogeneous relationships between language and social relations. The nature of such connections is often precisely what is contested. (I will discuss this point in greater detail later.)

Several other writers have contributed to this growing sense that conflict plays a key role in the production and reception of cultural forms. The relevance of Gramsci's (1971) concept of hegemony for the analysis of cultural forms has been articulated by Williams (1977). The work of Williams and other theoreticians has fostered a view of culture as contested and politically interested; culture thus emerges as a crucial means by which hierarchy is created, legitimated, and challenged. Habermas (1989 [1962]) has pointed to the emergence of a "public sphere" of cultural and political activity, which he deems a crucial facet of the emergence of modern societies. Anderson (1991 [1983]) has illuminated the ways that the symbolic structures that seem to be natural features of the *conscience collective* of modern societies were produced as means of generating the structures of feeling (Williams 1977) that form the cultural bases of nation-states. Appadurai (1990) has extended the search for connections between large-scale institutional relations and local cultural forms to embrace the transnational production of public culture. The study of conflict has thus come to be seen as a central facet of social scientific inquiry rather than the focus of specialized subfields (such as political anthropology).

The contributors to this volume demonstrate the centrality of a wide variety of forms of social conflict to social life in settings that range from Native American communities in Latin America (Basso, Briggs, and Haviland), East Indians in the Fijian Islands (Brenneis), and pastoral communities in Crete (Herzfeld) to such facets of American social life as family dinners (Ochs, Smith, and Taylor) and the

U.S. legal system (Mertz and O'Barr and Conley). By paying careful attention to the ways in which conflicts are created and mediated, they provide insights into the centrality of conflict to the constitution of social relations, institutions, and ideologies.

The contributions by Elizabeth Mertz and by William O'Barr and John Conley focus on the U.S. legal system—an institutional nexus dedicated to the production and reception of highly specialized conflict discourses representing conflicts that emerge in legal and other contexts. Mertz points to the way that textual features of U.S. Supreme Court opinions are tied to strategies for restructuring social issues—such as racial segregation and abortion restrictions—that divide substantial segments of American society. Her paper focuses on two celebrated cases: she contrasts *Plessy v. Ferguson* (1896), which sustained a "separate but equal" pattern of discrimination, with *Brown v. Board of Education* (1953), which held segregation to be unconstitutional. Her analysis details textual practices that enable U.S. courts to use legal narratives in playing an active role in accommodating social change and giving voice to conflict while reasserting the considerable authority of the legal system and its textual practices over social conflict.

Directing their attention to the opposite end of the legal hierarchy, O'Barr and Conley describe contrastive ways that litigants structure their narratives. They argue that weighting opposing narrative strategies differentially provides a crucial means by which the U.S. legal system limits access to the domain that appears to be most open to lay persons—small-claims courts. These writers suggest that familiarity with ways of talking about conflict that are compatible with legal canons of relevance and evidentiality emerges from increasing contact with "the culture of law and business" (page 189). Like Mertz, O'Barr and Conley argue that participation in conflict mediation is measured in more than simple zero-sum, win-loss terms. They suggest that litigants who are given a chance to tell their story in ways that they find fulfilling often feel satisfied with their involvement in small-claims court—even if the decision is unfavorable. Both the decisions and the way they are perceived by lay participants are closely related to the manner in which litigants' narratives locate conflict and mediation within social systems—in interpersonal terms, as instances in which the social contract has been violated, or as infringements of contractual relations, as defined in legal and impersonal terms. These essays also enable us to see how conflicts connect individuals and groups with broad social and institutional structures and ideologies. Mertz's assessment of the social functions of legal discourse is more guarded. Arguing against approaches that posit direct connections between semiotic structures and social effects, she claims that although parties who are successful in getting their stories told in legal proceedings are in some cases less inclined to sustain and extend conflict, the opposite outcome is also possible.

Although establishing links between individuals and institutions might seem to play a less direct role in the conflicts that emerge at the dinner table, Elinor Ochs, Ruth Smith, and Carolyn Taylor demonstrate that conversations that take place in this setting constitute a crucial site for creating knowledge and social (dis)order among American families. As stories focus on school, work, and other topics, narrators attempt to construct the way family members are situated within familial and institutional structures. Ochs, Smith, and Taylor reveal important connections between restrictions on individuals' powers of self-representation in both types of settings. Since personal experience narratives are co-performed, narrative collaborators can reshape the manner in which events are (re)presented; particularly in "detective stories," where co-narration focuses on revealing missing information that some participants see as vital to understanding the problem, narrators may be forced to reveal facts they would rather keep hidden. As they learn to co-narrate stories—and become aware of the power of such co-narration—children discover how broader institutional structures (such as those associated with schools) interact with structures of authority within the family (see also Ochs, Taylor, Rudolph, and Smith 1992).

Michael Herzfeld argues that thefts and counterthefts of sheep and goats play a crucial role in the social life of Cretan communities. Here, too, winning and losing is not simply a matter of coming up with more livestock: outcomes are also assessed in terms of the manner in which raids shape the identities and statuses of the participants and produce new social alliances. Raiding fuels a sort of moral discourse in which actions are not simply characterized as right or wrong but are carefully contextualized in terms of the performer's account of his own clever strategizing. Narrators accordingly position themselves, their allies, and their opponents with respect to idealized ways that men should act and speak (see Herzfeld 1985). Herzfeld argues that raiding provides rural Cretans with crucial discourses for attempting to oppose the hegemony of the nation-state. By characterizing bureaucrats' representations of animal thieves in highly ironic terms, narrators seek to expose the interests and contradictions that are hidden in the supposed impersonality and rationality of official political discourse (see Herzfeld 1992).

Don Brenneis' study of Fiji Indians also draws attention to the way that both individual identities and reputations, as well as social control and social organization, are constituted through conflict. On the face of things, *pancayat* dispute mediation sessions provide disputants with a chance to tell their stories and to make the outcome reflect, at least to some extent, their own interests, thus celebrating the prevalent egalitarian ideology (see Brenneis 1984b). Here again, the emergence of clear winners and losers is much less important than reasserting an egalitarian and solidary public culture. By limiting participation to males, selecting and rehearsing witnesses in advance, and claiming exclusive rights to ask questions, a "confidential committee" that consists of elected officers of a religious association ensures the production of "a single and non-contradictory account of crucial events" (Brenneis 1990:229).

Ellen Basso focuses on a trickster figure, Taugi, who provides an embodiment of disorder and conflictual social relations for Kalapalo storytellers and audiences in central Brazil. Taugi models both effective and ineffective strategies for creating and reacting to aggression. Basso argues that the construction of Taugi's character as a "scattered self" points to the limitations of Western assumptions regarding the need for selves to be fixed, unified, and consistent. She further suggests that trickster narratives provide Kalapalo audiences with resources for grasping the role of strategic thinking and for maintaining emotional detachment from personal goals in successfully dealing with conflict. She argues that these narrative performances also provide important contexts for socializing children and adults with respect to ways of responding creatively to social change. Basso associates this cultural dynamism with the relatively recent migration of the Carib-speaking Kalapalo from the north, arguing that these narratives may be of "adaptive value" in enabling Kalapalo to cope with a new environment and with hostile relations with neighboring Native American groups. Taugi's use of deception to counter deception would seem to relate as well to the colonial and postcolonial history of contact with non-Indians.

The essays by Briggs and Haviland discuss narratives in other Native American societies; here, conflict and attempts to control it are as apparent in the narrative as they are in the narrated events (that is, in the process of narration as well as in the events represented by stories).[5] In both cases, disputants compete for control over how conflict is represented, not only with each other but with the authoritative voices of individuals who act as mediators. These officials have access to exhortative speech styles that seem to embody social order. Mediators may help to "give voice" to disputants' perspectives, but the process of recontextualization layers these narratives with the discursive and social control exercised by male leaders.

In both cases, dispute mediation provides a context in which models of social order and the way they are embodied in everyday practices, including discursive practices, become both means and ends of strategic interaction. In the Warao example, three prevalent, hierarchically ranked modes of thinking/speaking provide bases for contesting control over the interpretation of conflictual speech. In Zinacantecan marital mediation, on the other hand, a single image of order—as embodied in parallel couplets—seems to predominate; constestations revolve around attempts to co-opt or disrupt this ritually charged speech. Haviland's analysis of Tzotzil-speaking communities makes reference to political institutions (as embodied in the local jail) and the socioreligious hierarchy of *cargos* with respect to how they enter into the structures of authority associated with counseling discourse. The challenges posed simultaneously by the predominantly Mayan Ejército Zapatista para la Liberación Nacional to progovernment leaders in Mayan communities (such as neighboring San Juan Chamula), to the national government, and to the Free Trade Agreement during the Chiapas insurrection of January 1994 suggest that the imposition of hierarchically based notions of order and efforts to resist them also extend to broader relations of domination.

Recent studies have advanced a number of competing perspectives regarding the ability of participants to conceptualize the nature of conflict and the factors that relate to its creation and mediation. The debate has been waged in many terms. A common formulation is the opposition between *hegemony*, framed as pervasive and unstated forms of control that simply seem to reflect the natural order of things, and *ideology*, defined as an articulated system of beliefs, meanings, and values (see Comaroff and Comaroff 1991:19–27). Gramsci (1971) similarly opposed hegemony to *resistance*, the capacity of the subaltern to gain critical perspectives on hegemonic practices and to formulate alternatives. Whereas many scholars have followed Scott (1985, 1990) in documenting popular acts of resistance, Harding (1975), Said (1989), Taussig (1992:37–52), and others have questioned the epistemology and the politics of such studies: Is resistance real if hegemony is not effectively challenged? If so, who gains from its revelation to elite audiences? Kaplan and Kelly (1994) have recently criticized the assumption that social forms must be fully conscious to be designated as acts of resistance; they also argue that such dichotomies as hegemony *versus* resistance or hegemony *versus* ideology are epistemologically questionable when used by scholars as binary and discrete categories in classifying social forms.

These essays contribute to this debate by virtue of the diversity of positions that the authors adopt, as well as the manner in which they reveal the complexities that arise from attempts to discern hegemony, ideology, and resistance in conflictive events. Basso, Brenneis, and Herzfeld argue that narratives of conflict provide privileged sites for reflexive examination of individual identities and the social order as a whole. Their essays share an interest in explicit models of the person, emotions, conflict, and the social order that is also evident in a collection edited by Watson-Gegeo and White (1990). Basso suggests that Kalapalo storytellers use trickster narratives in presenting models of social action and of the epistemological grounds that inform social interaction and accounts of events. It would be interesting to raise the question of reception: If hereditary leaders perform narratives concerning this ritually potent male ancestor in the socially privileged setting of the central plaza, do women and socially subordinate males challenge or at least resist the models of conflict—and social hierarchies—that are embedded in them?

Brenneis argues that the narratives of conflict that emerge in gossip sessions and *pancayat* dispute mediations produce culturally salient models of knowledge, reputation, and affect. In this as well as in two other essays (1984b, 1990), he suggests that the *pancayat* imposes a model of social equality and interpersonal amity on the process of narration and the events narrated. The structure of the *pancayat* lends a sense that all parties are able to represent their positions and that a consensus has been achieved through a process of give and take on all sides. As Brenneis notes, however, participation is limited to adult males, and the "confidential committee" that organizes the event not only decides who is granted the right to testify but also rehearses their testimony in advance. Thus, the celebration of culturally salient models of equality and amity can also provide means of naturalizing social hierarchy as well as individual interests.

As I noted earlier, Herzfeld suggests that both animal thefts and narrative representations of them provide rural Cretans with central means of challenging the hegemony of the nation-state. Narrative representations of politicians' roles in recovering stolen animals provide a means of criticizing the duplicitous attitude of the government toward both animal theft and rural communities. Herzfeld adds, however, that such acts of resistance emerge in the course of increasing willingness to cooperate with officials in suppressing raiding, a growth in the degree of dependence on agriculture, and an increase in the extent to which rural communities are incorporated into the national economy. One might ask as well if this rhetoric of resistance provides dominant sectors with rhetorical resources to maintain the social and cultural marginalization of rural Cretans. As Herzfeld himself comments (1985:208–9, 322), these assertions of resistance to the nation-state take the form of narratives that are created at the request of a scholar who will use them in representing Cretan communities to an international audience.

Since O'Barr and Conley are specifically concerned with lay ideologies of the law, it would seem at first glance that they share the conclusion that emerges from the essays by Basso, Brenneis, and Herzfeld, namely, that narratives presented in settings of conflict provide revealing insights into the social order. Rather, they argue that lay litigants fail to perceive the systemic and pervasive nature of the control that legal professionals exercise over their participation in the court system. O'Barr and Conley suggest that even as litigants learn to present their narratives in ways that reflect the ideologies and discursive forms that are predominant in the legal system, they may continue to be motivated by contradictory ideologies—such as the idea that courts exist to right social wrongs. When this discrepancy between lay and legal ideologies leads to discontent on the part of litigants, they are nonetheless more likely to blame a particular judge or other court official than to hold legal institutions and procedures themselves responsible. Small-claims courts accordingly play a crucial role in maintaining the legal status quo.

Mertz argues that Supreme Court opinions can simultaneously respond to changing historical circumstances and social pressures and maintain the dominance of legal institutions. She makes the interesting observation that social groups that seek to influence these opinions participate in this process as well—rather than simply seeking to make their voices heard, parties to these major social cleavages try to get their stories incorporated into authoritative documents that bear the Court's considerable influence.

Haviland suggests that disputants attempt to infuse mediation discourse with their own perspectives, thus incorporating multiple points of view. Although battered wives may have the opportunity to make their grievances known, their voices are ultimately silenced by the authoritative speech of male authorities. The differential distribution of authoritative speech forms reproduces social inequality. Haviland ends, however, with a fascinating case in which a woman replays a wife's angry denunciation in a highly articulate fashion, including the use of parallelism, while the official's response is characterized as dramatically inarticulate. This counterexample might suggest that space may be available in other settings and genres, particularly in gossip sessions (see also Haviland 1977), for offering ideological and stylistic resistance to the words of authoritative mediators.

Briggs similarly traces the relationship between the social distribution of discursive resources and social hierarchies. Not only is "counseling speech" far more accessible to senior males, but also the male "leaders" control access to the floor, ask questions, determine when each narrator must stop speaking, and impose decisions. Nonetheless, women who are parties to the dispute do generally get to tell their stories, and they can use a broad range of verbal resources in advancing their claims and undermining those of other disputants. Moreover, persons who are not satisfied with the mediation process can violate the officials' injunction to "never speak of this again." By incorporating their contestations into gossip narratives or even further "angry speech," they can challenge not only the leaders' interpretations but potentially their legitimacy as well (see Briggs 1992a). Such challenges may result in the de-legitimation of particular leaders; however, they do not seem to result in the sort of structural change that would place women in positions of leadership.

Ochs, Smith, and Taylor focus in their contribution primarily on what they term "centralized dinners," that is, those in which families eat and talk together. They argue that such dinners are conducive to longer stories with greater audience involvement. Participation in this process, which these authors deem an important component of socialization within family units, would seem to hold a double lesson for children. On the one hand, co-narration confers rights of co-ownership to stories, thus involving children actively in the process of constructing knowledge and social organization. As they share stories, children share power. In the long run, children develop competence in the use of narratives in creating and mediating conflict, the strategic representation of experience, problem solving, and theory building. On the other hand, rights to decide what sorts of consequences stories will have on family relations seem to be structured by age and, as is clearly evident in the second example, gender. Ochs, Smith, and Taylor suggest that although centralized dinners open up more space for narrative problem solving at dinnertime, they also enable adults—particularly fathers—to exert more social control over children (see Ochs, Taylor, Rudolph, and Smith 1992). Some families, on the other hand, do not eat together, or they devote more attention to watching television and other activities than to conversation. If such differences are structured, at least in part, by social class, variability in the coperformance of narratives at meals may help reproduce class-based differences in access to the social and linguistic skills that place individuals in broader social and institutional structures.

The contributors to this volume thus take a number of positions with respect to questions of hegemony, ideology, and resistance, and their essays point to several interesting facets of these issues. "Negotiation" and other metaphors that are often used in characterizing conflict talk raise difficult epistemological and political issues. Participants seldom enjoy equal access to the discursive resources that shape who can talk when, in what ways, and with which effects. When scholars appropriate such metaphors as "disentangling" from the discourses they study (see Watson-Gegeo and White 1990), they run the risk of ratifying images that give the sense that all participants have equal access to modes of waging conflict and that all seek to achieve consensus, even when these are the very tools used by the powerful to *limit* access to conflict talk and to advance their own agendas.

It is clear that conflict and conflict discourse are seldom aptly characterized as either hegemony *or* resistance, conscious *or* unconscious. One reason that scholarship in this area tends to be reductionistic is that analysts often read discourse in terms of its referential content; awareness of linguistic units rarely extends beyond lexical or clausal levels to include larger discursive structures. Since all discourses are multifaceted and multifunctional, dominant structures and processes can be naturalized, revealed, and challenged—all at the same time. For example, referential content and formal patterning often work in opposite directions; while the explicit content may accord a prominent role to assertions that all parties have equal rights to speak and be heard, restrictions on which speech styles are deemed to be appropriate or powerful may limit real access to authoritative voices (see later discussion). Similarly, while dissident voices may overtly (i.e., referentially) proclaim their acquiescence to the powers that be, subtle stylistic or generic subversions may disrupt dominant discourses and reveal ways that authority is naturalized.[6] Radner and Lanser (1993) argue that women often embed coded messages in their discourses, thus conveying meanings to other women that may be invisible or opaque to men. On the other hand, self-proclaimed dissident voices may water down or even undermine their subversive capacity by adopting the discursive trappings of the forces they are attempting (or purporting) to resist. Gal (1991) notes that while some scholars read women's silence as acquiescence, others regard it as embodying strategies of resistance.

As I noted above, analysts are now attempting to go beyond simplistic analyses that characterize social forms and processes as either hegemony or resistance. I believe that one of the reasons the contributors to this volume present provocative and nuanced approaches to this question is that they advance their analyses of conflict via close examinations of formal dimensions of discourse production and reception.

Narrative (and) Discourse

The preceding section suggested that the essays in this volume contribute to a growing body of scholarship which has demonstrated that conflict is not simply a departure from normal social processes but rather involves complex social forms that play a broad range of roles in constituting social life. It is particularly fruitful to examine the relationship between conflict and narrative at this juncture in that students of narrative and of discourse have similarly pointed to the complex ways that language shapes—rather than simply reflects—the social world.

One important departure in recent theory and analysis pertains to the social distribution of linguistic structures and meanings. With important exceptions, such as the work of Sapir (1921), linguists generally joined Saussure in assuming that the socially significant part of language constitutes a sort of cognitive lowest common denominator "which exists in the form of a number of impressions deposited in the brain of each member of a community, almost like a dictionary of which identical copies have been distributed to each individual" (Saussure, 1959 [1916]:19). Whether or not they agree with Lacan's (1977 [1966]) or Derrida's (1978 [1967]) formulations of difference as lying at the core of processes of creating and defending the Self, most practitioners would agree that discourse in general and narrative in particular not only reflect but also create social differentiation as based on race and ethnicity, gender, social class, and sexuality. Gumperz (1982, 1992) and Labov (1972a, 1972b) placed the relationship between social and linguistic difference at the center of their research. Paredes (1968, 1993) and Bauman (1972) similarly suggested long ago that verbal art provides resources not simply for celebrating shared identities but for discursively defining social and cultural boundaries as well. Clifford (1988) and other students of "the politics and poetics of ethnography" (Clifford and Marcus 1986) argue that such observations are equally true of ethnographic narratives in that ethnographers implicitly create a Self in the process of inventing an Other (also see Said 1978).

When one moves from theoretical models to situated narrative practices, it is clear that the manner in which stories are presented and used is often contingent upon their being framed as embodiments of shared beliefs and understandings. Recent studies of discourse have come to view such claims as situated social constructs; that is, such framings enter into strategies by which individuals and groups attempt to lend legitimacy or even hegemony to particular narratives. This statement captures important dimensions of the role of storytelling in the creation of social life from the smallest to the most inclusive social formations. Ochs, Smith, and Taylor argue that co-narration structures the way families perceive the relationship between competing versions of a story and between different stories; this process not only shapes how members perceive and evaluate events but entitles interlocutors to coauthor one another's biographies. Goodwin's (1990) research on African-American children points to the value of imposing a particular narrative representation of past events as a means of restructuring the social organization of an ongoing conflict. Bennett and Feldman (1981) argue that the narratives which emerge in testimony constitute a dynamic process of "reconstructing reality in the courtroom" rather than recollections of preexisting facts. Cretan narrators harshly criticize fellow members of their communities and kin groups when they collude with opposing animal thieves. Although the resulting failure to locate stolen livestock is clearly far from irrelevant here, it would seem that such perceptions that the social contract has been violated emerge in part from these individuals' refusal to assist their neighbors and relatives in constructing narratives that validate their material and social claims.

This process of legitimating particular narratives also plays a crucial role in constructing the nation-state. Herzfeld suggests that stories of animal thefts assert community solidarity and construct an image of rural Cretans in opposition to the institutions of the nation-state. Anderson (1991 [1983]), Handler (1988), and Hobsbawm and Ranger (1983) argue that the construction of narrative images of a glorious and unified past plays a crucial role in the creation of nation-states. Bauman (1993) demonstrates the role that such nationalist narratives can play in attempts to market national images globally. The traditional objects of folkloristic analysis, such as fairy tales, proverbs, ballads, and the like, are now seen by many researchers less as spontaneous and collective products of "folk culture" than as literary creations. Creating explicit images of the Other—based on class, ethnicity, and gender— provided an important and largely implicit means of constructing the cultural hegemony of the bourgeoisie in 18th- and 19th-century Europe (Briggs 1993b; Stewart 1991; see also Briggs and Shuman 1993). Mertz similarly points to the way that Supreme Court opinions that focus on race have shaped and reshaped images of African-Americans in the United States. These examples suggest that detailed examination of the discursive practices used in rendering particular narratives authoritative is of great value to the study not only of culture but also of the politics of culture.

Just as Saussure's assumptions regarding the homogeneity of the language system have been questioned, Jakobson (1971 [1957], 1960), Silverstein (1976), and others have drawn on Charles S. Peirce's (1932) semiotics in expanding the search for meaning in discourse to include indexical and iconic, in addition to symbolic, relations. Saussure's *langue* accords a central role to context-independent referential meaning. With respect to indexical meaning, however, contextualization is crucial. Indexes are established in particular events of speaking or writing, and they link words or other linguistic forms to contextual and, following Silverstein (1993:36), cotextual elements. In order to understand the meaning of the word *now*, for instance, one needs to know when a particular utterance was spoken, while decoding *here* involves knowledge of particular spatial relations.[7] Icons, on the other hand, relate a sign to its object of representation on the basis of perceptible similarities. Narrators often change their voice characteristics when reporting emotionally charged speech; for example, a rise in pitch, an increase in volume, and a breathless quality may suggest that the character was excited or scared.

This shift toward considering a range of different ways of creating meaning is crucial for the study of narratives. Stories generally focus the attention of the listener or reader on the plot; at the same time that narratives foreground what Jakobson (1960) referred to as the referential function, however, they provide access to vast indexical and iconic resources. Urban (1991, 1993) has argued that the ability of narrators to use indexical and particularly iconic relations as bearers of culturally central messages without drawing attention to them lies at the center of the "cultural functions" of myth (see also Parmentier 1993:263). While indexes and icons often enhance and expand referential content, they can also be used to contradict the overt message of the story. The articles in this collection present rich examples of the value of analyzing iconic and indexical relations in studying narratives.

The core of O'Barr and Conley's distinction between relational and rule-oriented ways of telling one's story in small-claims court can be characterized as contrastive means of indexically grounding the events that comprise the conflict; while relational litigants connect each step in the unfolding story to the social relations that surrounded them, rule-oriented narrators tie events to the legally significant discourses (such as contracts) that shape their juridical significance. Mertz demonstrates how Supreme Court opinions regarding major social conflicts tell two stories simultaneously: while the referential content of decisions like *Brown v. Board of Education* may explicitly link the Court's narrative with efforts to produce societal change, the manner in which decisions are constructed—by linking the legal implications of events indexically to judicial documents and institutions—would seem to tell a much more conservative legal tale.

The essays by Basso, Briggs, and Ochs, Smith, and Taylor show how narrators provide competing indexical groundings of key events. The Kalapalo trickster Taugi is constantly confronted with contradictory evidence regarding the world around him. His cousin and foe Kafanifani presents Taugi with situations in which the indexical underpinnings of speech are deceitfully displaced, as when words are heard but no speakers are to be seen. Taugi's ally, Akugi the Agouti, on the other hand, reminds Taugi that he possesses a special intelligence that enables him to reveal such hidden indexes. In Warao dispute mediation, narrators attempt to connect conflicts and the "bad speech" that is often seen as having given rise to them with the angry, jealous, or otherwise inappropriate speech and actions of their opponents. When families tell first person narratives at dinnertime, other individuals link the events described by the protagonist indexically to other stories or settings, thus potentially transforming the social impact of what has been said and done. In another essay, Ochs (1992) connects the way American mothers index gender and power with the underrating of their role in society.

A number of authors have recently demonstrated the powerful role that iconicity plays in shaping the form, meaning, and social significance of narratives. According to Tedlock (1983), narrators draw on a "poetics of verisimilitude" in fashioning the acoustic properties of stories into icons of the events they describe, thus making the imaginary seem real. Hymes (1981) argues that the core of indigenous American storytelling lies in complex iconic relations between the formal organization of lines, verses, and stanzas and the way that plot is structured by sequences of repeated actions. Parmentier (1987, 1993) argues for the importance of indexical icons, iconic (technically diagrammatic) signs that are contextually situated, in shaping political rhetoric and conceptions of history. Urban (1991) suggests that both acoustic and rhetorical aspects of the formal organization of indigenous South American narratives are iconically tied to basic elements of social organization, such that performances provide sensible icons of cultural models of sociability.

Of the essays included in this volume, Haviland takes up the question of iconicity most centrally. Like Urban, he points to crucial associations between the form of discourse and forms of authority; he suggests, in particular, that ritual Tzotzil speech, arranged in parallel couplets, is "a perfect icon of orderliness, control, sobriety, and proper public demeanor" (page 257). He characterizes this iconicity, however, less as a predetermined, normative relationship that pervades social and discursive order than as an accomplishment that is achieved in the course of performances; his analysis also points to how "dissident voices" attempt to disrupt this hegemonic process. For Haviland, grammatical parallelism is but one example of the importance of the linearization of discourse in dispute mediation. We can extrapolate from Coleman's (1957) observations on the developmental cycle of disputes to suggest that the sequential structure of such discursive events as Tzotzil dispute mediation can be constructed in such a way as to impose a particular view of the developmental progression that a dispute has taken—or, according to the narrator, should take. (I will return to this point shortly.)

Brenneis similarly suggests that narratives regarding the same conflictual events can iconically invoke the fluidity and contestation of everyday life when told as gossip and, when performed in *pancayat* dispute mediations, model the orderly and amiable give and take of ideal egalitarian social relations. His description of the *pancayat* opens up the possibility that competing iconic constructions of narratives may be possible: the explicit model of equality coexists with the manner in which *pancayat* discourse constitutes an implicit image of the power of the "confidential committee" to impose order. The *pancayat* iconically reflects not simply the conflictual events but the committee's rehearsing of testimony as well. Finally, Basso, Briggs, Herzfeld, and Haviland argue that reported speech provides narrators with the ability to embed their assessment of a character's affective and/or moral state in the way his or her words are replayed on the narrative stage.

One way in which many linguistic anthropologists and other students of language have continued to follow in Saussure's footsteps is to deem locating and decoding meaning as the central métier of their projects and of discourse itself. In contrast, Foucault has argued for "a refusal of analyses couched in terms of the symbolic field or the domain of signifying structures, and a recourse to analyses in terms of the genealogy of relations of force, strategic developments, and tactics" (1980 [1972]:114). It seems particularly apparent in the case of conflict discourse that conveying meaning, including the communication of referential content and speaker intention, may not be the central goal of interlocutors.[8] Bloch's (1975) work on political oratory suggests that the referential function may be highly subordinated to indexical and iconic elements when discourse is saturated with authority.

Nonetheless, positing some sort of blanket equation regarding the relationship between reference and the ritual or political "formality" of a communicative event (see Irvine 1979) would seem to provide a less useful point of departure for examining the construction of models of meaning than drawing on the insights provided by recent work on ideologies of language (see Joseph and Taylor 1990; Kroskrity, Schieffelin, and Woolard 1992; Woolard and Schieffelin 1994). Here, conceptions of meaning and its centrality to discourse are viewed as social, cultural, and historical products that are, like other social forms, often contested. Ideologies of language themselves thus become objects of empirical investigation. For example, contrastive perspectives of the meaning of "bad speech" and of how speech in general is produced and received form both means and ends of waging conflict in Warao dispute mediation. Opposing views of the nature of authority in discourse similarly characterize men's and women's gossip in Warao communities (see Briggs 1992a). Basso argues that Kalapalo narrators use the trickster Taugi in teaching their listeners to perceive alternative strategies for producing and receiving discourse by paying attention to deceit and disorder. Indeed, Taugi's example suggests that the apparent meaning of what is seen and heard is likely to be an illusion that is created by one party to further his or her own interests.

The specialized lexicons and discursive structures associated with high prestige occupations, such as law and medicine, are generally justified as means of creating precise meanings, but they also make nonspecialists painfully aware of the constraints they face when participating in the production and reception of such discourse. O'Barr and Conley suggest that the legal system's monopoly over the discourse practices through which meaning is generated produces confusion and alienation even in small-claims courts, where discourse is supposed to be maximally accessible to laypersons. Cicourel (1982) and Mishler (1984) have argued that serious midunderstandings often arise when professionals use specialized terminology and highly asymmetrical discursive routines while interviewing patients—and thus jeopardize the diagnostic process. Clearly, narrators often *do* seek to specify meanings and convey them to their interlocutors. When one set of interpretations comes to be accepted as the authoritative account of a conflict and as the basis for shaping outcomes, however, this outcome must be seen less as a natural product of communicative processes than as a particular social construction; attention can thus be directed toward grasping what types of material and symbolic capital (Bourdieu 1991) were mustered in achieving this result and the ways in which they were deployed.

Unfortunately, scholars who have followed Foucault on the question of meaning have generally dismissed detailed analyses of formal and functional patterning. This move effectively erases or at least subordinates the special skills that linguistic anthropologists as well as students of pragmatics, sociolinguistics, conversation analysis, and related areas can offer to the study of conflict discourse. It is thus important to explore the possibility of developing theoretical positions and methodological strategies that permit us to broaden and deepen the social, political, and historical thrust of analyses without abandoning a concern with discourse structure. I would like to suggest that the study of narratives presents an extremely fertile arena for developing such an approach. If we wish to grasp the role of discourse in the construction and representation of social life, narratives provide particularly intriguing objects of study in that they foreground not only the object of representation but the process of representation itself. In other words, narratives are powerful because they can focus attention on the events that constitute the story as well as the process of storytelling.

I would like to suggest that it is useful to discuss the representational power of stories as forming part of *metadiscursive practices*. An interesting point of departure for understanding the relationship between discourse and practices can be drawn from Foucault's (1972 [1969]:49) emphasis on "treating discourse [not] as groups of signs . . . but as practices that systematically form the objects of which they speak," as well as Silverstein's (1976, 1993) framework for analyzing the "metapragmatic" means through which this process is realized. Here, discourses consist less of messages generated within a circumscribed linguistic and social system than as means of determining the norms and limits regarding who can say what to whom and the relations of power created in the production and reception of discourse. In proposing the term metadiscursive practices, I draw on Foucault (1977 [1975]) in identifying discourses that seek to shape, constrain, or appropriate other discourses. By presenting discourse in narrative form, narrators and their audiences gain access to a range of metadiscursive practices for shaping *social interactions* as well as the *production and reception of discourse*.

Social Interaction

The work of Harvey Sacks (1972, 1992) stressed two implications of a simple but far-reaching observation: stories are embedded in conversation and interaction. First, the formal organization of narratives is shaped by indexical ties to the social interaction. Second, this relationship accords a great deal of weight to stories as means of structuring social interaction and social organization. Conversation analysts and other researchers have explored the significance of Sacks's insight. Thus, in his essay Brenneis urges us to see the process of contextualization as constitutive of narrative: "It is difficult to sustain the premise that there can be narratives independent of the situations in which they are told" (page 42).

One of the most obvious effects of opening up a narrative frame is a shift in ways that turns at talk are allocated. Beginning a story often grants one speaker access to more extended turns, even if the narrator is an individual who generally enjoys fewer rights to talk. Nonetheless, narration often takes the form of co-narration, involving a complex process of determining who tells what and how.[9] Brenneis argues that sharing the task of telling the story may provide a crucial means of sharing accountability for its contents, since no one participant bears sole responsibility for what is revealed (see also Briggs 1993c; Hill and Zepeda 1992; Schiffrin 1990:253). Ochs, Smith, and Taylor suggest that the ability of narrative performances to produce socially significant cognitive reframings, which they refer to as "paradigm shifts," emerges from the process of co-narration. Another essay that resulted from their research argues that the co-production of these narratives aids in the development of cognitive skills associated with scientific theorizing (Ochs et al. 1992).

The essays by Brenneis, Briggs, and Haviland suggest that the ability of dominant parties to create a sense of participation, balance, and harmony in the storytelling process, particularly with respect to turn taking, can iconically represent these individuals' power to manage conflictual social relations. Cases as widely separated in terms of geography and culture as Warao *monikata nome anaka*, Fiji Indian *pancayat*, and U.S. small-claims court all provide examples of the way that eliciting narratives in interrogative fashion enables authoritative speakers to use the power of the question-answer format in structuring interaction. In Tzotzil marital mediation, the sequential movement from a more competitive, heteroglossic, and "disorderly" mode of turn taking to an "orderly," hierarchical mode signals the imposition of social order. On the other hand, Ochs, Smith, and Taylor point to the crucial role that unpredictability can play: even though performing a first person narrative entitles an individual to display information over which he or she can assert special rights, the initial narrator cannot foresee who will have something to add and how such contributions will disrupt the impact on the social interaction that the initial narrator hopes to achieve. Subsequently told stories may similarly reshape previous interpretations of a personal narrative.

As work by Charles Goodwin (1984, 1986) and Marjorie Harness Goodwin (1990) demonstrates, telling a story has important effects on participation structures. An individual who is engaged in a conflict can use a narrative performance as a means of recruiting other persons' involvement, and non-narrators can use their evaluations of story elements in aligning themselves differentially to parties and positions. According to Deborah Schiffrin (1990), the expansion of participation frameworks invoked by narratives can reconfigure social relations in the course of an argument, including the responsibility for satisfying truthfulness and sincerity conditions. Work by both the Goodwins and Amy Shuman (1986) suggests that how the participants relate to story events and previous tellings (as principal characters, eyewitnesses, etc.) shapes each individual's entitlement to serve as narrator or audience member in retellings.

By virtue of the way that they unlock a broad range of metadiscursive practices, narratives constitute powerful means of shaping social interactions. Nevertheless, taking a narrow interactionist position overlooks the way that the interactional power of stories is tied to their capacity for *representing* social and discursive interactions positioned at some temporal and/or spatial distance. The use of reported speech foregrounds how narratives represent discourse, including the indexical relations that links words and settings.

In conflict settings, representing speech provides disputants with resources for

evaluating the role of discourse in social life. Briggs shows how in dispute mediations Warao participants attempt to characterize the words they uttered in conflictive
situations as well reasoned and sensitive to the sensibilities of their interlocutors,
whereas their opponents' words are characterized as inappropriate and provocative.
Like their Warao counterparts, Tzotzil mediators, as discussed by Haviland, provide
hypothetical models regarding who should say what in which types of situations.
Herzfeld focuses on narratives that show how rural Cretans should and should not
talk and act; while the words and actions of opponents are criticized, narrators
provide elaborate excuses that idealize the relationship between their own speech
and comportment. The Kalapalo trickster Taugi, on the other hand, embodies incon-
gruity in speech and action. Basso suggests that this lack of fit is used in constructing
opposing models: Taugi's superior intelligence sometimes enables him to use this
contextual gap in furthering his own interests, but on other occasions his susceptibility to being duped leads him to miss vital indexical links. Urban (1984, 1993)
argues that representing speech in relation to action constitutes not only an important
focus of mythic narratives but a crucial means of inculcating cultural norms in
indigenous South American groups.

Stories invoke metadiscursive practices that enable participants to present their
own evaluations of past conflicts at the same time that they are attempting to shape
the ongoing interaction. The examples provided by Briggs and Haviland suggest that
this process of discursive projection goes further still, linking prior to current to
future interactions in such a way that how participants spoke and acted in the past,
along with their current words and actions in the present, provides models for how
they will ideally talk and act in the future. Goodwin (1990) similarly observes that
narrative exchanges that ''instigate'' a he-said-she-said dispute include rehearsals of
what the speaker intends to say in a future phase of the conflict.

This process of tying narratives to social interactions that take place beyond the
spatiotemporal parameters of their performance points to the status of stories as
excellent resources for shaping broader dimensions of social organization, as Brenneis argues in his contribution. Ochs, Smith, and Taylor show how co-narrating
detective stories that focus on interactions outside the family shapes relationships
within it (see also Ochs et al. 1992). The role of dinner conversations in socialization
would seem to extend to teaching children how institutions such as schools shape
their rights and responsibilities. Mertz's essay provides a striking example of how a
powerful institution can create a document that seeks to preserve—or transform—
such crucial dimensions of social organization as race relations. O'Barr and Conley
similarly argue that by weighting competing models of how discourse is embedded
in social interaction differentially, small-claims courts help maintain the political-
economic status quo. These essays thus assist us in relating the ''micro'' view
associated with much linguistic research to discourse analyses that explore how
hegemony is produced in broader institutional and societal contexts. Beyond detail-
ing the metadiscursive practices that link discursive settings across time and space

and that connect individual experience with institutional constraint, these analyses open up important questions regarding the societal mechanisms that grant or withhold access to particular practices and that help shape the social effects that accrue from their situated use.

Discourse Form

The work of two Russian scholars, M. M. Bakhtin and Roman Jakobson, provides important insights into the power of the formal patterning of narrative in shaping social conflict. Bakhtin stressed the dialogic character of discourse, that is, the way that the words we utter are tied not just to the setting in which they are produced and received but to other discourses, texts, settings, and the like. Rather than being neutral vessels for conveying meaning, words are products of linguistic and social *heteroglossia*—words invoke the genres, styles, speakers, writers, settings, institutions, occupations, and ideologies with which they are associated (Bakhtin 1981; 1986; see also Medvedev 1985 [1928]). Vološinov (1973 [1930]) argued that discourse not only represents but is itself an object of representation. Although he was particularly interested in forms of dialogism that he believed to be tied to the emergence of the novel, Bakhtin's view of linguistic patterning as a product of the intersection of texts, textures, and contexts has proved to be quite stimulating to scholars interested in a wide range of narratives.

Jakobson (1971 [1957]), in his famous "Shifters" article, pointed to the importance of a particular form of dialogism that emerges in narratives, such that they simultaneously represent *narrative events* (the discursive setting of their telling) and *narrated events* (the words and actions that they relate). Bauman (1986) has stressed the particular importance of this dual orientation for oral narratives, arguing that formal manipulation of the relationship between narrative and narrated events provides an important base for launching social commentary in narrative form.

In the case of conflict narratives, this dual orientation enables narrators to focus on conflictual events, the circumstances that purportedly gave rise to them, past attempts at mediation, and the like, while linking them to the narrative process. Connecting events that are separated in time and often space involves an active social process of extracting discourse from one setting, which can be referred to as *decontextualization*, and inserting it in a new setting, which has been termed *recontextualization* (Bauman and Briggs 1990).[10] Let us use Kristeva's (1980) term *intertextuality* to refer to discursive relationships that are created through this process. As the contributions to this volume suggest, the narrated events can be hypothetical, projected future events, or generalized expectations regarding what people normally do in certain types of situations. Parmentier (1993) provides an example in which the "quoted" speech not only never was spoken but is drawn from a genre that the speaker is in the very act of creating.

The constructed nature of narrated events points to the importance of a notion articulated by Bauman (1986:5). He argues that narratives do not simply describe ready-made events; rather, they provide central means by which we *create* notions as to what took place, how the action unfolded, what prompted it, and the social effects of the events. This process of social construction also works in the opposite direction, such that narrated events contribute to the means by which narrative events are created. Just as narration provides a central forum for contesting the ownership and social control of representations of conflictual events, particular constructions of conflictual events position narrators and audiences in the contestations that take place as stories are told. In a recent article, Silverstein (1993:36–37) argues that the creation of events by linking sets of indexical signs to temporal phases constitutes a central means of creating the sense of cohesion that orders discursive interaction; it thus forms a crucial dimension of the metapragmatics of language use in general.

The referential function of language provides the basis for a wide range of connections between narrated and narrative events. Since the objects of reference and predication are the pragmatics of language use in such instances, we may refer to them, following Silverstein (1976, 1993), as examples of explicit metapragmatics. Silverstein defines metapragmatic signs in terms of their objects of representation, arguing that they "have pragmatic phenomena—indexical sign phenomena—as their semiotic objects; they thus have an inherently 'framing', or 'regimenting', or 'stipulative' character with respect to indexical phenomena" (1993:33). He goes on to distinguish "degrees and kinds of metapragmatic explicitness," that is, the extent to which the significance of a particular metapragmatic sign is based on the referential function of language. *Denotatively explicit* metapragmatic signs are tied to some discourse element by virtue of their semantic content. *Denotatively implicit* metapragmatic signs, on the other hand, designate some discursive element apart from their semantic content—if they possess semantic content at all.

Some metadiscursive practices delineate *degrees of closeness versus distance between narrated and narrative events*.[11] The introductory formulas that so frequently open narratives provide explicit means of relating narrative and narrated events; when Warao narrators situate a story in the time when *kaina mate hidoma* 'our world was still being formed', they create the maximum distance between the two orders of events. Narrators use disclaimers of performance to distance narrated and narrative events by calling into question their own command of the story (Bauman 1992). Mexicano elders in New Mexican communities explicitly create both distance and proximity by emphasizing their own firsthand knowledge of "the talk of the elders of bygone times" at the same time that they stress the ignorance of their audiences, who are products of "nowadays" (Briggs 1988). The orientational and evaluative components of narrative analyzed by Labov (Labov and Waletsky 1967; Labov 1982) provide important explicit means of relating narrated and narrative events. Even when reference is brought into play in creating relationships between narrated and narrative events, a broad range of dimensions of discursive patterning provide *implicit* metapragmatic tools for shaping these relationships. Here, subtle features of speech style, intonation, reported speech,[12] and grammatical patterning link the two orders of events in particular ways. The contributors to the present volume provide examples that illustrate the rich range of metadiscursive practices that narrators and audiences use in relating narrated and narrative events in conflict situations.

When the two sets of events are construed as being separated by time, space, participants, participation framework, type of interaction, and/or a vast range of other discursively significant features, the process of relating them that takes place in narration necessarily produces both links and gaps. Narrators and audiences can emphasize the *links* that exist between the two, or, alternatively, they can foreground the *gaps* that separate them.[13] The essays in this volume point to the way that narrators often attempt to stress *both* links and gaps in order to situate themselves and their positions in a conflict in a number of different ways simultaneously.

As Briggs's contribution to this volume and his research on Warao ritual wailing suggest, tense-aspect forms and other grammatical elements can be used in calibrating the distance between narrated and narrating events. Marking verbs for past + perfective places the narrated events in a realm that is bounded and separated from the present, while repeated use of non-past + durative forms affords the sense that the actions represented in the narrated events continue into the present (see also Briggs 1988). Work by Hopper (1979, 1982), Wallace (1982), and others suggests that tense and aspect are used in constructing the relationship between narrative and narrated events in a wide range of languages. Lucy (1993a) argues that contrastive *verba dicendi* provide different degrees of closeness and transparency between narrating and narrative events in Yucatec Mayan. Silverstein (1985) points to the importance of different syntactic constructions in creating culturally distinct configurations of reported speech in Chinookan. Hickmann (1993) argues that the acquisition of contrastive techniques for representing speech—and thus for regulating the boundary between narrated and narrating event—is an important developmental achievement.

One axis of comparison involves *the degree to which narrators and audiences focus on narrated versus narrative events*. Social groups sometimes possess strong preferences along these lines. Heath (1983) contrasts the tremendous concern with narrated events in oral narrative performances in working-class white communities in the Carolina Piedmont with the focus on the narrative event—particularly the narrator's skill—in African-American communities. Abrahams (1976, 1983) suggests that an orientation toward the performance event itself is a widespread feature of communication in African-American and Afro-Caribbean communities. Briggs (1988) argues that the degree of focus on narrative versus narrative events in Spanish-language Mexicano discourse in New Mexico differs widely from genre to genre; this contrast is associated with profound differences in the manner in which these two orders of events are experienced and in how they are used in shaping social interaction and discursive authority. Brenneis's contribution suggests that in gossip

sessions, Fiji Indian narrators and audiences focus on the sheer joy of co-partici-
pation in the narrative process, whereas the overt focus seems to be much more on
getting the story straight—or, better yet, straightening the story—in *pancayat* dispute mediations. In the latter, the "confidential committee" seems to go to great
lengths to ensure that narrators focus on "the facts" regarding one particular incident; suppression of topic shifting and explicit evaluations or interpretations would
seem to outlaw a broad range of strategies for linking narrative and narrated events
(page 45). Clearly, one would hardly want to accept "fact," "evaluation," or
"interpretation" as transparent and neutral categories; indeed, the committee's
power would seem to be nowhere more evident than in their control over the process
of constructing and imposing these categories.

A second axis of variation pertains to the way that *different narrators* calibrate
the relationship between narrative and narrated events. In the he-said-she-said disputes analyzed by Goodwin (1990) and Shuman (1986), narrators must link the two
sets of events closely enough to show that their involvement in the original incident
was sufficient to have gained the right to recount it legitimately. In the examples
reported by Briggs and Haviland, on the other hand, discursive authority is associated with a certain degree of distance between the two. In both Tzotzil and Warao
cases, mediators generally refrain from invoking directly the words and the passions
of the conflict. They keep their social and discursive distance by relying on generalized, indirect allusions to the conflict; by shifting to exhortation, they move even
further away from the scene of the dispute. Warao disputants link their narration to
narrative events closely enough to show that they not only know what happened but
can pinpoint the causes as well. Nevertheless, they attempt to avoid linking the two
so tightly that their voices as narrators directly embody the powerful emotions and
the angry words that are likely to be condemned by mediators and audiences. If they
are able to goad their opponents into losing their composure and reanimating their
"bad speech," so much the better. Directly invoking the words and actions of the
conflict seems to be used most often in Tzotzil mediations by participants who lack
discursive authority; Haviland suggests that replaying conflictual discourse provides
a means of resisting official voices.

The distance between narrated and narrative events also varies in keeping with
the positions ascribed to *different characters in the story*. With regard to the stories
of animal thefts in Crete, for example, narrators provide us with blow-by-blow
accounts of their own actions, including close-up glimpses into the circumstances
and psychological states that prompted particular events. Conversely, when recounting the words and actions of villainous members of their own communities—for
example, opposing animal thieves and politicians—narrators widen the gap between
narrative and narrated events by providing more abbreviated and much less detailed
descriptions. Some of the family dinner narratives analyzed by Ochs, Smith, and
Taylor seem to operate in precisely the opposite fashion. While Lucy, a young girl,
narrates in some detail the crime committed by one of her classmates and the

punishment administered by school officials, she attempts to maintain as much distance as possible from events in which *she* ran amuck of school authorities; her brother and parents, on the other hand, try to narrow the gap between narrated and narrating events precisely at this point. Although such character-based variation seems to be particularly prominent in the case of personal experience narratives, the Taugi tale described by Basso suggests that it is by no means restricted to such stories. Whereas Taugi's words, motives, modes of perception, and foibles are related in detail in the narrative, his rival Kafanifani receives much less close attention.

A fourth axis of comparison pertains to variation in the distance created betwen narrated and narrative events vis-à-vis the *different types of discourses incorporated into the narrative*. Herzfeld draws our attention to the creation of a heteroglossic texture in Cretan narratives through the use of High register terms. In diglossic communities, shifts in register constitute what Herzfeld refers to as "officializing strategies"; along with reports of the words of politicians, such shifts insert discourses connected with the nation-state into stories about animal thefts. In diglossic and multilingual communities, style shifting and code switching provide narrators with formal resources for creating complex relationships between competing perspectives on narrated events and different ways of connecting them to the narrative event. Mertz suggests that Supreme Court narratives use such features as direct discourse (quotation) and syntactic agency in linking a particular opinion to discourses previously produced by legal and legislative bodies. These connections present a legal chaining effect, as it were, when the narrated events reported in these opinions are other judicial narratives; such linkages present a sense of a historically deep continuous progression of events that are simultaneously narrated and narrative. The words of litigants who are not part of legal institutions—such as Brown and Plessy—are, on the other hand, held at much greater distance. Vološinov (1973 [1930]:122–23) argues that the use of reported speech in both judicial and rhetorical speech fosters clear-cut boundaries between narrated and narrative events; the higher the placement of an utterance in the social hierarchy, the more sharply defined the boundary. In Tzotzil and Warao disputes, mediators rely on the more rigid boundaries invoked by rhetorical speech in constructing the authority of their discourse.

As Goffman (1974) argues, narrators assume a wide range of roles in narratives. One of these is a *principal*, the party who is seen as standing behind the position being adopted. In the case of Supreme Court decisions, "the Court" commits itself to the legal stance that is written in the name of one or more justices; although the justices present themselves as the *author(s)*, much of the prose may be written by their clerks. In personal experience narratives, the narrator casts himself or herself as a *character* or *figure* while playing the role of *animator*, the person who brings all of these personages and their words and actions to life. The narrator can move between such guises as a participant in the narrated events, an eyewitness to their unfolding, a commentator on their social and historical location, an observer who can trace what happened later, an interpreter who can tell why events took a particular course, and a participant in the ongoing, narrative event who can thus point to the significance of these events for the narrating event.[14] In an example reported by Herzfeld, an older man situates himself as a character in a daring raid, as a person who knows the results achieved by the theft, and as a commentator on the moral character of the raid at the same time that he is the animator of the story; he is thus able to characterize himself simultaneously as brave and manly as well as dignified and thoughtful. Goffman's (1974) framework can provide us with a new appreciation of the Kalapalo trickster Taugi. Basso argues that Taugi possesses a "scattered self," which enables him to play a number of roles simultaneously and accordingly benefit from the special abilities of each. But Taugi is not alone in this respect; narrators in general construct scattered selves that enable them to position themselves in complex, multiple ways in relation to a range of persons and perspectives. Thus, one could say that there is something of the trickster in every narrator.

A broad range of comparative questions emerges when we consider the formal means by which narrated and narrative events are connected. The work of Bakhtin (1981) and V. N. Vološinov (1973 [1930]) stimulated a great deal of research on reported speech (see Lucy 1993c for recent examples). In the case of direct discourse, a chunk of speech is framed as being situated in both narrated and narrative events. Brenneis, Briggs, and Haviland show how reported speech enables narrators to embed characterizations not only of what was said but of how it was said, thereby attributing affective and moral qualities to the speaker (see also Besnier 1993). Warao disputants thus use reported speech as a running implicit metapragmatic channel for asserting the thoughtfulness and moderation of their own conduct, as contrasted with the rash and uncontrolled character of their opponents' words and actions.[15] Robert Moore (1993) documents the cultural salience of reported speech in Wasco narrative, arguing that quoted speech is not only constitutive of the genre of myth but also provides a core that is remarkably stable through the course of different performances of a narrative. Parmentier (1993), Sherzer (1983:213), and Urban (1993) suggest that reported speech provides authoritative speakers with powerful rhetorical devices for disguising normative messages as simple repetitions of the words of others. The use of reported speech turns narrators into ventriloquists (see Haraway 1992; Ritchie 1993), rendering their own positions both powerful and invisible by purporting to simply give voice to the discourse of others.

Stylistic dimensions of narrative discourse are not solely of importance in the case of reported speech. Certain ways of speaking are associated with authority; the examples included in the contributions include *special lexicons,* such as the legal terminology used in Supreme Court decisions; *diglossia,.* as is evident in Cretan animal theft narratives; *morphosyntactic patterning,* such as the use of grammatical agency and voice in Supreme Court opinions, evidentials in Kalapalo trickster narratives, and alternations between tense-aspect forms in Warao dispute narratives;

and *rhetorical patterning,* as in the use of question-and-answer chains and alterna-tions between narratives and exhortation in Tzotzil and Warao dispute mediation. In some settings, one feature bears singular weight as a means of constructing au-thority; the use of parallel couplets by Tzotzil mediators provides a striking case in point. Given the power of stylistic configurations as indexes of particular social relations and ideologies, narrators use them as means of embedding images of order and authority and structures of feeling into the very texture of their words. Herzfeld argues that the style of narration provides an icon of the social identity that the narrator wishes to establish for himself. Speech styles can also be linked to other participants in the narrative event (e.g., as appeals to dominant parties or denigra-tions of opponents), positions in the conflict, and possible outcomes, as well as to the larger discursive events in which stories are embedded. Speaking styles can also be connected to particular narrated events, characters, and perspectives.

Since narratives need not be stylistically unified, as both Bakhtin and the Rus-sian "formalists" have demonstrated, a single narrative can represent ideological contestations through heteroglossic juxtapositions of different styles and/or through multiple relationships between style and referential content. O'Barr and Conley are centrally concerned with the manner in which discourse patterning is tied to ide-ology. They focus on the grounds, in Peirce's (1932) sense of the term, that are used in connecting narrated and narrative events, that is, whether contractual formalities or interpersonal understandings lie at the center of both the conflict and its represen-tation. As the other essays in this volume suggest, any dimension of formal pattern-ing can be linked to ideologies. Several studies of ritual wailing argue that subtle acoustic features provide powerful tools by which wailers position themselves in social and ideological terms (see Briggs 1993c; Feld 1990, 1990 [1982]; Seremetakis 1991; Urban 1988). Moving from minute to macroscopic formal units, Hymes (1981) has pointed to the overall rhetorical structure of narratives as embodying repeated sequences of thought, speech, and action. In the case of conflict discourse, such progressions often extend beyond individual narratives to include the overall sequential construction of dispute events (as in the cases described by Brenneis, Briggs, and Haviland).

Such rhetorical structures are highly ideologically charged for a number of reasons. First, they structure the overall patterning of conflict discourse and of attempts to mediate it in keeping with situated and interested perspectives. If struc-tures are accepted, particular visions of the outcome—as consensus, imposed judg-ment, contestation, or the like—become practically unavoidable.[16] Second, such rhetorical patterns create hierarchies of metadiscursive practices and of the partici-pants who use them. When events begin with disputants' narratives and end with exhortations by officiants, as in the Warao example, the authority that accrues to political leaders and to their exhortations is asserted anew. It is, I think, not by accident that the final segment of such events foregrounds the authority of these individuals and the metadiscursive practices that they control. I suggest in my contribution that the ability to mediate disputes effectively is a sine qua non for these officials; repeated failure is likely to result in their removal from office. The discursive basis of this power provides, of course, a potential source of its undoing—challenging these rhetorical structures and hierarchical rankings of speakers can provide openings for resisting the ideologies that they construct and that empower them.

A third way in which such rhetorical structures—along with other formal dimensions of conflict narratives—are rich in ideological significance lies in their capacity to naturalize particular constructions of a conflict and of social relations in general. Sound symbols and other techniques of verisimilitude (Tedlock 1983), subtle features of grammatical patterning, and rhetorical structures can be used in creating the sense that the events unfolded naturally just as the narrator described them. Such theorists as Frederic Jameson (1981) and Raymond Williams (1977) have pointed to the power of narratives as means of imposing or sustaining not only particular ways of perceiving but also limits to perception. By weaving dominant social formations into the texture of descriptions of conflictual events, narrators can naturalize discursive and social hierarchies. Examining this process in detail provides us with a useful basis from which to pursue Foucault's (1977 [1975], 1980 [1972]) concern with the means by which truth, knowledge, subjectivity, and agency are produced and how particular individuals, institutions, and social groups (as defined by race and ethnicity, gender, sexual orientation, social class, and nationality) gain control over this process. The role of narratives in reproducing ideologies and forms of authority also springs from the way that their bounded and linearized structure facilitates decontextualization and recontextualization: stories are highly portable discursive units.

Close analysis of stylistic patterning is not merely of value in linguistic research; it also can tell us a great deal about the social organization and social control of discourse. Formal analysis is indispensable in developing a better sense as to why narratives often play such powerful roles in disputes. Who gets to establish the mechanisms that shape relationships between narrated and narrative events is of great significance in determining how narrative performances affect alignments between parties and positions. O'Barr and Conley's analysis suggests that contests between rule-oriented versus relational perspectives in small-claims courts form part of contestations regarding whose interests will be served by the larger institutions—those of legal and business institutions or those of individuals who depend upon them. Notions of "admissibility" and "evidence" similarly determine what types of stories can be told in civil and criminal courts. What is at stake is clearly not just what can be said, but also what cannot be said by whom, as well as differences in the social value attached to discourse produced by different parties.

Thus, narratives shape much more than just the narrative and narrated realms that they create. To cite two striking recent examples, the stories told by Anita Hill and Clarence Thomas in the latter's Senate confirmation hearings and by former Los Angeles Police Department officers in their trial for the beating of Rodney King have reshaped conceptions of race and gender in the United States. The many representations of what happened to Rodney King, particularly the televised screenings of the videotape that transformed the beating into a central image in transnational public culture, not only led to civil insurrections in Los Angeles and elsewhere but also catalyzed awareness of the profound social conflicts associated with race and racism in the United States. Veena Das (1994a, 1995) has written eloquently about the Bhopal disaster and the riots that followed the assassination of Indira Ghandi, pointing to the role of narratives in constructing authority in families, communities, and the nation-state. In celebrating narrative representations of the Mexican Revolution, the governing Partido Revolucionario Institucional (PRI) provided the indigenous Ejército Zapatista para la Liberación Nacional (EZLN) with the symbolic resources that is used in launching an armed struggle in January 1994 and in making its actions resonate for audiences around the world.

Close study of who controls the processes by which stories are told and retold, as well as how they are interpreted, challenged, and co-opted, is thus of central importance to social scientific and humanistic inquiry. In my introduction, I have pointed to a number of ways that the contributions to this volume demonstrate how detailed study of the production and reception of narratives forms an integral part of research on far-reaching social, cultural, and political questions. I have suggested that the authors provide us with insights into how we can explore discourse patterning without depoliticizing it and can study power and discourse without reifying them. I am thus pleased to bring my recontextualization of their words to an end and to present the reader with essays that offer both a rich range of perspectives and a fascinating set of narratives.

Notes

The essays published in this collection grew out of papers presented in a session entitled "Narrative Resources for the Creation of Order and Disorder," which took place under the auspices of the Annual Spring Meeting of the American Ethnological Society, held in St. Louis, Missouri, on March 25–26, 1988. I would like to thank the participants who are not represented in this volume: Alan Feldman, Robert Hayden, Keith T. Kernan, José Limón, and Brinkley Messick. These individuals, the contributors to this volume, and discussants W. Lance Bennett, John Comaroff, and Sally McLendon contributed to an extremely lively and productive exchange. Martha B. Kendall, past editor of *Anthropological Linguistics*, encouraged the initial publication of the papers, and Douglas Parks, the current editor, kindly granted permission to reprint the essays from *Anthropological Linguistics* (vol. 30, nos. 3 and 4, 1988). The interest and patience of series editor William Bright and our editor at Oxford University Press, Cynthia Read, are much appreciated. I acknowledge the support of a fellowship from the John Simon Guggenheim Memorial Foundation in providing me with the time necessary to bring this volume to completion.

1. The essay by Brenneis in this volume discusses the role of gossip in Fijian Indian disputing. See also Abrahams (1983), Besnier (1989), Brenneis (1984a), Briggs (1992a), Cox (1970), Gluckman (1963), and Haviland (1977).

2. See Anderson (1991 [1983]); for examples, see Bauman (1993), Bhabha (1990), Salas de Lecuna (1987), and Wilson (1976).

3. See Grimshaw's (1990) essays in *Conflict talk:* for commentary on why sociologists and other students of conflict have neglected the study of discourse. In a notable exception, anthropologist Victor Turner (1982) was long interested in the role of narrative in conflict, which he envisioned as a process of restoring cultural meaning and equilibrium.

4. See, for example, the contribution by Ochs, Smith, and Taylor to this volume as well as work by Brenneis and Lein (1977); Corsaro and Rizzo (1990); Goodwin (1990); Goodwin and Goodwin (1990); Maynard (1985); Ochs, Taylor, Rudolph, and Smith (1992); Schieffelin (1990); and Shuman (1986).

5. I discuss the relationship between narrated and narrative events in detail later in this introduction.

6. See Jones's (1986) study of women's writing in the Renaissance for an interesting example.

7. As Hanks (1990) suggests, however, the distribution of such deictics reflects more than simply spatiotemporal relations. See Silverstein (1976) for an in-depth treatment of indexes and their importance in language use.

8. Derrida (1974 [1967], 1978 [1967], 1985 [1982]) and others have criticized the philosophical implications of this ideology of language and thought. Such writers as Austin (1962), Grice (1957, 1989), Searle (1969, 1983), Sperber and Wilson (1988), and Strawson (1964) present theories of language that place much emphasis on intentionality. A great deal of recent work has criticized the theoretical and cross-cultural validity of Western notions of intentionality. See Du Bois (1992), Duranti (1992), Goodwin and Duranti (1992:16–19), Ochs (1984), Rosaldo (1982), and Silverstein (1979).

9. See Duranti and Brenneis (1986) for analyses of the nature and importance of co-narration and audience participation.

10. The terms *decentering* and *recentering* are used in Silverstein and Urban (1996). Note that new settings may include the reinsertion of stories at a later point in a conversation, or other discursive interaction, as illustrated in the essays by Briggs and by Ochs, Smith, and Taylor.

11. Silverstein (1993:48–53) provides a useful framework for analyzing the relationship between the event in which metapragmatic signs emerge and the events in which their objects of representation are situated, which he refers to as "pragmatic calibration." His discussion points to the broad range of linguistic features—including *verba dicendi,* deixis, tense, and poetic patterning—that can be used in creating various modes of pragmatic calibration.

12. As I noted previously, the *verba dicendi* and other aspects of the framing of reported speech also involve explicit metapragmatics. See Lucy (1993b).

13. This framework is described in greater detail in Briggs and Bauman (1992).

14. See Briggs (1993a) for an example of a personal narrative told by the Rev. Benjamin Chavis, in which he adopts all of these roles.

15. The distinction made by Mertz, as summarized earlier, between contrastive ways in which legal documents and plaintiffs' statements are reported in Supreme Court opinions is relevant here as well.

16. See Duranti's (1984, 1990) work on the Samoan *fono*, Keenan's [Ochs] (1973) early research on Malagasy oratory, and Sherzer's (1983) study of the Kuna "gathering-house" for other examples that point vividly to associations between the linear structuring of events and the creation of discursive and social hierarchies.

Works Cited

Abrahams, Roger. 1976. *Talking black*. Rowley, MA: Newbury House.

———. 1983. *The man-of-words in the West Indies: Performance and the emergence of creole culture*. Baltimore, MD: Johns Hopkins University Press.

Anderson, Benedict. 1991 [1983]. *Imagined communities: Reflections on the origin and spread of nationalism*. London: Verso.

Appadurai, Arjun. 1990. Disjuncture and difference in the global cultural economy. *Public Culture* 2:1–24.

Austin, John L. 1962. *How to do things with words*. Cambridge, MA: Harvard University Press.

Bakhtin, M. M. 1981. *The dialogic imagination: Four essays*. Austin: University of Texas Press.

———. 1986 [1979]. The problem of speech genres. In *Speech genres and other late essays*, ed. Caryl Emerson and Michael Holquist, pp. 60–102. Austin: University of Texas Press.

Bauman, Richard. 1972. Differential identity and the social base of folklore. In *Toward new directions in folklore*, ed. Américo Paredes and Richard Bauman, pp. 31–41. Austin: University of Texas Press.

———. 1986. *Story, performance, and event: Contextual studies of oral narrative*. Cambridge: Cambridge University Press.

———. 1992. Disclaimers of performance. In *Responsibility and evidence in oral discourse*, ed. Jane H. Hill and Judith R. Irvine, pp. 182–96. Cambridge: Cambridge University Press.

———. 1993. The nationalization and internationalization of folklore: The case of Schoolcraft's "Gitshee Gauzinee." *Western Folklore* 52:247–69.

Bauman, Richard, and Charles L. Briggs. 1990. Poetics and performance as critical perspectives on language and social life. *Annual Review of Anthropology* 19:59–88.

Bennett, W. Lance, and M. S. Feldman. 1981. *Reconstructing reality in the courtroom: Justice and judgment in American culture*. New Brunswick, NJ: Rutgers University Press.

Besnier, Niko. 1989. Information withholding as a manipulative and collusive strategy in Nukulaelae gossip. *Language in Society* 18:315–41.

———. 1993. Reported speech and affect on Nukulaelae Atoll. In *Responsibility and evidence in oral discourse*, ed. Jane H. Hill and Judith T. Irvine, pp. 161–81. Cambridge: Cambridge University Press.

Bhabha, Homi K., ed. 1990. *Nation and narration*. London: Routledge.

Bloch, Maurice. 1975. Introduction. In *Political language and oratory in traditional society*, ed. Maurice Bloch, pp. 1–28. New York: Academic Press.

Bourdieu, Pierre. 1977. *Outline of a theory of practice*, translated by Richard Nice. Cambridge: Cambridge University Press.

———. 1991. *Language and symbolic power*, translated by Gino Raymond and Matthew Adamson. Cambridge, MA: Harvard University Press.

Brenneis, Donald Lawrence. 1984a. Grog and gossip in Bhatgaon: Style and substance in Fiji Indian conversation. *American Ethnologist* 11:487–506.

———. 1984b. Straight talk and sweet talk: Political discourse in an occasionally egalitarian community. In *Dangerous words: Language and politics in the Pacific*, ed. Donald Lawrence Brenneis and Fred R. Myers, pp. 69–84. New York: New York University Press.

———. 1990. Dramatic gestures: The Fiji Indian *pancayat* as therapeutic event. In *Disentangling: Conflict discourse in Pacific societies*, ed. Karen Ann Watson-Gegeo and Geoffrey M. White, pp. 214–38. Stanford, CA: Stanford University Press.

Brenneis, Donald Lawrence, and Laura Lein. 1977. "You fruithead": A sociolinguistic approach to children's disputes. In *Child discourse*, ed. Susan Erin-Tripp and Claudia Mitchell-Kernan, pp. 49–66. New York: Academic Press.

Briggs, Charles L. 1988. *Competence in performance: The creativity of tradition in Mexicano verbal art*. Philadelphia: University of Pennsylvania Press.

———. 1992a. Linguistic ideologies and the naturalization of power in Warao discourse. *Pragmatics* 2(3):387–404.

———. 1992b. "Since I am a woman, I will chastise my relatives": Gender, reported speech, and the (re)production of social relations in Warao ritual wailing. *American Ethnologist* 19:337–61.

———. 1993a. "I'm not just talking to the victims of oppression tonight—I'm talking to everybody": Generic strategies in an African-American poetics of political engagement. *Journal of Narrative and Life History* 3:33–77.

———. 1993b. Metadiscursive practices and scholarly authority in folkloristics. *Journal of American Folklore* 106:387–434.

———. 1993c. Personal sentiments and polyphonic voices in Warao women's ritual wailing: Music and poetics in a critical and collective discourse. *American Anthropologist* 95:929–57.

Briggs, Charles L., and Richard Bauman. 1992. Genre, intertextuality, and social power. *Journal of Linguistic Anthropology* 2:131–72.

Briggs, Charles L., and Amy Shuman, eds. 1993. Theorizing folklore: Toward new perspectives on the politics of culture. *Western Folklore*, 52(2–4):109–400.

Chomsky, Noam. 1965. *Aspects of the theory of syntax*. Cambridge, MA: MIT Press.

Cicourel, Aaron V. 1982. Language and belief in a medical setting. In *Contemporary perceptions of language: Interdisciplinary dimensions*, ed. Heidi Byrnes, pp. 48–78. Washington, DC: Georgetown University Press.

———. 1992. The interpenetration of communicative contexts: Examples from medical encounters. In *Rethinking context: Language as an interactive phenomenon*, ed. Alessandro Duranti and Charles Goodwin, pp. 291–310. Cambridge: Cambridge University Press.

———. 1993. Aspects of structural and processual theories of knowledge. In, *Bourdieu:*

Critical perspectives, ed. Craig Calhoun, Edward LiPuma, and Moishe Postone, pp. 89–115. Chicago: University of Chicago Press.

Clifford, James. 1988. The predicament of culture: Twentieth-century ethnography, literature, and art. Cambridge, MA: Harvard University Press.

Clifford, James, and George E. Marcus, eds. 1986. *Writing culture: The poetics and politics of ethnography.* Berkeley, CA: University of California Press.

Coleman, James S. 1957. *Community conflict.* Glencoe, IL: The Free Press.

Comaroff, Jean, and John Comaroff. 1991. *Of revelation and revolution: Christianity, colonialism, and consciousness in South Africa,* vol. 1. Chicago: University of Chicago Press.

Comaroff, John L., and Simon Roberts. 1981. *Rules and processes: The cultural logic of dispute in an African context.* Chicago: University of Chicago Press.

Corsaro, William A., and Thomas A. Rizzo. 1990. Disputes in the peer culture of American and Italian nursery-school children. In *Conflict talk: Sociolinguistic investigations of arguments in conversation,* ed. Allen D. Grimshaw, pp. 21–66. Cambridge: Cambridge University Press.

Cox, B. A. 1970. What is Hopi gossip all about? Information management and Hopi factions. *Man* 5(n.s.):88–98.

Das, Veena. 1994. Moral orientations to suffering: Legitimation, power and healing. In *Health and social change in international perspective,* ed. Lincoln C. Chen, Arthur Kleinman, and Norma C. Ware, pp. 139–67. Boston: Department of Population and International Health, Harvard School of Public Health.

———. 1995. Suffering, legitimacy and healing: The Bhopal case. In Veena Das, *Critical events: An anthropological perspective on contemporary India,* pp. 137–74. Delhi: Oxford University Press.

Derrida, Jacques. 1974 [1967]. *Of grammatology,* translated by Gayatri Chakravorty Spivak. Baltimore, MD: Johns Hopkins University Press.

———. 1978 [1967]. *Writing and difference,* translated by Alan Bass. Chicago: University of Chicago Press.

———. 1985 [1982]. *The ear of the other: Otobiography, transference, translation,* ed. Claude Levesque and Christie McDonald, translated by Peggy Kamuf. Lincoln, NE: University of Nebraska Press.

Du Bois, John W. 1992. Meaning without intention: Lessons from divination. In *Responsibility and evidence in oral discourse,* ed. Jane H. Hill and Judith R. Irvine, pp. 48–71. Cambridge: Cambridge University Press.

Duranti, Alessandro. 1984. *Lauga* and *talanoaga:* Two speech genres in a Samoan political event. In *Dangerous words: Language and politics in the Pacific,* ed. Donald L. Brenneis and Fred R. Myers, pp. 217–42. New York: New York University Press.

———. 1990. Doing things with words: Conflict, understanding, and change in a Samoan fono. In *Disentangling: Conflict discourse in Pacific societies,* ed. Karen Ann Watson-Gegeo and Geoffrey M. White, pp. 459–89. Stanford, CA: Stanford University Press.

———. 1992. Intentions, self and responsibility: An essay in Samoan ethnopragmatics. In *Responsibility and evidence in oral discourse,* ed. Jane H. Hill and Judith R. Irvine, pp. 24–47. Cambridge: Cambridge University Press.

Duranti, Alessandro, and Donald Brenneis, eds. 1986. The audience as co-author. *Text* 6(3):239–347.

Eder, Donna. 1990. Serious and playful disputes: Variation in conflict talk among female adolescents. In *Conflict talk: Sociolinguistic investigations of arguments in conversations*, ed. Allen D. Grimshaw, pp. 67–84. Cambridge: Cambridge University Press.

Feld, Steven. 1990 [1982]. *Sound and sentiment: Birds, weeping, poetics, and song in Kaluli expression*, ed. 2. Philadelphia: University of Pennsylvania Press.

———. 1990. Wept thoughts: The voicing of Kaluli memories. *Oral Tradition* 5:241–66.

Foucault, Michel. 1965 [1961]. *Madness and civilization: A history of insanity in the age of reason*, translated by Richard Howard. New York: Random House.

———. 1972 [1969]. *The archaeology of knowledge*, translated by A. M. Sheridan Smith. New York: Harper and Row.

———. 1973 [1963]. *The birth of the clinic: An archaeology of medical perception*, translated by A. M. Sheridan Smith. New York: Random House.

———. 1977 [1975]. *Discipline and punish: The birth of the prison*, translated by Alan Sheridan. New York: Vintage.

———. 1980 [1972]. *Power/knowledge: Selected interviews and other writings, 1972–1977*, translated by Colin Gordon, Leo Marshall, John Mepham, and Kate Soper. New York: Pantheon.

Gal, Susan. 1989. Language and political economy. *Annual Review of Anthropology* 18:345–67.

———. 1991. Between speech and silence: The problematics of research on language and gender. In *Gender at the crossroads of knowledge: Feminist anthropology in the postmodern era*, ed. Micaela DiLeonardo, pp. 175–203. Berkeley: University of California Press.

Gluckman, M. 1963. Gossip and scandal. *Current Anthropology* 4:307–15.

Goffman, Erving. 1974. *Frame analysis*. New York: Harper and Row.

Goodwin, Charles. 1984. Notes on story structure and the organization of participation. In *Structures of social action*, ed. Max Atkinson and John Heritage, pp. 225–46. Cambridge: Cambridge University Press.

———. 1986. Audience diversity, participation, and interpretation. *Text* 6:283–316.

Goodwin, Charles, and Alessandro Duranti. 1992. Rethinking context: An introduction. In *Rethinking context: Language as an interactive phenomenon*, ed. Alessandro Duranti and Charles Goodwin, pp. 1–42. Cambridge: Cambridge University Press.

Goodwin, Charles, and Marjorie Harness Goodwin. 1990. Interstitial argument. In *Conflict talk: Sociolinguistic investigations of arguments in conversation*, ed. Allen D. Grimshaw, pp. 85–117. Cambridge: Cambridge University Press.

Goodwin, Marjorie Harness. 1990. *He-said-she-said: Talk as social organization among black children*. Bloomington: Indiana University Press.

Gramsci, Antonio. 1971. *Selections from the prison notebooks of Antonio Gramsci*. New York: International Publishers.

Grice, H. Paul. 1957. Meaning. *The Philosophical Review* 66:377–88.

————. 1989. Meaning revisited. In *Studies in the way of words*, pp. 283–303. Cambridge, MA: Harvard University Press.

Grimshaw, Allen D., ed. 1990. *Conflict talk: Sociolinguistic investigations of arguments in conversation*. Cambridge: Cambridge University Press.

Gumperz, John J. 1982. Discourse strategies. Cambridge: Cambridge University Press.

————. 1992. Contextualization and understanding. In *Rethinking context: Language as an interactive phenomenon*, ed. Alessandro Duranti and Charles Goodwin, pp. 230–52. Cambridge: Cambridge University Press.

Habermas, Jürgen. 1989 [1962]. The structural transformation of the public sphere: An inquiry into a category of bourgeois society, translated by Thomas Burger. Cambridge, MA: MIT Press.

Handler, Richard. 1988. *Nationalism and the politics of culture in Quebec*. Madison: University of Wisconsin Press.

Hanks, William F. 1990. *Referential practice: Language and lived space among the Maya*. Chicago: University of Chicago Press.

Haraway, Donna. 1992. Promises of monsters. In *Cultural studies*, ed. Lawrence Grossberg, Cary Nelson, and Paul Teichler, pp. 295–337. New York: Routledge.

Harding, Susan. 1975. Women and words in a Spanish village. In *Toward an anthropology of women*, ed. Rayna R. Reiter, pp. 283–308. New York: Monthly Review Press.

Haviland, John Beard. 1977. *Gossip, knowledge, and reputation in Zinacantan*. Chicago: University of Chicago Press.

Heath, Shirley Brice. 1983. *Ways with woras: Language, life and work in communities and classrooms*. Cambridge: Cambridge University Press.

Herzfeld, Michael. 1985. *The poetics of manhood: Contest and identity in a Cretan mountain village*. Princeton, NJ: Princeton University Press.

————. 1992. *The social production of indifference: Exploring the symbolic roots of Western bureaucracy*. Chicago: University of Chicago Press.

Hickmann, Maya. 1993. The boundaries of reported speech in narrative discourse: Some developmental aspects. In *Reflexive language: Reported speech and metapragmatics*, ed. John A. Lucy, pp. 63–90. Cambridge: Cambridge Univesity Press.

Hill, Jane H., and Judith T. Irvine, eds. 1992. *Responsibility and evidence in oral discourse*. Cambridge: Cambridge University Press.

Hill, Jane H., and Ofelia Zepeda. 1992. Mrs. Patricio's trouble: The distribution of responsibility in an account of personal experience. In *Responsibility and evidence in oral discourse*, ed. Jane H. Hill and Judith T. Irvine, pp. 197–225. Cambridge: Cambridge University Press.

Hobsbawm, Eric, and Terence Ranger, eds. 1983. *The invention of tradition*. Cambridge: Cambridge University Press.

Hopper, Paul. 1979. Aspect and foregrounding in discourse. In *Discourse and syntax*, ed. Talmy Givón, pp. 213–60. *Syntax and semantics*, vol. 12. New York: Academic Press.

————. 1982. Aspect between discourse and grammar: An introductory essay for the volume. In *Tense-aspect: Between semantics and pragmatics*, ed. Paul Hopper, pp. 3–18. Amsterdam: John Benjamins.

Hymes, Dell H. 1981. *"In vain I tried to tell you": Essays in Native American ethnopoetics*. Philadelphia: University of Pennsylvania Press.

Irvine, Judith T. 1979. Formality and informality in communicative events. *American Anthropologist* 81:773–90.

——. 1989. When talk isn't cheap: Language and political economy. *American Ethnologist* 16:248–67.

Jakobson, Roman. 1960. Closing statement: Linguistics and poetics. In *Style in language*, ed. Thomas A. Sebeok, pp. 350–77. Cambridge, MA: MIT Press.

——. 1971 [1957]. Shifters, verbal categories, and the Russian verb. In *Roman Jakobson: Selected writings*, vol. 2, pp. 130–47. The Hague: Mouton.

Jameson, Fredric. 1981. *The political unconscious: Narrative as a socially symbolic act.* Ithaca, NY: Cornell University Press.

Jones, Ann Rosalind. 1986. Surprising fame: Renaissance gender ideologies and women's lyric. In *The poetics of gender*, ed. Nancy K. Miller, pp. 96–116. New York: Columbia University Press.

Joseph, John E., and Talbot J. Taylor, eds. 1990. *Ideologies of language.* London: Routledge.

Kapferer, Bruce. 1988. *Legends of people, myths of state: Violence, intolerance, and political culture in Sri Lanka and Australia.* Washington, DC: Smithsonian Institution Press.

Kaplan, Martha, and John D. Kelly. 1994. Rethinking resistance: Dialogics of "disaffection" in colonial Fiji. *American Ethnologist* 21:122–51.

Keenan [Ochs], Elinor. 1973. A sliding sense of obligatoriness: The polystructure of Malagasy oratory. *Language in Society* 2:225–43.

Kristeva, Julia. 1980. *Desire in language*, translated by Leon S. Roudiez. New York: Columbia University Press.

Kroskrity, Paul, Bambi Schieffelin, and Kathryn Woolard, eds. 1992. Language ideologies (special issue). *Pragmatics* 2(3):235–453.

Labov, William. 1972a. *Language in the inner city: Studies in the Black English vernacular.* Philadelphia: University of Pennsylvania Press.

——. 1972b. *Sociolinguistic patterns.* Philadelphia: University of Pennsylvania Press.

——. 1982. Speech actions and reactions in personal narrative. In *Analyzing discourse: text and talk*, ed. Deborah Tannen, pp. 219–47. Washington, DC: Georgetown University Press.

Labov, William, and Joshua Waletzky. 1967. Narrative analysis. In *Essays on the verbal and visual arts*, ed. June Helm, pp. 12–44. Seattle: University of Washington Press.

Lacan, Jacques. 1977 [1966]. *Écrits: A selection*, translated by Alan Sheridan. New York: W. W. Norton.

Lucy, John. 1993a. Metapragmatic presentations: Reporting speech with quotatives in Yucatec Maya. In *Reflexive language: Reported speech and metapragmatics*, ed. John A. Lucy, pp. 127–57. Cambridge: Cambridge University Press.

——. 1993b. Reflexive language and the human disciplines. In *Reflexive language: Reported speech and metapragmatics*, ed. John A. Lucy, pp. 9–32. Cambridge: Cambridge University Press.

——, ed. 1993c. *Reflexive language: Reported speech and metapragmatics.* Cambridge: Cambridge University Press.

Maynard, Douglas W. 1985. On the functions of social conflict among children. *American Sociological Review* 50:207–23.

————. 1986. Offering and soliciting collaboration in multi-party disputes among children (and other humans). *Human Studies* 9:261–85.

Medvedev, P. M. 1985 [1928]. *The formal method in literary scholarship: A critical introduction to sociological poetics*, translated by Albert J. Wehrle. Cambridge, MA: Harvard University Press.

Mishler, Elliot G. 1984. *The discourse of medicine: Dialectics of medical interviews.* Norwood, NJ: Ablex.

Moore, Robert E. 1993. Performance form and the voices of characters in five versions of the Wasco coyote cycle. In *Reflexive language: Reported speech and metapragmatics,* ed. John A. Lucy, pp. 213–40. Cambridge: Cambridge University Press.

Myers, Fred R. 1986. Reflections on a meeting: Structure, language, and the polity in a small-scale society. *American Ethnologist* 13:430–47.

Myers, Fred R., and Donald Lawrence Brenneis. 1984. Introduction: Language and politics in the Pacific. In *Dangerous words: Language and politics in the Pacific,* ed. Donald Lawrence Brenneis and Fred R. Myers, pp. 1–29. New York: New York University Press.

Ochs, Elinor. 1984. Clarification and culture. In *Meaning, form, and use in context: Linguistic applications. Georgetown University round table on languages and linguistics 1984,* ed. Deborah Schiffrin, pp. 325–41. Washington, DC: Georgetown University Press.

————. 1992. Indexing gender. In *Rethinking context: Language as an interactive phenomenon,* ed. Alessandro Duranti and Charles Goodwin, pp. 335–58. Cambridge: Cambridge University Press.

Ochs, Elinor, and Carolyn Taylor. 1992. Family narrative as political activity. *Discourse and Society* 3:301–40.

Ochs, Elinor, Carolyn Taylor, Dina Rudolph, and Ruth Smith. 1992. Storytelling as a theory-building activity. *Discourse Processes* 15:37–72.

Paredes, Américo. 1968. Folk medicine and the intercultural jest. In *Spanish speaking people in the United States: Proceedings of the 1968 annual spring meeting of the American Ethnological Society,* ed. June Helm, pp. 104–19. Seattle: University of Washington Press.

————. 1993. *Folklore and culture on the Texas Mexican border,* ed. Richard Bauman. Austin, TX: Center for Mexican American Studies.

Peirce, Charles Sanders. 1932. *Elements of logic, Collected papers of Charles Sanders Peirce,* vol. II, ed. C. Hartshorne and P. Weiss. Cambridge, MA: Harvard University Press.

Parmentier, Richard J. 1987. *The sacred remains: Myth, history, and polity in Belau.* Chicago: University of Chicago Press.

————. 1993. The political function of reported speech: A Belauan example. In *Reflexive language: Reported speech and metapragmatics,* ed. John A. Lucy, pp. 261–86. Cambridge: Cambridge University Press.

Radner, Joan N., and Susan S. Lanser. 1993. Strategies of coding in women's cultures. In *Feminist messages: Coding in women's folk culture,* ed. Joan Newlon Radner, pp. 1–29. Urbana: University of Illinois Press.

Ritchie, Susan. 1993. Ventriloquist folklore: Who speaks for representation? *Western Folklore* 52:365–78.

Rosaldo, Michelle. 1982. The things we do with words: Ilongot speech acts and speech act theory in philosophy. *Language in Society* 11:203–37.

Sacks, Harvey. 1972. On the analyzability of stories by children. In *Directions in sociolinguistics: The ethnography of communication*, ed. John J. Gumperz and Dell Hymes, pp. 325–45. New York: Holt, Rinehart and Winston.

———. 1992. *Lectures on conversation*, vols. 1 and 2, ed. Gail Jefferson. Oxford: Blackwell.

Said, Edward W. 1978. *Orientalism*. New York: Vintage/Random House.

———. 1989. Representing the colonized: Anthropology's interlocutors. *Critical Inquiry* 15:205–25.

Salas de Lecuna, Yolanda. 1987. *Bolívar y la historia en la consciencia popular*. Caracas: Instituto de Altos Estudios de América Latina, Universidad Simon Bolivar.

Sapir, Edward. 1921. *Language: An introduction to the study of speech*. New York: Harcourt, Brace and World.

Saussure, Ferdinand de. 1959 [1916]. *A course in general linguistics*, ed. C. Bally and A. Schehaye, translated by Wade Baskin. New York: McGraw-Hill.

Schieffelin, Bambi B. 1990. *The give and take of everyday life: Language socialization of Kaluli children*. New York: Cambridge University Press.

Schiffrin, Deborah. 1984. Jewish argument as sociability. *Language in Society* 13:311–35.

———. 1990. The management of a co-operative self during argument: The role of opinions and stories. In *Conflict talk: Sociolinguistic investigations of arguments in conversation*, ed. Allen D. Grimshaw, pp. 241–59. Cambridge: Cambridge University Press.

Scott, James C. 1985. *Weapons of the weak: Everyday forms of peasant resistance*. New Haven, CT: Yale University Press.

———. 1990. *Domination and the arts of resistance: Hidden transcripts*. New Haven, CT: Yale University Press.

Searle, John. 1969. *Speech acts: An essay in the philosophy of language*. Cambridge: Cambridge University Press.

———. 1983. *Intentionality: An essay in the philosophy of mind*. Cambridge: Cambridge University Press.

Seremetakis, C. Nadia. 1991. *The last word: Women, death, and divination in Inner Mani*. Chicago: University of Chicago Press.

Sherzer, Joel. 1983. *Kuna ways of speaking*. Austin: University of Texas Press.

Shuman, Amy. 1986. *Storytelling rights: The uses of oral and written texts by urban adolescents*. Cambridge: Cambridge University Press.

Silverstein, Michael. 1976. Shifters, linguistic categories, and cultural description. In *Meaning in anthropology*, ed. Keith Basso and Henry A. Selby, pp. 11–55. Albuquerque: University of New Mexico Press.

———. 1979. Language structure and linguistic ideology. In *The elements: A parasession on linguistic units and levels*, ed. Paul R. Clyne, William F. Hanks, and Carol L. Hofbauer, pp. 193–247. Chicago: Chicago Linguistic Society.

———. 1985. The culture of language in Chinookan narrative texts; or, On saying that . . . in Chinook. In *Grammar inside and outside the clause*, ed. Johanna Nichols and Anthony C. Woodbury, pp. 132–77. Cambridge: Cambridge University Press.

———. 1993. Metapragmatic discourse and metapragmatic function. In *Reflexive language:*

Reported speech and metapragmatics, ed. John A. Lucy, pp. 33–58. Cambridge: Cambridge University Press.

Silverstein, Michael, and Greg Urban, eds. 1996. *Natural histories of discourse.* Chicago: University of Chicago Press.

Simmel, Georg. 1955 [1908]. Conflict. In *Conflict/The web of group-affiliations.* New York: Free Press.

Sperber, Dan, and Deirdre Wilson. 1988. *Relevance: Communication and cognition.* Cambridge, MA: Harvard University Press.

Stewart, Susan. 1991. *Crimes of writing: Problems in the containment of representation.* New York: Oxford University Press.

Strawson, P. F. 1964. Intention and convention in speech acts. *Philosophical Review* 73:439–60.

Taussig, Michael. 1992. *The nervous system.* New York: Routledge.

Tedlock, Dennis. 1983. *The spoken word and the work of interpretation.* Philadelphia: University of Pennsylvania Press.

Turner, Victor. 1982. Social dramas and stories about them. In *From ritual to theatre: The human seriousness of play*, by Victor Turner, pp. 61–88. New York: PAJ Publications.

Urban, Greg. 1984. Speech about speech in speech about action. *Journal of American Folklore* 97:310–28.

———. 1988. Ritual wailing in Amerindian Brazil. *American Anthropologist* 90:385–400.

———. 1991. *A discourse-centered approach to culture: Native South American myths and rituals.* Austin: University of Texas Press.

———. 1993. The represented functions of speech in Shokleng myth. In *Reflexive language: Reported speech and metapragmatics*, ed. John A. Lucy, pp. 241–59. Cambridge: Cambridge University Press.

Vološinov, V. N. 1973 [1930]. *Marxism and the philosophy of language*, translated by Ladislav Matejka and I. R. Titunik. New York: Seminar Press.

Vuchinich, Samuel. 1990. The sequential organization of closing in verbal family conflict. In *Conflict talk: Sociolinguistic investigations of arguments in conversation*, ed. Allen D. Grimshaw, pp. 118–38. Cambridge: Cambridge University Press.

Wallace, Stephen. 1982. Figure and ground: The interrelations of linguistic categories. In *Tense-aspect: Between semantics and pragmatics*, ed. Paul Hopper, pp. 201–23. Amsterdam: John Benjamins.

Watson-Gegeo, Karen Ann, and Geoffrey M. White, eds. 1990. *Disentangling: Conflict discourse in Pacific societies.* Stanford, CA: Stanford University Press.

Williams, Raymond. 1977. *Marxism and literature.* London: Oxford University Press.

Wilson, William A. 1976. Folklore and nationalism in modern Finland. Bloomington: Indiana University Press.

Woolard, Kathryn A. 1985. Language variation and cultural hegemony: Toward an integration of sociolinguistic and social theory. *American Ethnologist* 12:738–48.

Woolard, Kathryn A., and Bambi B. Schieffelin. 1994. Language ideology. *Annual Review of Anthropology* 23:55–82.

Young, Katherine Galloway. 1987. *Taleworlds and storyrealms: The phenomenology of narrative.* Dordrecht: Martinus Nijhoff.

Telling Troubles
Narrative, Conflict, and Experience

My recent participation on a college-wide personnel committee raised several critical questions for me concerning narratives. We were hiring for a position in economics, and my role included listening to "job-talks" by five candidates. Economics job-talks share remarkably consistent generic characteristics. A formula phrased in numbers, mathematical symbols, and Greek letters emerges slowly on the blackboard. Each letter represents a "proxy," that is, a measure standing in for a broader range of related variables. The formula indicates proposed relationships among these factors with an eye, ultimately, to predicting behavior. The formula drives the talk. Speakers invariably follow a completed formula with the same framing device, a rhetorical question in the strict sense: "Okay, what story does this tell us?" Such formulas—abstract and curiously achronic models of complex covariation—never told me a story. They did, however, speak compellingly to more knowledgeable members of the audience, who would often leap in with their own versions, challenging and correcting the candidates.

Apart from the striking notions of appropriate audience behavior characteristic of these events, such job-talks illuminate a range of questions central to an understanding of narrative. What must we take into account when we consider "stories"? Where can the narrative be found? Is it found in an abstract underlying set of relations, similar to that proposed by such structuralists as Chatman (1978), or is it found in the circumstances of a particular telling? Does meaning reside in an autonomous "story," in the intentions of the teller, or in whatever members of the audience choose to make of it? Further questions have to do with the nature and adequacy of narrative representation, that is, the relation between such elements as the economists' proxies and those assumed external realities that they are taken to encode. Finally, whose story is it to tell? When multiple voices, whether cooperative or contending, are heard, authorship, authority, and the right to speak are under active negotiation.

These questions are highlighted and therefore all the more compelling when we consider the various roles of narrative in generating and helping to manage social conflict. In this essay, I will suggest a range of issues critical to such a consideration, issues that also are relevant to some of the other essays in this book. I will then turn briefly to ethnographic data from the Fiji Indian community of Bhatgaon, examining two quite different kinds of narrative performance central to the course and management of conflict in the village. These two genres—*talanoa* 'gossip' and the *pancayat* 'mediation session'—both enable the telling of troubling stories, albeit through significantly different means and with very different consequences for participants. Finally, I will explore some of the ways in which these narrative events are effective, that is, how they both engender personal experience and construct particular social realities.

A first general point about conflict narrative is that it is difficult to sustain the premise that there can be narratives independent of the situations in which they are told. The content and conduct of conflict narratives are linked through the circumstances of a particular telling, and they are further intertwined with a particular web of narrator, audience, purposes, and expectations. Motives are usually patent rather than covert, and audiences are often clearly partisan.

Bauman's observations on the doubly anchored character of narratives are particularly relevant to conflict stories: "Narratives are keyed both to the events in which they are told and to the events that they recount, toward narrative events and narrated events" (1986:2; see also Jakobson 1971). Stories both draw upon experience and engender it. As stories about narrated events, conflict narratives raise critical questions of representation. What kinds of correspondence between texts and "the world" are possible, and how—and in response to what concerns—are they shaped? Over the course of a conflict, particular alleged events are represented and re-represented in various ways, reflecting different speakers, audiences, and goals. When a narrative is embedded in an ongoing conflict, analysts are unlikely to assume a one-to-one relationship between accounts and the events they are taken to portray. Nowhere is it more likely that there will be at least two sides to every story, neither of which can be taken as objective. The indeterminacy inherent in narrative representation may not be immediately evident in many contexts, but it cannot be avoided in cases of conflict.

Participants often speculate about events with which they are only partially familiar, in both senses of the word. They tell stories of what might have happened. Such speculative fictions provide insights into local views of character, motive, and logic. Furthermore, such stories are not always intended to provide clarity; they may also be instruments for "obscuring, hedging, confusing, exploring or questioning what went on, that is, for keeping the coherence and comprehensibility of narrated events open to question" (Bauman 1986:5–6). Finally, conflicts often prompt scenarios, that is, narratives concerning the possible future implications of particular courses of action. These are stories for which there are no antecedent "narrated events."

Conflict is a process, not a state. Disputes have beginnings, middles, and, occasionally, ends, or at least resting places. Narratives are used to stir up trouble, to further one's particular goals, and to help draw the dispute to a close. At each particular juncture, very different stories may be told, in very different ways and with very different implications. The processual perspective, so necessary in social anthropological studies of conflict, is equally important for a consideration of conflict-related narratives. Attention to intertextuality, that is, to relations between the different stories, is essential.

Over the course of a dispute, one narrative or another often assumes an authoritative role. In more or less standardized form it may be taken as a binding or reference account. Other contending stories are subsequently shaped and evaluated in terms of these valorized versions. How and through whose efforts such authoritative accounts are accomplished and the ways in which they constrain or frame subsequent discussion are critical variables in the politics of narration.

Turning to the narrative event, that is, to the occasion in which a particular story is told, other features of conflict-related narratives are evident. First, the taken-for-granted view that narratives are produced by single speakers or authors—an assumption central to many approaches to the genre—cannot be sustained here. In most of the cases discussed in this volume, the focus is on processes of co-narration, not individuals telling individual stories but rather people telling stories together. These are tales that emerge from a multitude of tellers, with a range of quite different relationships—cooperative, adversarial, negotiating—among tellers. As Briggs points out in his introduction to this volume, conflict narratives clearly represent a welter of contending voices and stories in the Bakhtinian sense. Such narratives also involve multivocality quite literally; the negotiation of co-narration and the privileging of one particular account over others are central to their tellings.

Such narrative events also have very complicated audiences—those present, those likely to hear the story in the future, and those waiting in the wings with barbed rejoinders or contradictory accounts. These audiences are more than targets. Although from a speaker's point of view they offer different constraints and incentives, they also make of the story what they will, interpreting and editing, attributing intentions and degrees of veracity, and acting in response to their own active hearings. A comprehensive account of conflict-related narratives must consider both the general local theories and understandings that inform such responses and the more individual opinions and interests guiding their application.

A final aspect of such conflict-related narratives is the question of entitlement: Whose story is it, and who has the right to tell it? These are particularly important questions given the multiple authorship of most conflict narratives. As Amy Shuman argues in her study of junior high school girls' narratives (1986), the relationship between one's personal experience and those stories that it might engender often figures critically in disputes. Unentitled narrators telling one's "own" story stir up considerable trouble. Over the course of a particular dispute, such entitlement may well be transformed. As authoritative accounts emerge, they often become more widely tellable. One's own story may become everyone's property or available only to particular privileged groups. In any case, entitlement and its transformation in conflict are entangled with power relationships within the particular community (see Shuman n.d.).

In the following section I will contrast briefly two types of narrative events closely linked to the course of conflict in Bhatgaon, a rural Fiji Indian community. The striking differences between these performance genres—gossip and mediation discourse—demonstrate the dangers of generalizing about conflict-related narratives. They also suggest ways in which patterns of conflict narrative reflect broader features of social life. I then turn to the question of the effectiveness of such narrative discourse. Why might we find such stories compelling, to what extent do they serve to constitute ongoing social realities, and how are such effects accomplished?

Conflict-Related Narratives in Bhatgaon

Among Bhatgaon males, an overt egalitarian ideology prevails. The roots of this outlook lie in the historical conditions of immigration and indenture and in the continuing relative similarity in wealth throughout the village. As one villager said, *"Gaon me sab barabba hei"* 'in the village all are equal.' It is, however, a rather tender and limited egalitarianism. First, not every villager is a potential equal. Women and adolescent males are not considered to have the same social stature as men. A second problematic aspect is the delicate balance between people who should be equals. Individual autonomy is highly prized; equals are those who respect each other's freedom of action. Obtrusive attempts to influence the opinions or actions of another violate this equality. The overt exercise of influence or informal authority leads rapidly to its decline. A consequent reluctance to intervene in the affairs of others has shaped patterns of conflict management in which most disputants are left to their own devices. Only in those cases seen as particularly consequential for the larger community are third parties willing to take a role, and then only in particularly guarded ways, such as through the *pancayat*. Avoidance remains the most frequent means of managing conflict in Bhatgaon. Finally, individual reputation is central to one's social standing. A man's *nam* 'name' or 'reputation' is subject to constant renegotiation through his own words and deeds and through those of others. In conflict, one's good name is particularly vulnerable; the stories that others tell directly threaten one's place as an equal.

These broader features of Bhatgaon social life—particularly the reluctance of third parties and the susceptibility of reputation—have directly informed the two varieties of conflict narratives I will consider here. One genre—*talanoa,* a loan word from Fijian that I translate as 'gossip'—figures almost inevitably in any village dispute. *Talanoa* provides a useful forum for toying with the reputations of others, as well as a unique opportunity for intimate sociability. The other genre, *pancayat* testimony, is the discourse of public mediation sessions, one of the few forms of third-party intervention in village disputes. Although infrequent, such events are seen as critical in the resolution of serious disputes, that is, those involving allegations of immoral behavior on the part of usually well-regarded village men.

Talanoa and *pancayat* discourse share one critical feature. They both require co-narration; one cannot tell the story by oneself. How such co-narration is effected, however, is quite different in the two cases. The underlying form of *pancayat* discourse is question and answer pairs (for a more detailed account, see Brenneis 1983, 1984a). The committee that has called the session asks questions; various witnesses respond under oath. In contrast to an American trial, this questioning is not adversarial because the committee is putatively neutral. Turn-taking rules are strictly observed. Although the event as a whole is multivocal, only one person speaks at a time.

In *talanoa* sessions, discourse is characterized by frequent overlap and simultaneous speech (for a more detailed account, see Brenneis 1984b). In contrast to the decorous and stately pace of *pancayat*s, *talanoa* talk is quick, raucous, and often characterized by short, metrically fairly regular chunks. This rhythmic quality provides entry points for new speakers and gives an ongoing pulse to the event as a whole. There are two or more speakers, but a satisfying *talanoa* session is stylistically very well integrated. Narratives are accomplished through the concatenation of known detail and speculation; each participant contributes in a chain of bits and pieces.

The topics of *pancayat* and *talanoa* may be similar, but the kinds of stories told vary considerably. *Pancayat* testimony is carefully confined to the details of one particular alleged incident. Witnesses are interviewed and their accounts compared and checked before the sessions so that only appropriate questions will be asked. What emerges in the session is an explicit, coherent, and internally consistent account of the disputed event. Such accounts usually exculpate the accused, while providing a credible explanation of how the misunderstanding might have come to pass. The committee is concerned with what is to be taken as "fact," not with evaluation or interpretation. *Pancayats* end with the last witness's testimony, not with an overt summary or decisions. Participants are left to draw their own conclusions, but they are carefully guided by the ways in which information has been presented.

Talanoa, on the other hand, involves far-ranging, if at times oblique, discussions of unseemly events, possible motives, and likely character flaws. Although they are clearly interested in learning more, gossipers also appreciate the chance to censure others with relative impunity and to enjoy an artful complicity with their co-narrators. *Pancayat* discourse is much more *about* events than is gossip. In *talanoa* the pleasures of somewhat scurrilous talk seem more important than its topic.

The characteristics of participants and audiences in the two kinds of events are a third area of difference. They do share one element: both are primarily adult male activities. In the case of the *pancayat,* only immediately involved parties, carefully prepared witnesses, and the organizing committee are present. It is expected, how-ever, that the entire religious group and, beyond that, everyone in the village, will quickly learn what has been said. *Pancayat* narratives are intended for the broadest possible audience, in large part because the stories they tell leave no one in too bad a light. Both individual reputations and, by implication, the reputation of the commu-nity are preserved. These cooperatively produced narratives further establish privi-leged and binding accounts of events in terms of which the subsequent behavior of all concerned may be evaluated.

The participants in gossip sessions are adult male intimates. They are allies, but often they are not partisans in the conflict that they are discussing, which is critical. One does not usually gossip about one's own case; gossipers are usually third parties who are critical of all the interested parties. The accused, whether implicitly or directly identified, is not present. In *talanoa,* the critical audience is provided by coparticipants in the gossip event itself. There is, however, always a secondary audience, that is, those who will seek revenge if they learn about the *talanoa.*

One of the criterial elements of *talanoa* sessions is that there is absolutely no entitlement to the stories whatsoever. Not having the right to tell the story makes it *talanoa.* Other villagers will happily suggest motives that might underlie the gossip. Similarly, when one is talking privately about his own experiences, others will pay careful attention to his possible intentions. The speaker is always recognized and questions of motive are taken into account in such private narratives, whether one is entitled to tell them or not.

In the *pancayat,* on the other hand, entitlement is transformed. No longer does a collection of private stories circulate more or less surreptitiously throughout the village. It has been replaced by a publicly owned story, an account that is taken as factual and retellable by all. Furthermore, a *pancayat* story has no apparent author. Not only does everyone have a right to tell the story, but it is no longer any one individual's story because it has become everyone's, jointly authored and broadly accessible. As such, the story is taken as objective and unmotivated, not inflected by personal interest or bias.

One of the goals of gossip is to have a good time. People enjoy *talanoa;* the combination of lively interaction and pleasure at someone else's expense is quite satisfying, even if it is publicly decried as worthless. For some gossipers, there is also the notion of bringing the conflict into the public arena, of making other villagers aware of potentially troublesome situations. In Bhatgaon, where most conflicts are left to the immediate disputants themselves, such public attention is often necessary if the dispute is to be resolved.

In discussing *pancayat* mediation, villagers quite explicitly stress the goal of letting a coherent and amenable account of disputed facts emerge, one through which troubled relationships can be worked out. Such accounts must suit everyone involved; all the parties are shown to have made some minor mistakes, but no one is seriously in error. Marked as they are by no conclusions or explicit evaluation, *pancayat* stories literally are made to appear to speak for themselves.

Finally, the implications and effects of *talanoa* and *pancayat* discourse are quite different. Gossip sessions are considered wild and worthless by both the people who engage in them and others. In many ways they are seen as the re-creation of other people's disorderliness. The processes by which that re-creation is accomplished, however, involve two or more men in a trusting and intimate sociability; gossip is fun. The story cannot be publicly retold; it is neither licit nor taken as "factual." The narrating event itself, however, serves as a bond holding people together in a kind of friendship often difficult to achieve in the perilously flexible social world of Bhatgaon.

In a *pancayat,* on the other hand, the implications are supposed to flow *naturally* from an emergent text. The narrated event—that account co-produced in an orderly and authoritative manner by disputants and third parties—is taken as true and useful. No one speaks for what the implications, moral or otherwise, might be, although the account presented leaves few real options; the record has been set straight. Beyond this, the decorous style and seriousness of the telling shape a shared experience of public amity, one in which individual concerns are downplayed and a sense of common purpose and interest is made possible (Brenneis 1990).

Narrative Realities

An underlying question in looking at conflict-related narratives is, quite simply, whether or not they make a difference. Are they effective in shaping both the future course of the conflict and the broader contours of social life? My intention in this final section is to argue that such stories—and such joint storytelling practices—are indeed consequential. Narratives are not epiphenomenal reflexes of sociopolitical relations, solely mirroring apparently real action going on elsewhere. Rather, they constitute both important opportunities for and means of carrying out such action. I would like to suggest four areas in which dispute narratives help effect and transform social realities.

First, disputing narratives often serve to constitute knowledge; they create for us the narrated event. Bauman has argued that "events are not the external raw materials out of which narratives are constructed, but rather the reverse. Events are abstractions from narratives" (1986:5). As Sudnow's (1965) classic study of "normal crimes" for charge reduction in plea bargaining demonstrated, categorizing and labeling practice—and the narratives that they implicate—create new, consequential, and at times obviously fabricated types of knowledge. One way of characterizing adversarial modes of conflict management is in terms of rival narratives of how particular events came to take place; each side tries through a variety of linguistic and rhetorical means to present a more coherent and compelling account. Bennett and Feldman's monograph on such contending narratives in American courts focuses on what they term the "reconstruction of reality" (1981), but one could argue that a quite consequential reality is indeed being constructed for the first time. In nonadversarial events as well, the sometimes cooperative construction of binding accounts of past events is a critical function of many conflict narratives—as in the *pancayat*. The relationship between such new knowledge and some externally verifiable reality is usually of secondary importance; the fact of having arrived at these accounts and their likely impact on the future course of events are considerably more salient.

The importance of such narrated events in defining new realities is of course not limited to conflict; Goodman has suggested, for example, that a scientific law represents "the nearest amenable and illuminating lie" (1978:121). A number of recent studies, however, clearly demonstrate the remarkable salience of such fact making in legal and other conflict situations (see, for example, Bennett and Feldman 1981; Brenneis 1983; Geertz 1985; Goldman 1986; Just 1986; Strathern 1974; Sudnow 1965).

A second way in which conflict-related narratives work constitutively has to do with the relationship between this produced knowledge and its creators, audiences, and subjects. The two critical elements here are entitlement and authorship. One recurrent feature of the role of narratives over the course of a dispute is a transformation of entitlement to the experiences being represented. Privately held stories become more or less public; one's sole right to recount one's own activities or grievances is often lost. As long as only the disputing parties are considered entitled to tell their own stories, illicit uses such as gossip—while pleasurable—may become the topics of appropriately censorious narratives. When others gain legitimate access to such stories, however, personal experience becomes public record, serving as explanatory information, moral example, or informal precedent. As such, these tales redefine one's relationship to others and one's moral and political stature.

Authorship—the notion of who is considered responsible for the narrative—may also shift over the course of a dispute. A clear example is the shift in Bhatgaon from *talanoa*, where individual participants are assumed to be playing out their own agendas, to *pancayat* testimony, where a jointly performed, public account not linked to personal goals "emerges." In other societies where issues of autonomy and equality are not as salient as in Bhatgaon, particular individuals' stories may well be taken as authoritative while others' stories are rejected or simply not heard. The consideration of cross-cultural variations in the attribution of authorship, intention, and "veracity" can provide an instructive perspective on the articulation of power and discourse.

These two ways in which conflict-related narratives serve constitutive roles have to do with what the stories are about, that is, with narrated events. Such stories help participants define, clarify, and comprehend troubled relationships and troubling events. The privileging of one account over others, attributions of authorship, and shifts in rights to tell the story all shape and politically inflect this ongoing interpretive process. Narration is not solely referential, however; it does more than help us make sense of conflict. In the telling, that is, in narrative events, it also engenders and transforms social experience.

If "events are abstractions from narrative" (Bauman 1986:5), one way of viewing narrative events is as particularly concrete and clearly framed instances of interaction. Telling a story is an inherently social activity, one in which, as Maynard (1985) suggests in his study of children's arguments, discourse produces local social organization (see also Goodwin 1980, 1982). Individuals do not simply fit into clusters of a priori roles when they relate as speaker and hearer or (particularly significant in the case of conflict narratives) when they relate as co-performers. These relations rather derive from complex interactions between antecedent conditions and organizational features of the narrating events themselves.

On a somewhat different but complementary tack, a range of recent studies argue that, for a number of relatively egalitarian Pacific communities at least, "society" above the level of the coresident family is instantiated only through shared participation in various speech events (Brenneis 1984a; Brenneis and Myers 1991; Myers 1986; Myers and Brenneis 1984). The apparent outcome of such an event does not matter as much as the fact that the event occurs at all. Although a range of discourse types might help structure such occasions, it is clear that narrating is often the focal activity. Schwartzman's (1984, 1987) accounts of how "meetings" and "stories" define an American mental health center provide strong evidence that the socially constitutive role of narrative events is as evident in complex institutions as it is in small-scale societies.

Finally, it is critical to consider the ways in which such narration might catalyze personal experience. How do participants feel as they tell or listen to such stories? What elements might contribute to a sense of pleasure, anger, amusement, or injustice? Just as conflict narratives are not solely about disputes, it is unlikely that they serve solely instrumental ends. As Spacks has suggested for gossip, "pleasure is the activity's primary value . . . it unites the sweet and the useful" (1983:159). What satisfactions do various kinds of narrative events offer?

Answering such questions about experience is difficult. Sentiments are not as easily assumed as political motives, particularly when working in another culture; we generally feel on safer ground with calculations than with feelings. One increasingly apparent finding in ethnopsychological research is the recognition that a relational dimension is often critical in local emotion theories (see, for example, Abu-Lughod 1985, 1990; Brenneis 1987; Myers 1979). "Feelings" often provide a social rather than an individual idiom, a way of commenting not so much on one's internal state as on oneself in relation to others. As Lutz (1982:113) suggests for the Pacific, "emotion words . . . [are] statements about the relationship between a person and an event." Although she is writing only of Oceania, attention to those features of events linked to particular emotions may prove useful in gaining access to "experience" in a much wider range of cultures.

The usual formal and interactional features of various kinds of co-narration are often conventionally associated with particular sentiments. In Bhatgaon, for example, the raucous tone and fast pace of *talanoa* are considered definitive elements of having "fun"; *pancayats,* with their decorous and orderly organization, are taken as prime instances of public amity. The intense and intimate co-performance of fellow gossipers both enacts a particular social relationship and allows for the experience of slightly culpable pleasure. Similarly, the *pancayat* embodies a mutually respectful sociability rarely possible at other times in village life.

Although the Bhatgaon situation is clearly singular in its details, its general implication—that narrative events not only create local social organization but may also engender specific culturally defined experiences of it—points to a fourth way in which conflict narratives help construct social realities.

The brief ethnographic discussion suggests some tentative answers to the questions raised earlier. If we want to consider the relationships between narrative and conflict, a great deal must be taken into account. Of central importance is the nature of the narrative itself, the knowledge of events and character that it claims to represent, and the ways in which such representation is accomplished. Many conflict narratives may well be reducible to underlying structural relations. Such analyses as Ortner's (1989:59–81) discussion of a recurrent cultural schema in Sherpa historical accounts and Basso's essay in this volume compel our attention to the "meanings" internal to stories themselves. My concern in this article, however, has been to illuminate some of the ways in which conflict narratives draw both meaning and social force from the particulars of their telling, that is, from the circumstances, styles, intentions, and understandings that shape them in performance. In Bhatgaon such issues as the transformation of entitlement and the surreptitious circulation of illicit accounts are clearly critical, as are the varieties of sociable co-narration and the experiences for which they afford an opportunity. Narrative event and narrated event are inextricably embrangled.

Note

An earlier version of this paper was presented at the Symposium on Narrative Resources for the Creation of Order and Disorder during the 1988 Spring Meeting of the American Ethnological Society. I would like to thank Charles Briggs for organizing the panels and for his subsequent editorial energy and vision. Thanks also to all participants for a very stimulating two days. John Comaroff, Charles Briggs, Michael Herzfeld, Lance Bennett, Daniel

Horowitz, Richard Bauman, Ronald Macaulay, Daniel Segal, and Amy Shuman provided insightful, friendly, and much appreciated commentary on that emergent if somewhat disheveled presentation, though they bear no responsibility for its subsequent transformations. Colleagues in the Text and Power Seminar at the Center for Psychosocial Studies have provoked many of the questions raised in this essay and helped shape some of the better answers; I am very grateful for our conversations.

Works Cited

Abu-Lughod, Lila. 1985. Honor and the sentiments of loss in a Bedouin society. *American Ethnologist* 12:245–61.

———. 1990. *Shifting politics in Bedouin love poetry: Language and the politics of emotion*, ed. Catherine Lutz and Lila Abu-Lughod. New York: Cambridge University Press.

Bauman, Richard. 1986. *Story, performance and event: Contextual studies of oral narrative.* New York: Cambridge University Press.

Bennett, W. L., and M. S. Feldman. 1981. *Reconstructing reality in the courtroom: Justice and judgment in American culture.* New Brunswick: Rutgers University Press.

Brenneis, Donald. 1983. Official accounts: Performance and the public record. *The Windsor Yearbook of Access to Law* 3:228–44.

———. 1984a. Straight talk and sweet talk: Political discourse in an occasionally egalitarian community. In *Dangerous words: Language and politics in the Pacific*, ed. Donald Brenneis and Fred R. Myers, pp. 69–84. New York: New York University Press.

———. 1984b. Grog and gossip in Bhatgaon: Style and substance in Fiji Indian conversation. *American Ethnologist* 11:487–506.

———. 1987. Performing passions: Aesthetics and politics in an occasionally egalitarian community. *American Ethnologist* 14:236–50.

———. 1990. Dramatic gestures: The Fiji Indian *pancayat* as therapeutic event. In *Disentangling: Conflict discourse in Pacific Island societies*, ed. Karen Watson-Gegeo and Geoffrey White. Stanford, CA: Stanford University Press.

Brenneis, Donald, and Fred R. Myers, eds. 1991. *Dangerous words: Language and politics in the Pacific.* Prospect Heights, IL: Waveland Press.

Chatman, Seymour B. 1978. *Story and discourse: Narrative structure in fiction and film.* Ithaca, N.Y.: Cornell University Press.

Geertz, Clifford. 1985. Local knowledge: Fact and law in comparative perspective. In *Local knowledge: Further essays in interpretive anthropology*, by Clifford Geertz. New York: Basic Books.

Goldman, Laurence. 1986. The presentational style of women in Huli disputes. *Papers in New Guinea Linguistics* 24:213–89.

Goodman, Nelson. 1978. *Ways of worldmaking.* Indianapolis: Hackett.

Goodwin, Marjorie H. 1980. He-said-she-said: Formal cultural procedures for the construction of a gossip dispute activity. *American Ethnologist* 7:674–95.

———. 1982. "Instigating": Storytelling as social process. *American Ethnologist* 9:799–819.

Jakobson, Roman. 1971. Shifters, verbal categories and the Russian verb. In *Roman Jakobson: Selected writings*, vol. 2, pp. 130–47. The Hague: Mouton.

Just, Peter. 1986. Let the evidence fit the crime: Evidence, law, and "sociological truth" among the Dou Donggo. *American Ethnologist* 13:43–61.

Lutz, Catherine. 1982. The domain of emotion words on Ifaluk. *American Ethnologist* 9:113–28.

Maynard, Douglas W. 1985. On the functions of social conflict among children. *American Sociological Review* 50:207–33.

Myers, Fred R. 1979. Emotions and the self: A theory of personhood and social order among Pintupi Aborigines. *Ethos* 7:343–70.

———. 1986. Reflections on a meeting: Structure, language and the polity in a small-scale society. *American Ethnologist* 13:430–47.

Myers, Fred R., and Donald Brenneis. 1991. Introduction. In *Dangerous words: Language and politics in the Pacific,* ed. Donald Brenneis and Fred R. Myers, pp. 1–29. Prospect Heights, IL: Waveland Press.

Ortner, Sherry. 1989. *High religion: A cultural and political history of Sherpa Buddhism.* Princeton, NJ: Princeton University Press.

Schwartzman, Helen B. 1984. Stories at work: Play in an organizational context. In *Text, play and story: The construction and reconstruction of self and society,* ed. Edward M. Bruner, pp. 80–93. Washington, DC: American Ethnological Society.

———. 1987. The significance of meetings in an American mental health center. *American Ethnologist* 14:271–94.

Shuman, Amy. 1986. *Storytelling rights: The uses of oral and written texts by urban adolescents.* New York: Cambridge University Press.

———. n.d. Redescribing literacy. Unpublished manuscript. Dept. of English, Ohio State University.

Spacks, Patricia Meyer. 1983. In praise of gossip. In *The pleasures of anthropology,* ed. Morris Freilich, pp. 153–70. New York: New American Library.

Strathern, Marilyn. 1974. Managing information: The problems of a dispute settler (Mount Hagen). In *Contention and dispute: Aspects of law and social control in Melanesia,* ed. A. L. Epstein, pp. 271–316. Canberra: Australian National University Press.

Sudnow, David. 1965. Normal crimes: Sociological features of the penal code in a public defender office. *Social Problems* 12:255–76.

The Trickster's Scattered Self

Hailed as "the spirit of disorder, the enemy of boundaries" (Kerenyi 1972), tricksters have long fascinated anthropologists for their pervasive ambiguity and independence from all social order. In keeping with this spirit, the elusive character of tricksters has resisted explanation during the entire course of theorizing that has emerged since the time of Boas. Then, as now, scholars and literary writers were impressed above all by what Boas called the "troublesome psychological discrepancy" between the apparently incongruous attributes of the "culture hero," who makes the world safe and secure for human life, and the "selfish buffoon," who in a compulsive and ludicrous manner acts in violation of the most fundamental social values (Boas 1982 [1898]). For Boas, Lowie (1909), and Radin (1972), these epithetical roles subsumed personal habits and proclivities: on the one hand, there were a trickster's creative insight and inventiveness in the service of human beings; on the other, his compulsive and thoughtlessly excessive behavior, his lust, his gluttony, and especially his greed for unsuitable objects and relationships.

Nearly all attempts to understand tricksters assume that they represent abstract cultural entities or categories that reflect broader social concerns and interests. Such studies have been directed toward specifying the logic of the category definitions. (This orientation is seen in Beidelman 1980; Carroll 1984; Evans-Prichard 1966; Paulme 1976, 1977; Pelton 1980; and Street 1972.) Examining the logic of trickster categories independently of the narrative discourse in which they seem to be most often presented, writers focus on "themes" and "elements" of character, those attributes of a trickster's demeanor or identity that seem to make him different from others in a corpus of texts. In this way, we learn a good deal about the more sensational and shocking attributes of trickster stories—what Kerenyi called their "drastic entertainment." But by singling out such elements, these attempts to understand tricksters tend to distort—indeed, to fragment—the intelligence of such characters and to emphasize only those mythological scenes and activities in which a character's actions are especially peculiar insofar as they are inversions of idealized personalities, of "normal" behavior, and of a society's fundamental values.

A Narrativized Self

An alternative strategy is to turn away from the Maussian concern with categories, the logic of definitions, and epistemological issues connected to the universality of the phenomenon of personal categories (represented, for example, in Carrithers et al 1985) and to consider how ideas of subjectivity (or the "self") are realized in and through discourse. We need to look more carefully at the manner in which a trickster's action, enacted and transacted, is developed as a biographical narrative that evokes responses from a listening, contemplating audience. J. Barre Toelken (1969, 1987), in his sensitive essays on Navaho Coyote narratives, shows us that the discursive, narrative representations of personality development that constitute the mythological stories of these imagined lives are important objects for interpretive scrutiny and linguistic analysis. This is because myths are "studies of self," in which subjectivity (a character's emotional actions, motivations, choices, interpretations, feelings, and goal orientations) contributes to the narrative formulation of personality processes, character development, and consistencies and changes within the operations of life. Myths intrigue us because they are analyzable by methods that unite a language-oriented focus on matters of discourse with a psychologically informed, interpretive focus on palpable symbolic forms, including, of course, linguistic forms used by narrators of myths.

By considering tricksters as narrativized selves, it is possible to ask how what appear to be the elements of a trickster's subjectivity are conceived and rendered apparent in discursive ways. Such a question orients us to the interpersonal and interactive dimensions of what are more likely to be developmental processes than states. Additionally, one might shift the focus from a trickster's moral ambiguities and pervasive liminality to address more concretely how a trickster's curiously decentered self can constitute a kind of personality. What are the implications of a trickster's undertaking contradictory and incompatible courses of action, of exploring the consequences of radically different feelings and attitudes? Does a trickster, in fact, act in such ways without experiencing distress or a sense of dilemma or absurdity? How are compromises made, that is, how are problems resulting from those contradictory and incompatible courses of action solved? Is there any sense of conflict in a trickster, or is there no experience of disorder, personal or otherwise? Does this capacity for inconsistent action imply that the trickster essentially disclaims responsibility for his actions? And if so, how is his disavowed action represented? Are tricksters completely free and uninhibited experimenters? I refer here not to the presence or absence of a sense of moral responsibility but to the consequences of the ability of a trickster (or a person, for that matter) to act inconsistently and experience inconsistencies—in other words, to actively participate in what Bersani (1984) calls a "dissolving" or "scattering" of the self. Does such a scattering result in a new understanding?

By asking questions such as these, we come to focus attention on what are clearly special qualities of intelligence in the actions of these preeminently deceitful characters. The playful subterfuges of tricksters, their wildly speculative thought, concrete inventiveness, fascination with tinkering, and seemingly capricious and uninhibited experimentation (that is, their "disorderly" nature) are often belied by the careful planning and cunning foresight that accompany their experiments. The very attributes that make tricksters inventive heroes and clownish fools in the first place are, after all, natural necessities of human intelligence, operating in practical, concrete, face-to-face relations that people negotiate all the time, sometimes with considerable immediacy. Moreover, the distressing hatred, envy, greed, and jealousy that so often shape the trickster's activities are also fundamental ingredients of human life. What is the connection, then, between these fearful attributes and the more positive trickster actions in service to humanity?

The Carib-speaking people called Kalapalo, who live in the central Brazilian Alto Xingu area, tell a great variety of trickster stories, although, as far as I know, there is no suggestion of such a category in their thinking about storytelling. The richness of these stories, both with regard to the ways in which tricksters are described and the audience-teller relationships that are effected through the tellings, offers the opportunity to explore the kinds of questions posed in the preceding paragraph. My approach is one that draws attention to the developmental aspects of a particular trickster character. Rather than abstracting theme and image from settings and activities, I begin by looking at the emergent structure in trickster stories. My concern is not with emergent patterns per se, but with how storytellers use them to construct rhetorical clues that help listeners understand the action of characters. I suggest that narrative patterns created by people telling stories have considerable significance in keying certain feelings that are not explicitly stated by the narrator, but that are crucial to comprehending the personal distinctiveness of a story's protagonists.[1]

Following the psychologist Roy Shafer's (1976) understanding of a psychoanalytic narrative, I regard a developmental pattern as a story of the consistencies or changes in a character's responses to situations of decision and choice. This is especially useful for understanding trickster stories because it allows us to see superficially ambiguous or outright peculiar actions of trickster characters as consistent with respect to a developmental process in trickster psychology, part of a general pattern developed by a storyteller, and also consistent with intended functions of the telling. When I write of the trickster's "scattered self," I am referring to both a narrative representation of a trickster character's action, comprehensively defined, and to a performative process in which the speaker tries to do something to the listener through the rhetoric of a particular representation. If we then consider "the scattered self" as not just a "fact" about tricksters (as a character "type") but as a way of thinking about the character, then the different things that a trickster is said to do have as much to do with the storyteller's different didactic and performative purposes as they do with some categorial notion of a "trickster." This helps us identify trickster stories in which there are no tricksters other than the storyteller, and to see in other stories that appear to be very different thematically from trickster stories certain human characters who are being "tricksterish," that is, behaving in many of the same ways that the mythological tricksters behave. We might say, then, that those other stories are figured through trickster tropes.

Lies About Himself

The Kalapalo trickster character I focus on in this paper is called either by his adult name, Taugi (derived from the word *taugiñe* 'lies about himself'), or his childhood name, Giti, meaning 'sun'. An epithet that some Kalapalo use for this trickster is *tikambïngïfïngï* 'a secretive person', 'someone who doesn't tell about himself'; another is *enggugikïgiñe* 'the baffler'. His twin brother, the younger of the pair, is called Aulukuma, or Ngune 'moon'.

There are at least 16 separate stories about Taugi, some very long, most rather short. Only the shorter ones are told together, as episodic clusters that apparently occur independently of any rules about order. The longer stories usually are heard in fragments, told over several days, months, or even years. Storytellers are frequently interrupted by the press of their, or their listeners', more urgent work, as well as by their own and their listeners' weariness. Consequently, storytellers often have to wait some time before resuming their tales. The longer stories in which Taugi is presented as the central figure are usually told by hereditary leaders, men and women who are considered the repositories of traditional knowledge inherited from their ancestors. Men often hear stories told in the central plaza when hereditary leaders entertain them during work parties. Stories are also heard inside houses, where they are told to young men and women in puberty seclusion. Fragments of these stories, or shorter ones, are also told by parents and grandparents to their children in less public and less formal settings, whenever people are relaxing during a break in the day's work. Although stories are often told directly to children, they are usually listened to by anyone who is close by, and it is not unusual for adults to ask to hear particular stories themselves.

To the Kalapalo, Taugi is a dangerous and angry *itseke* ('powerful being'), showing how unpredictable, capricious, absurd, and even extremely dangerous the world is. The disorderly, unpredictable, and dangerous nature of Taugi is the source of all human difficulties, particularly the troubling experiences of interpersonal contact that are shaped by bitter hatred, envy, jealousy, and the terrible grief imposed by the finality of death. Taugi's worst inventions are the evil, occult tools people use to kill one another.

On the other hand, Taugi is called the "father" of humanity, the *itseke* whose hyperanimate power created human beings, separating the different kinds of people by placing them (with their distinctive technologies and emotional dispositions) in their various habitats. He managed (after some false starts) to acquire erections from Lizard, to create menstruation, and to rid females of castrating vaginal monsters; his actions resulted in preventing the Dead from returning to visit the living. He is the inventor of male musicality, the most powerful ritual force. Finally, he is a technological innovator, inventing techniques for cooking corn and piqui fruit.

In the stories, Taugi acts as a husband, brother, lover, grandfather, father, son, leader, healer, and occult killer or witch. As a "grandfather" to the first humans, the Dawn People, he seems to be a commanding figure, dangerous and immensely destructive. Dressed in a gleaming headdress of oriole and macaw feathers, his fearful appearance signals to people that he is about to confront and intimidate them. So frightening is this potent anger that in the stories about Taugi, his future victims sense they are "done for" the moment they see him entering their settlement. And yet, in his guise as a "father" to humanity, he is portrayed as kind and helpful, winning respect for the advice he gives. His empathy is such that Taugi is said to be present at people's funerals as a father, mourning the death of his children. It is in such contexts that he enacts the complex feelings the Kalapalo associate with grief: sadness, anger, lust for revenge, ultimate resignation.

We see Taugi's acute self-consciousness when, as a small child (a "son" or "grandson"), he manifests a particularly complex and implacably self-contained personality. In these stories, Taugi's self-consciousness arises as follows: first, in connection with his acquisition of names (when he deliberately seeks names for himself and justifies them to his father, thus reversing the usual process); second, in the way he puts himself forward by demanding to be seen and heard (in other words, to be recognized as a distinctive individual); third, the exceptional manner in which he easily penetrates the verbal deceits of others; fourth, during his outrageous acts of revenge motivated by an intolerance of unpleasant emotions like mourning and depression; and fifth, through his invention of occult ways to make his own mother—who is in a half-dead limbo and whom he is tired of crying over—die. Taugi appears to be his most uncompromisingly unique, destructive, and disorderly self in stories in which he is a small child. It is then that he is particularly forgetful, thinking in a disorderly way, trying out alternative roles, and otherwise seeming flighty and unpredictable. The older Taugi becomes, the less directly violent and antagonistic he is and the more tolerant of stressful emotions. He is then apparently also less capable of revealing other people's deceits to themselves—that is, he is less aggressively insightful.

Many stories about Taugi describe his deliberate attempts to destroy other beings more dangerous than he, which he does for the good of humanity (that is, when he acts in the interests of his "children"), through the use of his maliciously inventive or imaginative intelligence. Thus, when he seeks the elements essential to human life—light, fire, and water—he overcomes their diffident *itseke* owners or guardians or source. But Taugi is a failure, or is even duped in turn, when he acts so compulsively as to be stupidly consumed by obsessive greed, envy, or sexual jealousy. The effective functioning of his powers of creative insight and imaginative cunning is hindered by the excessiveness of these feelings. For Taugi never overcomes his adversaries by overt force or moral persuasion. Mainly, he acts through concealment and deception, using verbal and visual subterfuges.

Compared with virtually all the other characters in Kalapalo myths, Taugi almost never tries to repeat an action. When he does, he fails. It is almost as if repetition for Taugi has a hindering, limiting effect, just the opposite of what it accomplishes for human beings. In Taugi's case, creative imagination that is successful is connected to his erratic, unpredictable ways. In other words, Taugi is most successful when he operates without planning, that is, as if he had no goal in mind. In contrast, other characters need to repeat their actions, each repetition often being accompanied by validation from others, in order to be successful. Normally, this repetition occurs five times. Of course, repetition by itself is not enough. When such repetition continues after the character is admonished or harmed, the one repeating the action begins to look eccentric, foolishly compulsive, even stupid. (The narrator typically uses a special grammatical particle to indicate this.) In some trickster stories, the trickster persists in such a context, and invariably fails or is turned into a dupe himself.

Kafanifani: A Kalapalo Trickster Narrative

The special relation to repetition is nicely developed in the story the Kalapalo call "Kafanifani," which was first told to me by the hereditary leader Muluku one February evening in 1987.[2] In this story, Taugi is pitted against his cousin and rival Kafanifani. Taugi invites the Dead to return to visit the living, since people are "being used up." The Dead agree and come to the settlement just as Taugi's wives rush to get water for the manioc drinks they are preparing to present to the guests. At the waters edge, the women are captured by their lover Kafanifani, who carries them away underwater. Extramarital relations are commonplace in Kalapalo life, so the fact that "even" Taugi's wives have lovers is not particularly interesting in and of itself. However, it does prepare listeners to think about Taugi much as they would a Kalapalo husband, that is, as a person whose jealousy will most likely disorient him. As Muluku described the events to me, Taugi forgets his guests and begins to search for his wives, without success. The Dead, angry at being kept waiting outside the settlement, where they are supposed to be formally greeted by their host, and realizing he has forgotten about them, return home, never to return. Taugi does not seem to worry about this very much, because he almost immediately begins to search for his wives in earnest. He travels to Kafanifani's house, where he sees his wives sitting in the doorway, laughing about having deceived him. But when he comes closer, all he sees are cooking pots leaning against the house wall. Puzzled, he returns home, where he encounters his friend Agouti. Agoutis are large, guinea pig– like rodents, typically found in Kalapalo settlements rummaging in the garbage dumps behind houses (a private region for residents, where men often go to signal to their lovers). Agouti, who is thus portrayed as a sneak and a spy, urges him to "use his power" (that is, to think intelligently about deception). When Taugi realizes the cooking pots are his wives in disguise, he goes back to Kafanifani's house. Pretending he is still unable to figure out where the women have gone, he sneaks up on the pots and painfully snaps his finger on them until they cry out. His wives turn back into womanly form and Taugi leads them back home. He avenges himself on Kafanifani by throwing him onto the sky.

Muluku opened his story with a characteristic thematic summary, introducing the focal characters, Kafanifani and Taugi, and describing the most important reasons that the events occurred the way they did. In the excerpt given here, Muluku has Taugi specify what he wants to happen and why (lines 6–9). This goal is validated by Aulukuma (lines 10–11). This is the only story in which Aulukuma validates Taugi, possibly because Taugi's goal is one that seems to be right for human beings. Aulukuma is always feeling sorry for people.

I. Summary.

> Listen. Kafanifani ran away with Taugi's wives, Kafanifani did that. He did that because Taugi was trying to return those of us who had died, he was trying to return those of us who had died. [5]
> "Something does have to be done, Aulukuma. I'm doing this so that our Dead will return to us," he said. "I do want our Dead to return, because the mortals are being used up, that's why I want the Dead to return." "You're right, that shouldn't happen, [10] you're right, that shouldn't happen."

II. Taugi puts his plan into action.

> "Come here, everyone, something has to be done," and so a messenger went on, the messenger went on. We went to Añafïtï, the Place where the Dead Congregate. *Titititi.* [15] *Titititi.* That was all.
>   Then, right away he arrived. He arrived, their messenger did arrive. [20] "Everyone should hurry. In fact your followers must do that tomorrow, they must do that." "All right, that will be fine." They were all so excited! "Tomorrow Taugi's guests will arrive, Taugi's guests will arrive!" "The Dead are really returning, the Dead are returning!" [25] Then, shouting out, the Dead were coming back this way, the Dead were coming back. "We should all hurry," there were so many doing that! "The Dead are really trying to return, the Dead are trying to return, [30] the Dead are trying to return." "We must keep returning so we can remain here, we must keep returning." They were the Dead, those people who had died. Yes. Then, I'm told, that was all.

III. The women prepare to greet the guests with food.

So then cold manioc soup was being made, it was being made for the guests'
entrance, [35] it was being made for their entrance. A huge quantity of it! His
wives, Taugi had five wives, Taugi's wives. They were getting it ready for when the
visitors were seated in the plaza. [40] That was all.

"They're almost here!" So now, the Dead were appearing. Then *tititi* . . . it
ended. They were right there near the house circle, [45] near the house circle. "Go
on," they were occupied with their preparations. His wives, Taugi's wives went to
get water for mixing up the manioc drinks. "Quickly now, go get it!" Kafanifani
was there. Kafanifani was there. [50] Since he just happened to be coming back
from some place where he had been fishing, from where he had been fishing. "I'm
wondering, what you're all up to? What are you all up to? What are you all up to?"
[55] "Nothing," they answered. "This is for the drinks we're mixing that will be
given out, we're mixing the drinks that will be given out. Taugi's guests are just
about arriving now, Taugi's guests are arriving." [60] "I see," he answered, "I
see." "Where were you?" "Fishing." "All right," they replied. "Give me some
fish." [65] "Give me some fish." [the women seductively ask for fish, a sexual
overture] "Get it if that's what you want. Here, they're right here, get into my
canoe." Into his canoe, the canoe. [70] *Buk buk.* So he stole them from him without
further thought, Kafanifani did. He stole Taugi's wives. *Buk* and away they went.

IV. Taugi misses his wives, forgets about his guests but fails to find the women.

A. The women are missing.

"Come here, all of you." Nothing. "Come. Come here, all of you." By then the
Dead had nearly reached the houses, [75] they were close to the houses. Nothing
happened. "Come here!" But now people were already talking about it. "It seems
as if Taugi's wives have just been stolen! [80] Kafanifani has stolen Taugi's wives,
Kafanifani did that." "Yes, he left right away!" That's all.

B. Taugi looks for his wives.

Then Taugi sped off to look for them, [85] on the path to the water's edge. Then at
the path to the water's edge, *mbii* they had vanished, they had vanished. "Where in
the world did they go? [90] I think they're really deceiving me as usual."

C. Kafanifani flees to his own settlement.

"I've got to do something," so he went on. As he went further on into the water, he
took them under with him, Kafanifani did. And he carried them away beneath the
water, he carried away Taugi's wives, [95] he carried away Taugi's wives. So he
stole them, he stole them. *Pupupu* . . . far away and so he brought them up to the
surface at some place, who knows where, he brought them up to the surface. [100]
As he did that, their husband kept following behind . . . nothing. He was following them from far behind. Nothing. Next they went on and he carried them off
through a submerged log, [105] Kafanifani made it happen. He wasn't a human
being, Kafanifani. He was a powerful being. Nothing. [110] Afterwards, because
Kafanifani had carried them away, Taugi saw nothing. So he rested, he rested.

D. The Dead are insulted and leave, cursing the living.

Then, "We're being made to go back, aren't we? It looks like we should go back,
doesn't it?" [115] Next, "You've really kept us standing in this place for a long time.

We're definitely going back. We're definitely going back right now.'' They turned right around. ''We'll stay just the way we are, we'll never reappear, [120] we'll never reappear, we'll never reappear. Let them stay the way they are,'' they said to each other. They turned right back, they turned back, [125] they turned back. And the Dead turned back.

E. *Taugi returns to find the Dead gone. He curses them.*

Then he arrived home, Taugi arrived home. ''Have you found your wives?'' [130] ''Not a trace.'' And so he arrived home. ''What a shame that happened. All your guests have left.'' ''They will stay the way they are, [135] they will stay the way they are. Now the mortals can't turn back, the mortals can't turn back. But I tried to do all that so the mortals would have to keep returning to us,'' he said. ''To return to us always. I did it so that would happen to them, they would always return to us,'' he continued. [140] ''To return to us always.'' Yes. ''So they will remain, I say, so they will remain.'' I suppose by now the others had left because of what he had done, and they all went back the way they came, [145] the Dead went back the way they came.

V. Taugi keeps looking for his wives.

A. *The first time.*

Then he went once again to look for his wives, Taugi went *titititi* to the other person's settlement, to his settlement. To Kafanifani's settlement. [150] He was at his house, his house, Kafanifani's house. Yes, I guess Kafanifani was fishing. Next he came up to his wives, Taugi came up to Kafanifani's wives. So *tikii*. ''Why, Taugi's here.'' [155] ''Taugi. What's the matter, Taugi?'' ''Nothing, nothing, I just came to see you, I came to see you.'' ''All right,'' they answered, ''All right.'' [160] ''Perhaps you've seen those who make my food around here? Those who make my food?'' ''We haven't, we haven't. They haven't come here.'' ''All right,'' he said. [165] So he went on.

B. *The second time.*

Then the next day he searched around, the next day he went, to look for them, to look for them. [170] The next time, nothing.

C. *The third time.*

Again he kept going to look for them, to look for his wives, Taugi kept going, Taugi kept going. [175]

D. *The fourth time.*

The next time he arrived they were seated in the doorway laughing at him, as Taugi arrived. ''Ha ha,'' they were laughing at him, they were laughing at him. ''Here's Taugi,'' they whispered excitedly to each other. [180] ''Here's Taugi!.'' They went over to their hammocks, they went right over to their hammocks. Next they turned themselves into large cooking pots, they became large cooking pots. [185] They hid themselves from him.

Then, *tikii* he came inside. No one was there, the place was empty. ''Where can they be going all the time? Where are they?'' [190] There was no one there. Since Kafanifani was fishing, Kafanifani had gone to do that. Then, that was all. Afterwards, he went away without those things of his, [195] without his things. Taugi went on.

VI. Agouti gives the women's secret away.

There was someone else who concerned himself with them, his informer, his informer. Taugi's informer. That was Akugi the Agouti. [200] That was Agouti. "Well, my friend," he said, "Friend. Have you found your wives?" "No I haven't. I haven't." [205] "Now see here, see here. Look, you're not like me, you're powerful. You're powerful. What was it like when you would go there? [210] What?" "When I went to them just this way, they would start to laugh. Then as soon as they saw me, they would get up and go away. They would get up and go away." [215] "Now look, think about it. What do you remember seeing there?" "Cooking pots, cooking pots." "I see," Agouti answered. "I should go back. I'll go get them. I'll be going, I'll be going," Taugi said. [220] So he went. "I'll go tomorrow without fail, I'll go tomorrow."

VII. Taugi goes for the fifth time.

He came to where they were. [225] They kept laughing, they were still talking. He was ready. "Well, Taugi's here again, Taugi's here again." He had come to where they were. [230] Nothing! "Well, where are they? Oh, where do they keep going? Where? Oh, why is it so easy for you?" he said to them. This time, he snapped his finger on the pots. *Pisuk, pisuk, pisuk, pisuk, pisuk.* [235] "Ouch, don't Taugiii." Now they began to speak to him, I'm told. Yes. Now, that was all. "Well, come along all of you, come right along." He had found his wives, [240] Taugi had. "Come along now, all of you, come along now." And so he carried them off, his wives, [245] Taugi did. The one who had run away with his wives, that was Kafanifani, Kafanifani did it. Taugi had kept trying to return to us . . . he had kept trying to return to us those of us who had died. [250] Kafanifani didn't want that to happen. He didn't want that to happen. Otherwise, they would have always returned to us. That was what Taugi wanted to have happen to us. Afterward, [255] afterward. But no, it didn't happen, it didn't happen.

VIII. Taugi learns a lesson from Agouti.

Listen. Afterwards they all returned home, [260] so they all returned home. "Taugi just found his wives, he's found his wives." "Now look, do think now. When you don't use your intelligence you're a failure." [265] That was all.

IX. Taugi takes revenge on Kafanifani.

Following that he threw him onto the sky. Taugi caused him to be on the sky, Taugi did. He threw Kafanifani [270] onto the sky. That's all. Then it was over. That's all, that's just all there is.

Discussion

In his version of the story, Muluku emphasizes in a somewhat didactic manner why the Dead no longer visit the living. The underlying idea—usually associated with Taugi's exploits but here also involving his cousin Kafanifani—is that deception and trickery can serve as the cause of some condition of life now experienced by the Kalapalo. It is the Dead who actually decide never to return, establishing their future conduct in utterances that are also present in Taugi's own speech: Let them stay the way they are (or, "So they will remain."). (The word is *laitsani,* a performative effecting the future condition of whoever is the referent; it is usually spoken angrily.) So, although Kafanifani initiates the conditions that lead to the final effect (his deception is to steal Taugi's wives so the Dead will no longer return), it is Taugi himself who declares in the end that the Dead will "stay the way they are" (lines 104–5). A hierarchy of power is suggested: at the summit are the Dead, followed by Taugi, then Kafanifani, and finally ordinary Mortals. Kafanifani's relative weakness is suggested by the fact that Taugi throws him onto the sky, where he becomes the stars that we know as Beta and Gamma in the constellation Hydra. (The Kalapalo see these rather prominent stars as Kafanifani's two hands flung over his head.)

Taugi fails to bring back the Dead because he forgets to use his magical power. Similarly, he fails to find his wives because he tries to achieve success as an ordinary person would, through persistence and bluff. Also, in "Kafanifani" sexual jealousy comes between Taugi and the Dead. His feelings are excessive in that he is too committed to finding his wives, thereby selfishly neglecting his more important aim of returning the Dead to the living. His exaggerated selfishness inevitably diminishes his insight and precipitates failure. Becoming detached from his goal of returning the Dead, however, he declares in frustration that they will forever remain as they are. (Actually, it is the Dead who really decide to do this.) Only at the climax of the story does his acute embarrassment at his failure to find his wives cause him to begin to think more carefully about what others are doing to him. But it is the rather insignificant Agouti who reminds him to think with his special power, not as an ordinary person would. There are limits, then, to Taugi's powers of insight and creativity. Taugi sometimes neglects to use his special intelligence—his particular success at penetrating deception—as if, unlike other powerful beings, he must constantly develop his special power through active mental work.

Emergent Structure in "Kafanifani"

Examining the structure of the story as it emerges in this telling, we see that there are nine major segments (or "verses"). The first verse is the beginning story-line summary. The second describes the successful invitation to the Dead, and the third describes what is being done to prepare for their visit. The fourth relates Taugi's preoccupation with searching for his wives, an action that inadvertently insults the Dead, who return home never to return to the living. (This is a complex verse with five subsidiary segments; the number itself indicates that a certain goal has been successfully accomplished.) In the fifth verse, Taugi continues to search for his wives, unsuccessfully four times (the number four indicates a complete set). In the sixth verse, Agouti reveals what is wrong, following which, in the seventh verse, Taugi returns for a fifth and successful attempt to find his wives. In the eighth verse, Taugi returns home where Agouti repeats his lesson about using power. Finally, the ninth verse describes how Taugi avenges himself on Kafanifani.

Wherever these motivated numbers appear in Kalapalo stories, as in the structure of nine verses and five segments, they metaphorically allude to completion, resolution, and successful accomplishment of a goal. What is interesting here is that simple repetition in Taugi's case does not work; he only succeeds by sudden insight, by penetrating illusion—that is, by using his power. Mere repetition in Taugi's search for his wives does not help him, although the storyteller uses the five-segment organization to encourage his listeners to anticipate success after the fifth try.

Traveling in "Kafanifani"

Another important and particularly effective structuring device in this story is provided by descriptions of traveling or, rather, the way characters somewhat frantically run back and forth. At the start of the story, Taugi instructs his messengers to invite the Dead to return. The Dead are urged to hurry by these messengers (whom they are supposed to follow back to Taugi's settlement). Then the women rush off to get water for the guests' drinks; at the place where water is drawn, Kafanifani quickly bears them away in his canoe. Taugi then rushes around looking for them, in vain. The Dead leave in a huff. Taugi runs about looking for his wives, back and forth to Kafanifani's place, but again in vain. Finally, after Taugi learns the truth from Agouti, he travels once more to Kafanifani's house, and brings all his wives home. In a final burst of angry energy he throws Kafanifani onto the sky. This somewhat undirected running around is characteristic of Taugi, in contrast to the more deliberate back and forth motion between two places on the part of other characters in Kalapalo stories.

Taugi's Forgetfulness

Finally, Taugi is portrayed as a trickster who is easily tricked because of his forgetfulness. Although he initially speaks with considerable warmth of the need to return the Dead to the living, he is actually more concerned with his wives and so is easily duped by Kafanifani (who doesn't want the Dead to return). Taugi's wives easily trick him by turning into cooking pots because they realize he is too consumed by his anxiety about their disappearance to think carefully about how they might have deceived him. Only Agouti, an animal easily able to penetrate deceptions because of his spying habits (not, as he says, because of any special intelligence like Taugi's), figures out what they are doing. So Taugi learns a lesson about using his power from the animal who knows everyone's secrets.

Evidentials in "Kafanifani"

Quoted conversation is also an important structuring device in Kalapalo storytelling, as well as the means for realizing ideas of emotional action, planning, and goal orientation. Language plays a distinctive role in modifying interpersonal relations during Taugi's deceptive action. In the first place, Taugi's verbal deception is marked here (as elsewhere) by the virtual absence of significant evidential particles in his speech. In "Kafanifani," the only evidentials Muluku the storyteller has Taugi use are those expressing doubt. For example, in (1) Taugi uses the simple questioning form *nika* (indicating uncertainty about hearsay) when he asks Kafanifani's wives for information.[3]

(1) line 161*

anginika	*inde*	*wokungita*	*ingilefa*	*efekeni*
be-UE	here/now	1p-liquid food-?	3p-see-MT	2p-ERG-pI

"Perhaps (as others say) you've seen those who make my food around here?"

Taugi uses *ma* (as expression of strong doubt and confusion) deceptively, while pretending he still does not know where his wives have gone. In (2), an unusual instance of Taugi's use of the "experience confirmation" evidential *aka* is (perhaps tellingly) linked to Taugi's recognition of his wives' deception.

(2) lines 90–91

una̱ma	*kuteluko*
where-DE	we incl-go-PRM-pl subject

"Where in the world did they go?"

ah,	*awïndakosuaka*	*igey*
EMPH	lie-pl sub-derogatory-CE	NDP

"Why, they're really deceiving me now, the way they always do."

Taugi's speech lacks challenging, counterclaiming, confirmatory, or (with the exception mentioned earlier) asserting forms, such as would occur when a shared interpretation is sought or where it is being thwarted: for example, in moments of intitial contact between persons, poor insight, negotiation, resistance to an interpretation, and especially outright denial of shared experience. In contrast, evidentials of this sort often appear in the speech of human characters in stories (see Basso 1992, 1995). In "Kafanifani" we see such forms in sequences of dialogue where human beings engage in persistent persuasion, as in (3), where the messengers urge the Dead to visit the living, using the emphatic *aketsange* 'should'.

(3) line 20

ogiñafe	*okogetsiko*	*aketsange, okogetsiko aketsange*
HORT-DIR-IMP	tomorrow-pl sub	should

"Everyone should hurry. In fact, your followers must do that tomorrow, they must do that."

Similarly, in (4), when the Dead, disgusted with being kept waiting, respond to Taugi's failure to greet them, we again find evidentials. In this sequence, the Dead

*See "Key to Linguistic Notation" (p. 70)

first use the evidential *nifa,* which conveys a relatively weak attempt at confirmation that is becoming stronger, as they are appealing to other's experience. Initially, they seem to feel that something is wrong, but they do not openly blame Taugi until several lines later. The sequence of lines ends very strongly as the Dead begin using the more assertive *kudya* (suggesting a strong positive confirmation of a prior suspicion) and the emphatic *aketsange.*

(4) lines 114–18
lepene   tisogopitsanifa,   Aña   kilï
next   we excl-go back-ADV-SE   the Dead   speak-PRM
"Then, 'We're being made to go back, aren't we?'"

tisogopitsanifa
we excl-go back-CRM-SE
"It looks like we should go back, doesn't it?"

tisogopitsa   aketsange
we excl-go back-CRM   should
"We're definitely going back."

tisogopidyï   aketsigey
we excl-go back-PRM   CE-be-NDP
"We're definitely going back right now."

Elsewhere (Basso, 1989, 1992, 1995), I have shown that evidentials in Kalapalo are, on the one hand, constitutive of independence, individuality, or open conflict, and, on the other hand, help to form the most intense kinds of solidarity of which Kalapalo are capable. In all cases, claims are being made about shared interpretations of experience. Moral boundaries and personal allegiances are being drawn through these claims. The absence of evidentials in Taugi's speech (especially when he speaks to others) is thus of considerable significance in understanding the peculiarly indeterminate nature of how he comprehends (or more exactly, how he shares) experience.

Taugi (and less frequently and successfully, his younger brother Aulukuma) is not only verbally disposed to deceive, he is also corporeally deceptive and visually misleading. One way to interpret this is to say (as some have said about tricksters) that Taugi is an ambiguous character, exhibiting the classic features of liminality (Babcock-Abrahams, 1975). A stronger interpretation, however, focuses on Taugi as an active agent, which is to say that his sensory or bodily qualities reveal the variety of potential in both how he can interpret experience, and his ability to use such interpretations to influence the actions of others. For example, both Taugi and his twin Aulukuma have the ability to conceal their sex and their age. They trick their grandmother (who has killed their mother) by turning themselves into cute little children, so that she is moved to cuddle and sing to them. They know how their grandmother will respond to them when they appear to her in this particular way, which, in turn, enables them to crush her to death by suddenly becoming very tall, grown-up, as she holds them in her lap. In another story, the twins appear to Nakika, a powerful being whose house Taugi covets, as beautiful women who offer themselves to him as brides. Stimulated by his lust, he is almost poisoned to death by the scheming "women" who have prepared ceremonial soup as a wedding present. They know Nakika will be unable to resist drinking this soup when Taugi, holding a gourd dipper close to his face, seductively urges him to drink. (Unfortunately for Taugi, Nakika realizes something is wrong and takes only a sip.)

In several stories, Taugi is described as being able to appear in more than one form simultaneously. He can create a second self—for example, an alligator, a tapir, a cricket, or a catfish—while pretending to watch innocently as the creature violates or destroys something the owner has refused Taugi. In these instances, Taugi exists side by side with an objectified agent who foregrounds his destructive envy, gluttony, lechery, or vengeful hatred. At the same time, such action becomes (through objectification) disclaimed, so that Taugi appears guiltless. Taugi also appears extremely detached from his goals, so that when he fails, he appears not to become particularly angry, vengeful, or upset. Sometimes, he takes on a second, objectified form to actually mock (and perhaps attempt to get rid of) such feelings in himself. In a story called "The Original Piqui," Taugi is unable to get enough of the fruit (which aids digestion). He turns into Cricket, who mocks himself for being constipated. Taugi then assumes the form of wind and causes a piqui to crush Cricket.

To summarize, through narrative discourse Taugi's personality is constituted as poorly oriented toward and easily detached from his goals. He cannot successfully repeat an action, and he readily abandons plans when they do not work. Furthermore, Taugi's feelings and interpretations cannot be easily (or at all) confirmed by human beings. This is because he is so changeable, creating visual illusions about himself. In all these stories about Taugi, we learn of a trickster intelligence that is speculative, eccentrically playful, idiosyncratic, and guiltless, possessed of an imaginal consciousness in which the things of the world, including Taugi's own self, can never be taken for granted, trusted, or assumed to be fixed and assured. The Kalapalo trickster's contradictions or inconsistencies are closely connected to a very positive kind of psychological grounding: a highly creative and detached imagination in which propositional truth is irrelevant to judging the validity of action. The positivist's concern with differentiating truth, genuineness, naturalness, normality, honesty, and the morally good, on the one hand, from falsehood, deception, paradox, and evil, on the other, is absent here. Put somewhat differently, the trickster's scattered self is a *contingent* self, acting strategically in full independence of rules.

Cohesive Versus Scattered Selves

My model of Kalapalo storytelling allowed me to reorient the problematic notion of "self" in the direction of action-oriented narrative process. I have moved away from thinking of the "self" as a structured, fixed, unified, and (as is often hoped in the psychological literature) consistent and harmonious "thing." Such ideas are common, whether the "self" is thought of as a mental structure, a set of bodily images, or a semiotic relation. Although a trickster narrative is occasionally contradictory and even incoherent, its very nature corresponds to the Kalapalo notion of a trickster "self." Put somewhat differently, the trickster has at least as many subjective possibilities as those revealed in the narratively ordered action in which he appears. This is clearly a very different idea of "self" from the usual objectification and reification of mental structures, and it is particularly useful because it is oriented toward the actual strategies appropriate for representing and contextualizing emotional and cognitive processes.

I have argued that the superficially "disorderly" scattering of the trickster's self is developed through narrative devices that emphasize the relationship between uncertainty, lack of focus, incohesiveness, and creative experimentation by reminding Kalapalo listeners of the positive aspects of unanticipated consequences and by showing why it may be necessary to be emotionally detached from goals. This narrative biography of Taugi is so complex and potentially varied that I propose to call him a "scattered" self.[4] This term suggests that his actions take on many different forms, measured above all by the fact that Taugi often has no predetermined goals and no ultimate fulfillments; he exists only as the emergent structure of pure narrative and the effects of chance. My sense of the trickster as "scattered" comes from what he does and what happens to him in interpersonal situations, where he and others respond to each other's words and acts.

The trickster's self is a deliberately scattered one, and I suggest that the very fact of scattering and deconstructing the self has a precise value, as well as functional consequences, with which storytellers are especially concerned. These scattered selves make psychological sense, and they are not chaotic. For example, one general possibility in Taugi that is also present in human beings (who are very much aware of it and even perhaps anxious about it) is what Jung called *imaginal* consciousness—the ability to speculate, invent, be flexible, and resist the status quo, as well as lie and conceal. All these attributes are closely connected to human language, which, as the Kalapalo represent it in their stories, is inseparable from human action, feeling, goal orientation, planning, and the constant process of making decisions and choices.

I now turn from this conclusion about the meaning of one mythical Kalapalo trickster to another question: What is the adaptive value of such a view of language and illusion? Or, put differently, Why do the Kalapalo place such emphasis on—

indeed, give such overwhelming importance to—the role of illusion in human consciousness? My response can, of course, be only speculative, but I suggest that the answer lies in the fact that the Kalapalo are a relatively "new" culture. Not only are they recent refugees who have occupied their territory for less than two centuries, but as a community within the more comprehensive society of the Upper Xingu Basin, they are also a very "new" people. We know this from their own histories, which include biographies of warriors and of communities that describe people living in a not very distant past of perpetual blood feuding, cannibalism, hostility toward neighboring communities of so-called fierce people, and murderous incursions by outsiders of European culture. In these stories, people are also moving around and into new and unknown territory.[5] Under conditions in which new interethnic relations were being formulated at the same time that new environmental/sensory experiences were being enacted, is it strange that the need to remain flexible, detached from goals, and suspicious of anything fixed and ideologically secure would be narrativized? What may appear to some to be an ambiguous sense of flux and indeterminacy in trickster stories can be understood more positively as a kind of stroboscopic sense of multiple possibilities. This vision fixes in a didactic narrative frame the complex transience of experience and the sense of many different experiential worlds existing side by side.

Scholarly puzzlement over tricksters' anomalous and paradoxical characters seems to be connected to an implicit application of this positivist notion of personality as a self that "holds still," one that is stable, regular, and consistent, and therefore definable. And if we are to assume that truth is an objective and describable quality that can be contrasted with falsehood, we necessarily come to define the trickster's self as an inconsistent, unstable, or simply ambiguous one tinged with a dubious morality. Thus, at least by implication, a scattered self is an incoherent, unstructured self, a false or even a psychotic selfless chaos, or an evil self that orients the person toward self-destruction.

To conclude, anthropologists have been accustomed to working with an idea of fixed psychic structure, generalized over all situations and goals. However, if the idea of fixed psychic structure is questioned along the lines suggested here, the contradictions in the patterns of a trickster's action need not be viewed as anomalous or paradoxical. In fact, to the Kalapalo, characters whose actions are stable and fall into a general pattern and whose goals and modes of orientation to goals seem not to vary are in danger of being regarded as excessively compulsive and inflexible and, ultimately, as failing in imagination. Pragmatic creativity and flexibility, the ability to conceive of more than one kind of relationship with other people, and the ability to fashion or invent a variety of thoughts about one's capacity as an agent are, on the other hand, entirely human. These skills, after all, are learned by most people everywhere as they come to understand how to experiment strategically and tactically with personal experience. For a people who have lived for centuries as refugees, only temporarily residing in communities with fixed and assured territories, such attitudes about illusion and deceit seem most appropriate.

Key to Linguistic Notation

ADV	Adverbializer
C	Copula
CE	Experience confirmation evidential
CRM	Continuous aspect, reportive mood
DE	Doubt evidential (firsthand)
DIR	Directive
EMPH	Emphatic expletive
ERG	Ergative
EX	Existential auxiliary (reportive)
excl	Exclusive we
HORT	Hortative
IMP	Imperative mode
incl	Inclusive we
MT	Metonymic taxis
NDP	Near deictic pronoun
pl	Plural
PRM	Punctual aspect, reportive mood
SC	Strong confirmation of experience evidential
SE	Evidential appealing to another's experience
sub	Subject
UE	Uncertainty about hearsay evidential

Notes

1. See Basso (1987) for a more developed presentation and analysis of Kalapalo trickster stories.

2. The translation I present here is a slight revision of one in Basso (1987).

3. See the "Key to Linguistic Notation" (above). In the examples, tokens of the form in question have been underlined.

4. Stories about Taugi constitute the largest single group of Kalapalo narrative mythology.

5. These stories are discussed in Basso (1995).

Works Cited

Babcock-Abrahams, Barbara. 1975. "A tolerated margin of mess": The trickster and his tales reconsidered. *Journal of the Folklore Institute* 11:147–86.

Basso, Ellen B. 1987. *In favor of deceit: A study of tricksters in an Amazonian society.* Tucson: University of Arizona Press.

———. 1989. Kalapalo biography: Psychology and language in a South American oral history. *American Anthropologist* 91:551–69.

———. 1992. Contextualization in Kalapalo narratives. In *Rethinking context,* ed. Alessandro Duranti and Charles Goodwin, pp. 253–69. Cambridge: Cambridge University Press.

———. 1995. *The last cannibals.* Austin: University of Texas Press.

Beidelman, T. O. 1980. The moral imagination of the Kaguru: Some thoughts on tricksters, translation and comparative analysis. *American Ethnologist* 7:27–42.

Bersani, Leo. 1984. *A future for Astyanax. Character and desire in literature.* New York: Columbia University Press.

Boas, Franz. 1982 [1898]. Introduction. In James Teit, *Traditions of the Thompson River Indians,* pp. 1–18. Memoirs of the American Folklore Society. Vol. 6. Rpt. *Race, language and culture: Collected works of Franz Boas,* 407–24. Chicago: University of Chicago Press.

Carrithers, Michael, Steven Collins, and Steven Lukes, eds. 1985. *The category of the person.* Cambridge: Cambridge University Press.

Carroll, Michael P. 1984. The trickster as selfish buffoon and culture hero. *Ethos* 12:105–31.

Evans-Pritchard, E. E. 1966. *The Zande trickster.* Oxford: Clarendon Press.

Kerenyi, Karl. 1972. The trickster in relation to Greek mythology. In *The trickster: A study in American Indian mythology,* by Paul Radin. New York: Schocken Books.

Lowie, Robert. 1909. The hero-trickster discussion. *Journal of American Folklore* 22:431–33.

Paulme, Denise. 1976. Typologie des contes africains du décepteur. *Cahiers d'études africaines* 60:569–600.

———. 1977. The impossible imitation in African trickster tales. In *Forms of folklore in Africa,* ed. Dan Ben-Amos, pp. 64–103. Austin: University of Texas Press.

Pelton, Robert D. 1980. *The trickster in West Africa: A study of mythic irony and sacred delight.* Berkeley: University of California Press.

Radin, Paul. 1972. *The trickster: A study in American Indian mythology.* New York: Schocken Books.

Schafer, Roy. 1976. *A new language for psychoanalysis.* New Haven, CT: Yale University Press.

Street, Brian V. 1972. The trickster theme: Winnebago and Azande. In *Azande themes,* ed. A. Singer and Brian V. Street, pp. 15–28. Oxford: Oxford University Press.

Toelken, J. Barre. 1969. The "pretty language" of Yellowman: Genre, mode, and texture in Navaho coyote narratives. *Genre* 2:211–35.

———. 1987. Life and death in the Navajo coyote tales. In *Recovering the work: Essays on Native American literature,* ed. Brian Swann and Arnold Krupat, pp. 388–401. Berkeley: University of California Press.

Embarrassment as Pride

Narrative Resourcefulness and Strategies of Normativity Among Cretan Animal-Thieves

The phrase "honor among thieves" suggests the paradox faced not only by thieves, but by all those (e.g., anarchists) whose principled defiance of the norms of an encompassing society requires that they, too, develop their own forms of normativity: ethical rules of conduct, organizational coherence, and social predictability. These "alternative normativities" generate modes of excuse-making that ironically echo the standardized pieties of the encompassing order. Linguistic clues provide the rhetorical armament for these tecnhiques of legitimation. In this essay, I examine certain narrative strategies, not so much for the evidence they may provide of the creation of order in any "official" sense, as for the strategic deployment of some of the signs of respectability that allow actors to mask acts of moral subversion.

Respectability is a categorial system, embodied in the forms of etiquette (lit. "label"). Actions that violate its prescriptions are, in Douglas's (1966) felicitous phrase, "matter out of place." But such a set of rules for correct and decorous comportment may not, in practice, be as precise or rigid as its very status as a normative "system" seems to require. Its precision is largely an impression successfully "managed" (Goffman 1959) by powerful actors with vested interests in maintaining a status quo. Conversely, actors of lowly position may find it most advantageous to emphasize subversive strategies, so that, by an alchemy of paradox, strategic action itself reflects a kind of normativity. It acquires the formal coherence of an ideology. Analyses that deny the ideological character of apparently antiregulatory social formations such as anarchism and social banditry simply endorse the encompassing hegemonies—usually those of the nation-state—by refusing to recognize local-level ideologies on equal terms (e.g., Hobsbawm 1959:23; but cf. Mintz 1982:274; Herzfeld 1985a:29).

The normativity of the subversive—"honor among thieves" again—has its distinctive embarrassments quite as much as any bourgeois respectability. But it is consistent with the logic of social marginality that these embarrassments, more often than not, should be occasioned by excessive obedience to the dictates of the law. They violate an intimate sense of community because they give authority to intrusive ideologies of conformity and good manners, or because they entail obedience to the law courts (explicitly called *prodhosia* 'betrayal'); moreover, no less than offenses committed against the larger order, such actions elicit a rhetoric of self-justification.

Here, Austin's (1971 [1956–57]) penetrating if programmatic discussion of excuses has particular relevance. Austin based his plea for more serious study of excuse-making on an essentially anthropological proposition, that is, that excuses, because they must always satisfy local concepts of decorum in order to succeed, provide an unusually effective basis for deciphering what Douglas (1975) has subsequently seen as the "backgrounded" implicit rules of a given society. The part of Austin's argument that interests us here can be summarized succinctly: excuses succeed to the extent that they are acceptable rather than convincing, since nonrelative notions of truth have little or no bearing on the extent to which members of a given society are prepared to tolerate each other's prevarications and peccadilloes. Moreover, if we accept that the presence or otherwise of belief is something on which an anthropologist is poorly equipped to pronounce (Needham 1972),[1] the question of conviction is irrelevant. What counts is the extent to which the performative style of the excuse (or of any other kind of disclaimer) protects the speaker from any public charges of untruthfulness, whatever people may actually think.

Austin's (1971 [1956–57]:80) distinction between justification and excuse also helps us here. Justification is essentially what happens when "we accept responsibility but deny that it was bad"; excuses occur when, admitting that the action was objectionable, we nonetheless disclaim responsibility for it. In the present essay, I shall be concerned with people—highland villagers from Crete—who use narrative devices to suggest that they fully recognize the objectionable properties of what they have done but want to convey that they had no real choice. What is more, since these particular people live in a social world that constantly pits them against larger, usually state-mandated forms of authority, they have to excuse some actions in terms of a morality that makes very little sense from the outside but perfect sense from within. Theirs is the dilemma faced, for example, by modern college students who excuse their formal way of dressing or their respectful politeness toward their teachers—both conventions approved by the larger society—on the grounds that the power structures governing success leave them no choice. When a Cretan shepherd acts in a way that a town lawyer or policeman would find thoroughly correct, he may have to excuse himself to his immediate peers in exactly the same fashion.

Even in such cases, however, the important thing is to show that one knows the rules, not that one is necessarily innocent of wrong intentions or deeds. The limiting case on Crete may be that of the shepherd who swears on a miraculous icon that he has not stolen his enemy's sheep; the enemy may not believe him, but can no longer challenge him since—even amongst these aggressively agnostic shepherds—it is socially inappropriate to challenge what is, in essence, a divinely sanctioned disclaimer of guilt (Herzfeld 1990). To return to the college context for a moment, a teacher may not believe the student who claims that a family funeral delayed the homework assignment, but would hardly be so tasteless as to say so. There are also aspects of excuse performance (in the dramaturgical sense) that are extrinsic to the linguistic basis of their performativity. Excuses are governed by an aesthetic of social interaction, and the creative artists in this genre are those who know when to use their pleas and how to pace them—timing (''tempo'') is vital here (Bourdieu 1977:7)—and who can for a brief moment turn the plausible-as-glib into the plausible-as-credible.

People who live in the margin of nation-state societies often have particularly well-developed skills for the management of social time. For them, aggressively creative performance is not only a permissible mode of interaction; it is the primary arena of social contest both within the community and between the community and the law. For such people, illegality usually needs no excuse. But justifications for obeying the official law and for disobeying the standards of the local society are bluffs that others delight in calling. It is time to turn to some examples.

Cretan Shepherds, Cretan Sheep-Thieves

In this essay I use the example of sheep-thieves living on the geographical and political margins of a centralized nation-state (Greece) to show how these strategies operate. The specific ethnographic locale is a village (here pseudonymously called ''Glendi'') in the mountains of west central Crete, in the northern foothills of Mt. Ida. It is a community in which verbal as well as athletic skills are constantly tested in the arena of male contest. Paying close attention, above all, to the narrative conventions of the sheep-thieves themselves, particularly with respect to one incident that involved a senior national politician whose origins lie in the area and in the culture of these unruly shepherds, I suggest that the tactics of excuse-making can perhaps best be described as apologetic—in the technical sense of that term, meaning modalities of self-explanation—and that, by plundering the rhetorical idiom of official values, they effectively subvert those selfsame values. Thus, the narratives they tell about illegal exploits may adopt official phrases and ideas about freedom, individuality, and pride to produce accounts of illegal activity—such as animal-theft, smuggling, cheating, or gambling—that are immensely embarrassing to officialdom. Conversely, they may also use the local social idiom of cynical opportunism in order to excuse acts of obedience to the state and its despised functionaries.

In approaching the Cretan material, we must pay at least precautionary attention to the role of the ethnographer in the production of ethnographic data.[2] It will become abundantly clear that the audience the speakers are most often addressing is not one of co-villagers, who might be supposed to share their views, but rather the ethnographer, an outsider, sympathetically received, but always at least potentially the target of various devices intended to minimize and counter the several forms of cultural embarrassment that Greeks evince in dealing with foreigners (especially Western Europeans).[3] At the same time, the existence of such a stock-in-trade suggests, in a community where few foreigners stay even as long as a single night, that the strategies have been ready and waiting. That, in turn, suggests that on the smaller stage of village interaction people have not been uniform in their evaluation of each others' actions; that, in short, cultural embarrassment occurs at many levels of social identity below that of the relatively novel nation-state. It is not a novel reaction to the novel situation that my presence afforded the villagers, although I almost certainly caused embarrassment at times merely by hearing stories that contravened official morality so dramatically.

Cultural embarrassment has, in fact, long been a staple of the ethnographic literature on Greece. It has appeared in this guise, however, as the Mediterraneanists' notion of "shame," a translation of indigenous terms (usually *dropi*) that only weakly conveys their structural implications. *Dropi* is the sense of appropriate concealment that, in any given context, plays on the social boundaries of cultural sharing by defining a fairly specific limit between intimacy and formality. When people hold several different kinds of allegiance, however, what constitutes appropriate concealment at one level may be better revealed at another. Thus, in a society that (1) knows its local values to be frequently at odds with those of the encompassing nation-state and (2) nonetheless identifies with that larger entity in opposition to all external criticisms and attacks, we should expect to find a sense of ambivalence born of these morally concentric but pragmatically conflicting allegiances (cf. also Meeker 1979:185).

This accounts for the phenomenon, which we shall observe in the texts given later, of modes of expression that are quite coyly bourgeois in their rush to self-exoneration, but that also appear in the ways in which sheep-thieves justify their failure to conform to a local code. The thieves apologize for their failure, above all, to steal in the right way, using the language of a worldview that animal theft violates ethically and legally. This is paradoxical, however, only in a state-centered view of the social world.

A very brief and schematic account of the ethnographic context must suffice here (but see Herzfeld 1985a; and cf. also Saulnier 1980 for a neighboring and very similar community). Glendi, once almost exclusively a pastoral village whose sole investment in agriculture was for immediate subsistence, has gradually, and more rapidly since 1963–64,[4] been moving toward a mixed economy in which agriculture (mostly vines and olives) has begun to predominate. Village men engage in highly agonistic duels in word and deed. In addition to a tradition of teasing exchanges in assonant verse and to rambunctious coffeehouse card games, villagers recognize as characteristic both the institution of bride theft (now more usually a form of consensual elopement) and that of reciprocal animal theft. It is this latter practice that provides young men with a tough testing ground for their masculinity. As with marriage, which unites in an affinal relationship households that previously may have been hostile and competitive toward each other, animal theft is often directed at establishing mutual respect and eventually alliance—sealed by the creation of a relationship of spiritual kinship—between the parties. This is what village men mean when they explain that they raid in order "to make friends."

Theft is a chancy business, and the real test of a man's social agility lies in his ability to seize opportunities with creative verve. This is as true of the verbal agility displayed in verse duels and narrative as it is of the thefts that the second of these genres in particular may celebrate. Such agility consists, in part, in rendering acceptable those acts that seem to contravene local ethics. The double-edged sense of "outrageous" (as in "outrageously funny") in English usage nicely captures this semantic and moral ambivalence: the issue is never whether a particular action flouts the rules but whether its very audacity garners approval for it. This holds as true for acts and words that violate the local canon by too great an apparent adherence to official law as it does for those that violate the law itself.

Embarrassing Conformities: A Textual Example

Two narrative texts will help concretize some of these rather general assertions. The first is a brief account by an elderly man of his last raid, which he carried out at the unusually advanced age of 65. It illustrates the potential ambiguity and embarrassment of a situation where the claims made flout the local code—in this case, the assumption that once a man has reached a certain age he becomes ridiculous by indulging in the habits of raiding that won him respect when he was young. Even this infraction of local morality is negotiable, however, and we shall see that recounting the event provides narrative resources for doing that. In the second and much longer example, conversely, we shall see that when actions that break the local code seem to agree with the state morality that circumscribes it, apologetic devices provide an escape from the locally no less disturbing implication that one has failed to behave as a good animal-thief should: one has had recourse to the law and to the official political establishment. For the paradox is that unconventionality also possesses—indeed, requires—its own conventions.

The Old Man's Last Raid

The first narrative is quite brief—its brevity is a matter of some interest in its own right—and is given here in its entirety.[5] The context is a discussion about raiding; I had asked the old shepherd about his last exploit.

> *Efighame ap' to Spiloti sta eksindapende mu xronia. Če pighame*
> We left from Spiloti when I was 65 years old. And we went
>
> *na me pari, lei, ya teleftea fora na pame se klopi. Epighame,*
> so he could take me, says he, for the last time raiding. We went,

idhame to vosko, ki aftos efovithiče ke efiyene, ce strimoksamen
saw the shepherd, and he was afraid and left, and we gathered

istera ta provata če piramene dhio, tria, tessera, dhen ksero m-
afterwards the sheep and took two, three, four, I don't know

posa, če epighame ke ta molarame ke ta 'kana zondaria če mu
how many, and we went and let them loose and I kept them and for me

kamane ke polla oza! Afti itone i teleftea mu klopi. [Esi či o
they made many animals. This was my last theft. [You and

Menelaos mazi dhiladhi?] O, če o Menelaos mazi. { Aftos . . .
Menelaos together, that is?] Yes, together with M. He

                    [{D/iladhi
                    [That is,

pateras ke yos dhen ine ligho asinithisto?] Asinithisto ine, ma
father and son isn't a bit unusual?]   It's unusual, but

lei ya teleftea fora prepi na se paro na pamene.
he says for the last time I must take you along.

In further discussion, he went on to say that he had not, in fact, done the actual stealing himself: he was no longer capable of the energy required for this arduous exercise. His disclaimer is important as a key to what has gone before and gives a sense of the double negotiation that is taking place: on the one hand, he must justify the odd behavior of a dignified elderly man who goes raiding when sensible men of his age would avoid such returns to youthful indiscretion; on the other hand, in that very process he gains for himself the right to do it. It is, in any case, his son's "fault": the reversal of the rule that prohibits father and son from raiding together— more strictly even than it forbids two brothers to do the same—requires an excuse, and the constant reminder that he would not have gone without his son's insistence lets him out. At no point does he try to justify his behavior in terms of the state's opposition to raiding; rather, his pride in undiminished manly spirit appears as a final act of resistance to the decay that, in the androcentric ideology of this community, gradually saps the manly energy and unbridled sexuality of youth and reduces senescent men to the same tame, fearful condition as that of old women.

From the state's point of view, the entire nexus of values and activities entailed in animal theft is a subversion of order. As Glendiots are fond of remarking, however, their village entertains two distinct kinds of order: that of the state, which is extrinsic and intrusive, and that of the local community. Every violation of the state order is a celebration of communal solidarity; the latter is a paradoxical kind of order in that it is morally congruent, yet pragmatically at odds, with the values of the nation-state. There is a delicate equilibrium in the complementary opposition of these moralities. The state's superimposition of order ("laws" or "rules") over strategy contains the paradox that laws are themselves strategies—what Bourdieu (1977:37–40) calls "officializing" strategies—that present themselves as standing outside the "tempo" (1977:7) of actual social interchange. Conversely, rather like the oxymoronic notion of an "anarchist organization," the villagers' strategies paradoxically entail the potential subversion of strategy-in-general by the at least tacit implication of an ultimate local social morality. This morality is what, with delicate irony, they call "unwritten law"—again an oxymoron, given the authority symbolically ascribed throughout Greece to the act of writing.

Notice, then, the characteristic social ambivalence of the thieves' cultural identity as they try to achieve a balance between national pride and local ferocity. It is narratively reproduced in oxymoron. In recounting his final theft, the old man embeds his almost aggressively nonnormative action in a set of assumptions about the right way to raid. First, he makes it clear, through the device of a string of numbers ending with "I don't know," that he has not counted the sheep. This is important in establishing his legitimacy as a brave and moral thief, since it demonstrates that he has not had his mind on the purely economic aspects of the raid—the dimension to which most official attempts at suppression try to reduce the practice. On the other hand, he emphasizes that he kept the stolen animals and "for me they made many animals," meaning that he did not conduct this raid as a means of making new alliances, as a young man would have done, but achieved closure of the event in a manner that also secured a large patrimony for his sons; this, too, is a claim to social legitimation. (Even for an ambitious young raider, the addition of fertile ewes to his own flock is a good second best to the raid that leads, through discovery and exposure, to the creation of an alliance based on a balance of mutual fear and respect.)

Narratives about theft are part of the social technique that includes the raids themselves. Like the raids they celebrate—both are called *istories*—they are interactional strategies, designed to shunt responsibility for infraction elsewhere (here, onto the younger generation) while glorying in the rebelliousness that this infraction entails. In other words, the speaker implicitly apologizes for having acted out of character for an old man, while at the same time taking credit for getting away with it. His success derives particularly from the fact that, in the process, he has provided for his sons, however unconventionally, as a father should. Moreover, the narrative devices he uses constitute one of the ways he avoids blame. They are performative in both senses.

One device that the speaker uses to establish the absolute validity of his actions is the brief and matter of fact tone of his account. In our second example, we shall find the young speaker reveling at times in the fine particularities of his actions, though at others he too reverts to an apparently factual and dispassionate account. Through such variation, he reproduced the changing tempo of his actions, especially their calibration with a cycle of revenge, with a narrative precision that enables the hearer to enjoy the dramatically timed climax of eventual vengeance. In the old man's account, by contrast, the only kind of chronology mentioned is his own age. The sequence of events is described quickly and without elaboration; the termination of the story matches the termination of his raiding career. A simple comparison with the second story will show how the sense of closure is here anticipated from the very beginning: this is his last raid, and the narrative moves decisively toward that conclusion.

The old man's narrative contains several indications that a reversal of the "order of disorder" is in train. First, the narrator's apparent failure to remember the number of stolen animals is relevant. It is not so unusual that a thief should fail to remember, but much odder that he should deliberately "fudge" the number of stolen animals rather than resorting to some symbolic device, such as a stereotypical series like "7–17–27. . .n7," to indicate a rising number of captured animals in a sequence of raids and counterraids. Second, the retention of the animals is definitive. Since a thief often hopes that his victim will discover his identity and require restitution of the animals, as well as initiating a counterraid that should culminate in an alliance between two well-matched, erstwhile foes, the boastful cry, *ke ta 'kana zondaria če mou kamane ke polla oza* 'and I kept them and for me they made many animals', emphasized in narration by a sudden slowing of speech and an increase in volume, turns the speaker symbolically and practically from a thief into a *nikokiris* (householder, man of substance and order). But, paradoxically again, he achieves this effect by using—and here even exaggerating—the measured precision of male speech that is the mark of the good thief. It is also paradoxical in that it belies his refusal of numerical precision: he has replaced the calculus of revenge with the expansive vagueness of property ownership, in a manner that suppresses the thievery necessary in this society to arrive at that estimable condition.

To understand the operation of this discourse, we must view as "shifters" (see Silverstein 1976), not only the pronouns of person and place, but also the evanescent rhetorical markers of right and wrong. In slightly different terms, we can say that the semantic lability characteristic of shifters is not confined to the semantic interpretation of lexemic elements in narrative, but also appears in the relationship between named concepts and their social connotations. Shifters are essentially properties of a social relationship. In that the moral content of an abstract social construct like honesty, manliness, or membership in the community is ceaselessly negotiated, not given, the interpretation of particular acts is similarly labile. Glendiots do not say that theft is good or bad in general, and indeed for them to do so would be incompatible with their emphasis on the performativity of the very role of being a thief. Instead, they represent acts of stealing as parts of a restless negotiation of status in which the disapprobation of the state is merely a surface that provides some of the rhetoric of regulation through which norms of disorder (from the state's point of view) are ordered and contested.

The operation of these moral shifters may perhaps best be seen in my own exchange with the speaker at the end of the narrative. In the dynamics of fieldwork, I found myself arguing the case for local norms, by asking whether it was not perhaps unusual for father and son to go raiding together. The question, simply by being a question, had the perlocutionary consequence of eliciting in response a rhetoric of self-justification before authority (see also Briggs 1986:56)[6]: "It's unusual, but he says, 'For the last time I must take you along.'" Note that it is "he," the son, who says this; he is thus made to assume the burden of moral responsibility for what has happened without diminishing the speaker's pride in either his own toughness at age 65 or his son's audacity and pride in him. That this was also the last time the speaker went raiding is stressed anew. The speaker thereby joins the ranks of the officially respectable as befits an elderly man[7]—if there is anything morally objectionable about his actions it now attaches to the son—and at the same time somehow "explains" the anomaly of father and son going on a joint raid. The speaker so effectively recasts local morality and its infractions in terms of an officializing discourse that a momentary sense of identity of interest is created between two kinds of "moral community"[8] that are, as we have already noted, structurally congruent but pragmatically at odds.

Protracted Vengeance

In the next example, we shall be looking at a narrative in which the violation of a local sense of order is created by the notion of "betrayal," that is, of co-villagers' treachery in covering up the theft of people from the neighboring community of Ossidhi. Glendi and Ossidhi have a long history of mutual distrust. The story is especially germane to this attempt at showing the parallels between social and discursive practices in that, toward the end, the narrator introduces the role of a member of the national parliament. From the point of view of the villagers, just about the only time that politicians appear in a favorable light is when they bail sheep-thieves out of prison or use their influence to get their sentences commuted. This does not occasion gratitude (as one might expect from the surface rhetoric of "obligation" and "social worth") so much as cynicism. The villagers understand that politicians' actions are motivated by venality and that they contradict the larger moral code that public figures are ideally supposed to support. They can thus morally "englobe" (Ardener 1975:25) the politicians on whom they depend as clients, using the politicians' violation of the national code as the ostensible basis for their more immediate distaste for the politicians' manipulation of local values. Here, narrative resources are vitally important (see also Herzfeld 1985a:107, for a comparable example). But this is to anticipate the analysis. Because the narrative is a very long one, I have divided it into episodic segments, quoting the text only where the narrative resources that interest us are especially well illustrated. This allows us to concentrate on selected discursive devices that mediate the relationship between the two principal levels of moral identity (state and village) through the use of self-justifying narrative tactics.

(1) Introducing the story. This segment is given in its entirety.

So, once, on the thefts I'm talking about now, it was, we had two lambs which (*ta opia* [a formalism]), let's say, my father had captured and they were suckling. And we had another that was sick. So my father takes one and takes it down to the village, to the house, and we take as you say we feed [them] together with my brother, my second oldest [brother], we fed them, let's say, we watch them here in the village, as . . . that is, like house animals (*martarika*), *koutrouvaria* we call them. So these lambs grew bigger, fatter, we fed them well! Good care! One day, my brother Ghrighoris, the oldest, takes them, and he takes them to the mountains. What's the upshot? The same evening, so to speak, they take ten sheep off my father again and it happens also to be [i.e., that this includes] the three lambs we had here in the village. That night, when he took them there, they stole them. Thirteen in all. Which they stole here in Ossidhi.

Telling stories of animal theft is the quintessential male mode of speech in a community where measured speech is itself often treated as a sign of male identity. The goal of such utterances is thus to "unman" the other side: the discourse of the narrative ideally reproduces and reinforces the discomfiture of one's foes. The present example is no exception. The speaker introduces an entire sequence of thefts and counter-thefts with a device that will, as the story progresses, suggest that his enemies are generically unmanly. By "converting" the stolen livestock into nonflock animals, he suggests that these enemies have not the courage to attack the flock proper, as real men do. Instead, they steal "house animals," a category of rather dubious moral purity.[9] The ambiguous nature of the deed is given emphasis here by the use of two synonyms for nonflock animals and by the speaker's careful distinction between the three stolen *martarika* and the other ten animals.

(2) Deception—successful at first. The speaker's father sends emissaries to all the surrounding villages in the hope of locating his animals before they are all slaughtered. He is unsuccessful; the emissaries—his own co-villagers—report back from the community of Ossidhi and mendaciously tell him that he can rule Ossidhi out. But his wife is unconvinced and sends the speaker's two older brothers back to visit an aunt there and through her to contact a man she thinks may know something.

. . . they knock on the door. What happens? Then of course it was lamps, we didn't have electric ones, he lights his lamp to get up, so to speak, and open the door. But as he approached the door he recalled that he had the meat hanging in the bag. So, now, we could hear his footsteps arriving near the door. But then, they went away, so to speak, he remembered the meat, he wanted to hide it before opening the door. But my second brother, so to speak, Enetaros, wondered why he hadn't opened. He got suspicious. He was then seven or eight years old, maybe? And he peers in through the keyhole, and sees this Ossidhi type going to take down a bag from the center beam. Center beams, in those days: old houses! Yes, earthen [houses]. And he took down the bag and stashes it away.

The Ossidhi man's crime was arguably the less heinous; the real offense was committed by the co-villagers whose betrayal violated the ideal of communal solidarity:

> But our co-villagers made fools of us (*mas ekoroidhepsane*), so to speak. And our own kin, even, made fools of us. [Saying] that they're not in Ossidhi, [when] meanwhile they were in Ossidhi.

When the Glendiot victims did discover the truth, they stole 20 animals from the Ossidhi shepherd. Notice that they did not bother to take revenge on the co-villagers who had cheated them. The speaker called them "animals," whose goal was to remove from competition shepherds such as himself and his brothers who were *apo mikro soi* 'from a small patrigroup' and were therefore an embarrassment as long as they owned larger flocks than did these hostile, large-patrigroup co-villagers. Co-villagers whose actions are so despicable are simply not worth the compliment of a counterraid. There is also a play on symbolic categories here: animals are the objects rather than the agents of manly theft, often being compared to women in a variety of complex metaphors, so a proud man does not risk demeaning himself by engaging with even "human animals" on terms that suggest any kind of equality.

(*3*) *Accidental raiding: initiating reciprocity.*   Shortly thereafter, some shepherds from Psila, a village in the opposite direction from Ossidhi, stole 12 goats, and then 5 more, from the speaker's father. The latter goes to his spiritual kinsman (the speaker's godfather) in Psila. The latter tells him to search in the other villages: "If your goats are in Psila and I can't find them for you, I'll give you back the oil with which I've baptized my godson!" It turns out that the thieves were indeed from Psila, and had only consumed three of the stolen animals. This was a normative theft; it happened by "chance." In other words, the thieves had not intended a deliberate act of revenge, but had merely seized a good opportunity to initiate a new cycle of reciprocal raiding as manly shepherds are expected to do. They owned up when challenged, surrendering the animals they had not yet slaughtered and being thereby absolved of any requirement to compensate the victims for the ones they had already succeeded in disposing of.

> But they, so to say, didn't go to take revenge on us, they happened by, so to say, to go and find a chance one (*ton dixonda*), that is, they didn't go for revenge. They went looking for a chance to steal. Eh! and they found ours and stole them. So. Well, naturally, of course, we stole from them too afterwards, and we came out all square.

The sense of partial closure here results from the fact that such raids are not only acceptable, but because they occur by "chance," they are also a fair demonstration of real manhood—of being, in short, a worthy adversary. For it is the thief's capacity for improvisation, like that of the singer of competitive jesting verses or indeed of the narrator, that defines his prowess.

(*4*) *And on to the next raid.* There being nothing abnormal here, the narration continues straight on without a break. The use of a year ("1975") suffices to mark the repetitive transition between episodes, and it also lends an air of historicity, almost of official reporting, to what now becomes a tale of grievance.

> In 1975, we had a, we had our goats still, and we had a he-goat. A red he-goat, a
> flock-leader (*ombrostari*). Eh! and we had the goats arranged up there, and in the
> morning we go and the he-goat is missing. Which (*o opios* [a formalism]), however
> (*dhe* [another formalism]), had been "eaten" by a co-villager of ours.

Revenge, however, had become impossible as well as inappropriate, because the thief was meanwhile killed in a tractor accident: "So, eh, what vengeance can you take on this fellow then?" Along with the opportunity for revenge, the chance of creating new alliances through reciprocal theft had also disappeared. One could presumably raid those of the deceased's close agnates who had substantial flocks of their own, but this might be interpreted as excessive or as disrespectful to the dead. Having thus shown himself to be a reasonable fellow, philosophical about lost opportunities, the speaker continues his enumeration of raids with two more uses of the chronological marker.

(*5*) . . . *And the next . . . and the next after that . . .*

> In 1976, we again had the goats here, put 'em in the winter pasture and again they
> steal from us seven goats. From the mountainside again; we of course failed to
> locate them, that is, we didn't, so to say, for sure, learn who'd stolen them, because
> we got a bit of information, let's say, that the So-and-so's, we suspect, let's say, the
> So-and-so's, but we aren't sure. [Mm.] Anyway, that is, we haven't found out
> about them yet, not a thing. In 1977, they stole 70 she-goats from us. Eh, so, so to
> speak, my father went and my brother, in the morning, to count the goats and found
> that 70 goats were missing.

It later transpired that only 34 of these had been slaughtered. Now, however, the story turns quickly into an account of grievance and redress. For the co-villagers who ostensibly went to "ask"—in other words, to inquire of their spiritual kin in other villages whether they knew anything about the missing animals—turned out to be traitors, motivated by the same hostility to small-patrigroup shepherds as those who had tried to ruin the speaker's side on that first occasion. Now that a series of smaller incidents have established the moral ascendancy of the speaker's group, the narrative returns easily to its original theme.

> These same (*i opii pali*), so to speak, villagers who'd "sold" them (*ts' ixane
> pulimenes*)—that is, they'd betrayed them (*ts' ixane prodhomenes*). They told, let's
> say, the thieves that "In such-and-such a place there are 300 goats, come take as
> many as you want! No one watches them at night. They're unguarded (*adhespotes*)
> at night. So come and get them."

Some linguistic features in the above deserve comment. First, the introduction of the first sentence with a formal or H-register[10] relative pronoun (*i opii*) serves as an "officializing strategy," and is reinforced by the use of pali, "again"—not only in the sense that we are hearing again about these same fellow villagers, but also as a reminder that this is a repetition of a theme from the beginning. Those who betray co-villagers, whether to other shepherds or to the authorities, are beneath contempt. The emphatic use of formal language here provides an "official" idiom for justifying a totally local form of morality. The latter also appears in discursive practice: the use of the passive participle (lit. "had them stolen"), which is local dialect (i.e., nonstandard from the standpoint of official usage) indicates a degree of possession and involvement that invites retaliation (see Herzfeld 1985b:32–34).

(6) *The conflict spreads: political ramifications.* The conniving of these co-villagers was a double blow. Not only had they betrayed a normatively sacred trust, but they had brought the speaker's family to the edge of ruin. In order to pay off the expenses of the *arotixtadhes* (the 'asker', kin who had—ostensibly—gone to the other villages to locate the stolen animals with the help of their spiritual kin there), they had to sell off 50 more animals. If one adds the 34 already slaughtered, and recalling that a small but just viable flock consists of a mere 50 head (with about five hundred the standard for a "large" flock), the magnitude of the damage becomes immediately apparent. Something had to be done, and fast.

That something was the involvement of a senior politician, here pseudonymously called Meghalostomos. This man, the scion of a shepherd family with strong Psiliot connections, was generally believed to be a willing and active patron of animal-thieves; in this way, according to a pattern common in the area, he could rely not only on their households' collective votes but also on those of a substantial range of their agnates. Politicians of this stature—Meghalostomos had held high government office—are also in a position to exercise some pressure on the police and judicial bureaucracies.

Of particular interest in the passage that follows is the speaker's rather embarrassed account of how his father was able to put pressure on Meghalostomos to act. Politicians and local shepherds are entangled in a nexus of reciprocal needs (see Campbell 1964). The values of obligation and reliability that sustain the resultant social relationships conflict with the larger ideals of disinterestedness forstered by the ideology, if not the practices, of the nation-state. For the politician, in an era of increasing public resentment against older forms of patronage and discomfiture with their "un-European" ethical base, the charge of protecting animal-thieves constitutes a dangerous embarrassment. One local leader, accused of playing an active role in perpetuating the entire system of protection (*rousfeti*) locally and on the national stage, announced in his election propaganda that he "did not want a single animal-thief as a voter [i.e., as a supporter]." Such disclaimers, greeted on the whole with derision, nonetheless increase the villagers' awareness that these patron-client relationships are viewed negatively in the larger world beyond the village, and thereby also fuel their resentment of the politicians' ability to manipulate them through superior control of legal resources. That patronage continues to pervade the bureaucratic system that ideologically rejects it (see now also Shore 1989) provides particularly rich opportunities for a local discourse that delights in mocking official pretensions and especially in showing how it fails to live up to its own, much advertised moral standards.

From these increasingly negative perceptions of patronage, then, there results a growing ambivalence about the value of such connections. Whereas it used to be commonplace for shepherds to boast proudly of their powerful political patrons, today they are more inclined to express resentment at a system of political values that makes such dependency possible and even necessary; to give evasive answers to questions about their own sources of influence in high places; and to be extremely vague about the exact nature of such connections. The following narrative exemplifies this ambivalence.

> The business went to Meghalostomos, went to all, then, the big guys, the Commander [of police]. . . . [MH: How do you mean, that you . . . ? That is, that is, what role did he play?] He played a role, he was at all the police authorities. If they couldn't find the animals, so to speak? But he knows . . . now, because they're a lot of animals. . . .
>
> [MH: You have a connection with Meghalostomos to. . . .] Yes, that is, my father [does]. Yes. My father has links, that is, with Meghalostomos.
>
> [MH: Are they *sindekni*, anything (of that sort)?] They aren't, let's say, [direct] *sindekni*, that is, Meghalostomos baptized a first cousin twice removed of my father's and from there. . . .
>
> [MH: But a Thiriouris (i.e., of the same patrigroup), still. . . .]
> Yes, a Thiriouris. From there, so to speak, we have a link and he's also a rightist (Karamanlikos [one who voted for Karamanlis, a famous conservative leader]), that is, he votes for him, let's say, as a person, for Meghalostomos, he doesn't vote for him, so to speak, as, because he's right-wing (Karamanlikos). Whatever party he [Meghalostomos] joins he'll vote for him.
>
> [MH: Mmm.]
> Yes, as a person (*atomo*), that is.
>
> [MH: They have connections, let's say.]
> They've connections.
>
> [MH: Yes.]
> That is, they are fraternal friends, *sindekni*. Incense-wafted (*merodhiči*) *sindekni*, as we say—incense-wafted.

In order to understand the tactics used in this segment of the narrative, it is helpful to turn back to Austin's useful insights into the pragmatics of excuse-making. Specifically, Austin (1971 [1956–57]:97) reminds us that the stylistics of excuses must be recognizably conformist at some level. For these shepherds, who make a virtue out of social nonconformism, the disclaimers of actual political influence are a necessary "excuse" for invoking such connections. The father is not closely connected to Meghalostomos because the link of spiritual kinship is through another member of the speaker's family; but he is able to conjure up his services. Again, he is not subject to the nastiness of political party affiliation, but does recognize a personal tie as binding and would also—and indeed only—vote for him on that basis: personal loyalty stands opposed to the ethos of the official world. There is a further ambiguity in his being "fraternal friends" with the politician; the phrase is a virtual oxymoron, in that brothers are always nominally equal, whereas friendship—an instrumental and asymmetrical relationship amongst non-kin[11]— inevitably implies the dependency that goes with patronage. The "incense-wafted" status of their relationship is also ambiguous: incense, as a sacramental substance, implies sanctified closeness, but it can also be taken as a confirmation of the indirect kinship basis of the relationship. Everyone is touched, metaphorically at least, by the sacramental incense of the baptismal ritual.

In short, a series of internal contradictions is paraded here so that the listener can appreciate not only what a good fellow the speaker's father is, but above all how well he manipulates those who think they are manipulating him. The clever management of contradiction in the narrative serves, I suggest, as a model for the social dexterity of the speaker and his father. One knows, after listening to this elaborate display of ethical fence-sitting, that these are people who understand the intricacies of social strategy.

(7) *The work of deception and counterbluff.*   At this point, in response to a question, the narrative abruptly switches back to the 1975 raid and the theft of the red he-goat. This is something of a diversion, but it allows the speaker to emphasize his side's cleverness still further and to "steal" meaning from the narrative form by subverting its linear constraints in order to bring the earlier event into direct juxtaposition with the now increasingly apparent evidence of that cleverness. This exemplifies the point just made about the creative use of narrative conventions to model social dexterity.

> The day when we lost the he-goat, ed, that guy has a balcony, and the meat he had on the balcony was he-goat. He-goat! Eh, from that, we understood, so to speak, and also found the bell of the goat, we found it in his sheepfold. Two or three years later, we find it, the bell of the goat, so to speak.

The enemy's (formally admirable) audacity in using the speaker's own animal in order to offer his side hospitality is balanced by the latter's cleverness in figuring out what has happened.

> Yes, and they treated [us], so to say, from the meat of the goat, and we saw that it was he-goat, whereas no: even from the butcher he didn't buy he-goat, nor did he have he-goat himself! He had sheep.

It is important to this narrator that he establish the high intelligence of his side. Although the 1975 raid is properly irrelevant to the later and more complex event in which this reversion is embedded, it serves here to switch the narrative thrust away from the always rather humiliating implications of Meghalostomos' patronage and toward the cleverness of the speaker and his family. In the process, narratively and pragmatically, the speaker regains control of the situation. Meghalostomos is eased out of the equation altogether, and as we move in the direction of the denouement we begin to see how the speaker's side will achieve a double triumph.

(8) *Revenge and pity: parallel humiliations.* That triumph consists in both a definitively final series of vengeance raids and the speaker's side's refusal to take advantage of the law to effect its revenge any further. By thus humiliating their enemies twice over, and by also rejecting the sanctions of the official world, the speaker's side also removes the no less humiliating taint of patronage that has brought them to this point. The narrative does briefly return to the subject of Meghalostomos and his intervention, but now emphasizing again the cleverness of the speaker's side. Finally, the initiative returns to the shepherds—thieves and avengers alike—since the moral authority of the law courts must not be upheld in the uplands.

Meghalostomos got involved, so to speak, and they say, let's say, "They must be found!" And says the Commander of Police of Crete, they must search, he says, inspect, let's say, all the butchers' shops of Crete, even the smallest [police] station of Cre-, says he, and even in the most mountainous village, here where there's a Cretan Police station they were notified that: from such-and-such a village have been lost so many head of goats; and they have such-and-such an ear-mark (*samia*). Eh, and they search, so to speak, it can't be found. So, some 20 days had gone by, and they call us on the telephone from Meropatas, the police do. And my father ups and goes with my brother, the oldest one, and he tells him, "Here were found," says he, "hooves," says he, "here, and horns. These wood-hard bits, so to speak," he tells him, "perhaps you recognize them?" he asks my father, the police chief does. Says he, "Let me see it, I'll know it." So in goes my father first, in [he goes], and they had them on a table, in a sack, inside it they had them, and the policeman goes and lays them out on a table. He spreads them out, so to say, and tells him, "Tell me," he says to him, "do you know them?" And my father takes a, one of its feet, tells him, "This is the brown goat's, this is the hoof of the brown goat with the twisted horn. This horn belongs to such-and-such a goat, the black one. This hoof belongs to the one that we put in front (lit. 'header', *čefalopis*). This one, this one— he told [i.e., identified] them all, let's say, in order, my father [did]. So he tells him, "Go outside." And he mixes them up again, and calls my brother Ghrighoris, and tells him, "Do you know these hooves and horns?" Says he, "I know them." And my brother Ghrighoris too picks them up and ?sees them in his turn and says, "This is the brown [goat's], this is the header's, this is the black one's. That is, he named them just as my father named them. That is. Yes. He said, let's say, that he recognized them. And the police chief tells him, tells my father, says, "How did you recognize them?'' he asks, "uncle?" Says he, "Is it possible," he asks him, "Mr. Police Chief, to be," says he, "from when I was born a shepherd, and not to know," says he, "the hooves of my goats or their horns? I even know," says he, "their every hair, I'd know it." So he, now, of course, they had taken them from him.

Apparently, a thieves' exchange had taken place.

. . . that is, the Meropatas man gave away stolen animals again from Meropatas to Ossidhi, that is, they did a give and take, an exchange, he gave sheep, so to speak, stolen ones, and they gave him goats. That is, he did a deal! And slaughtered them there, without fear or passion, and they could slaughter them here too without fear or passion. So, says he, so to speak, finally, "Are the goats yours or aren't they?" says the Police Chief to my father and my brother, "Are they yours? Would you take an oath that they're yours?" Says he, "We would! With our hands and feet!" So, we go, then, and the police filed a charge, made a charge against him. They found on him, of course, they found on him stolen sheep, and a charge is issued by the police and it comes to court. And he's sentenced, let's say, for this business, he got five years in jail, and did them too. Eh, afterwards, then, there went my brother, Enetaros, with another person from the village here, so to speak, and I don't know who he is, let's say, I've not been told by my brother even yet, so to say, he hasn't told me, so to speak, with whom he went to take revenge. [MH: Is it deliberately he doesn't tell you, then?] What? [Is it deliberately he doesn't tell you, then?] He doesn't tell me because, you see, so to speak, [he thinks, "It might inadvertently escape him [i.e., me]." That is, this must be kept secret as long as there are people [in the know] in existence, it mustn't be learned with whom he went. Yes. He told me, let's say, that "I went myself with one other, but who [it was] he didn't tell me. So. They got up then and go and steal from him the first dose: 40 sheep! *Maropa*. Meat animals. And he gets up the second time and goes, it was another 40! He was in jail, but his brothers looked after the animals. And he gets up for the third time and goes and they take 20 off him. That is, they stripped him of a 100, for the 34 goats they robbed him of 100 sheep! And these goats they found on him he hadn't stolen himself, but he'd gotten them from others, let's say. That is, the thieves (let's say) do a give and take (*pare-dhose*), that is, give me and I'll give you. That is, take some stolen sheep, Eftixis, to Glendi, and give me some from Glendi, stolen goats for me to give in Meropatas. As they say. Eh. Time was passing, was passing, so to speak, he'd done three and a half years jail and one and a half exile, that is, in all it was five years. He did the three and a half years in jail, you see. Afterwards, he was to do his exile. Meanwhile, what happens? In order not to do the exile, my father had to sign that "What the hell and, let's say, it doesn't matter, that he was paid, ah, he's paid me for the goats, their value," so he wouldn't do exile. Now he explains. They came and found him, people from Meropata [found] my father and tell him, "Sign," so to speak, so that, as he has children, he has five or six children, this guy, he has his flock, his animals, so to speak, as he was a poor person, anyway, and he signed so to speak so he wouldn't go into exile. And he didn't go into exile.

This final passage is very revealing. Having demonstrated their cleverness, the speaker and his kin can now afford to be magnanimous. They have sailed perilously close to the wind of association with the law and with political patronage, and the closing segment is mainly concerned with demonstrating their "innocence" of such ethical impurity. The vastness of the hue and cry has been well anticipated; how could the police have failed to succeed when Meghalostomos—who is implicitly the real cause—put pressure on them in this way?

Above all, the speaker is now able to represent his father as a man of charity. By making the Meropatas delegation speak the words of their co-villager's humiliation—"Sign, so to speak, so that, as he has children, he has five or six children, this guy, he has his flock, his animals, so to speak . . ."—he utilizes the narrative to reinforce that fall from pride. The plea that a culprit is "poor" and should therefore be forgiven, or at least not reported to the authorities, serves the same end in another narrative, in which it is again the wife of a farmer-turned-thief who begs for mercy for her errant husband (Herzfeld 1985a:224).[12] And since signing a document is the ultimate expression of symbolic authority, bureaucratic as well as cosmological,[13] the legalistic act that closes the tale is also an act of social closure.

Excusable Proprieties

The texts we have examined here both illustrate the uses of narrative to generate a sense of self-justification. The search for exoneration is always complex in societies such as that of Glendi, where the values of state both conflict with local mores and yet also provide the rhetorical materials for defending the latter. In the first text, the problem was relatively simple: an elderly man, by going on a raid, flouted the local norms and yet by presenting himself as a limiting case also exemplified them. The careful yet concise language of his account suggests a finely tuned attention to the management of such ambiguities in order for the speaker to present himself in the most favorable light he could.

In the second text, the techniques of self-justification are both more varied and more unpredictable. But essentially the narrator's verbal dexterity suggests the virtuosity of his side in all the other areas of contest in which masculine skills are aggressively deployed. Moreover, where the old man of the first tale must merely justify a slight internal bending of the social expectations appropriate to his age, the narrator in the second narrative must confront a potentially far more serious infraction of local values: by appealing to his patron, he has brought in the repressive authority of the police and the law courts. Yet even these potential "betrayals" of local morality are redeemable through skilled apologetics. By vacillating on the nature of the patron-client relation and especially by admitting that his father was cajoled into a merciful action at the end of the narrative, the speaker demonstrates superb control over the interpretations that others might apply to what happened. He uses the structure and language of the narrative to perform acts of self-exoneration and thereby to maintain and even increase his reputation as a real man.

It may be useful at this juncture to lay out the key segments of the narrative in order to pinpoint the major uses of the excuse for actions that violate both the national and the local codes. From this more analytical overview, it becomes apparent that consistency exists only at one level: the need to represent "our" side as manly and heroic. Whose terms these are, the state's or the local community's, is a choice determined by circumstance in each case.

CONTENT	EXCUSE
1. Stolen sheep are not flock animals.	Anticipates special revenge by emphasizing inappropriateness and unmanliness of stealing house animals.
2. Period of "asking" reveals act of betrayal by recipient of the stolen animals.	Again anticipates special revenge by emphasizing nonnormative betrayal; defines perpetrators as "animals" in contrast to poor but norm-observing victims.
3. Normative theft (by "chance"); cf. 1, 2.	Absence of excuse rhetoric (cf. 1, 2).
4. Another raid against the speaker's side.	Animals "eaten" by a co-villager (datum introduced by H-register pronoun [*o opios*]); death of perpetrator becomes excuse for inaction, which would otherwise violate local norms.
5. More raids.	Reappearance of H-register pronoun (*i opii*) and use of 'again' (*pali*) index major theme of grievance.
6. Political ramifications.	Use of a patron requires excuses both because bureaucratic system officially rejects such acts and because of local attitude of contempt for politicians.
7. Enemy offers "us" hospitality, but we discover our own meat is being used.	Our recognition of the trick played on us, which is laudable when played on the police, becomes despicable when used against fellow shepherds.
8. Discovery.	Speaker excuses father's generosity to enemy— thereby humiliating the enemy while enabling himself to do something "nonmanly" that still, at yet another level of excuse-making, thwarts the state of its prey in the name of a value it cannot object to.

The speaker basically faces two situations in which he will need excuses: (1) when he must excuse his own side for acts against the official morality, and (2) when he must excuse acts that violate local morality. He can use official language to validate acts that contravene official rules (as in his use of the formal relative pronoun), and obviously local terminology (e.g., *koutrouvaria* for the house animals) to signal his adherence to local values. What turns some of his self-justifications into real excuses (to use Austin's distinction) is the implication of force majeure. That usually comes from the state, which has no means of redressing insults to the person and does not easily sanction acts of violence by private citizens. Thus, the trick at the end of the tale was to re-represent an act of mercy as a clever act of revenge. In each case, the speaker recognizes that his side has done something bad according to one code or the other, but uses the various fragmentary excuses to suggest that there is no reason for his side to accept responsibility for it. There is always someone else to blame, especially when one can play off two moral codes sharing a partially common rhetoric against each other.

When I began thinking about the nexus of acts and norms that surround animal theft in Glendi, I was puzzled by an apparent paradox: villagers regarded any dealings with the authorities as a "betrayal," yet demonstrably there were times when well-regarded shepherds did, in fact, involve the law in their affairs. During the nearly 15 years since I first visited Glendi, moreover, shepherds have become increasingly willing to cooperate with the law on a more regular basis, for example—through the formation of committees for the suppression of the practice. How did this come about?

There are obvious material causes of this kind of change, notably the increased availability of agricultural land and the greater integration of the community into the national and regional economies. But I suggest that no account of material relations is complete without the dimension of rhetoric. This is exactly what any transitive notion of performativity must mean. Effective deployment of the services of officialdom depends on the shepherds' concomitant ability to render such hitherto traitorous actions as acceptable in the sense that Austin's exploration of excuses suggests. A poetics of social life, by thus addressing the palpable consequences of self-presentation, supplies the missing dimension of rhetoric to accounts of social change—a dimension hitherto lost in the false opposition between the material and the symbolic in the anthropological division of labor (see also Herzfeld 1988). In the narratives we have inspected here, the first suggests only a personal eccentricity that is unlikely to have far-reaching effects. The second, however, affords us a glimpse into social change effected through the agile re-presentation of violations as norms—through, in short, a restless dialectic that exploits the ambiguities inherent in the relationship between state and local community.

Notes

I would like to express my very considerable gratitude to Charles Briggs for including me in this endeavor and for his excellent editorial comments on my essay.

1. Indeed, the focus of the best studies of "sentiment" (eg, Abu-Lughod 1986) remain studies of its representation.

2. This is the "critical," "reflexive," or—what is perhaps more relevant here—"dialogical" turn in recent anthropology. Used carefully, this approach actually yields more empirical data than the canonical impersonality espoused by most self-styled empiricists.

3. The tension between introspective and extroverted cultural stereotypes, and their deployment in everyday life, represents a wider range than the phenomenon first recognized in linguistic analysis as "diglossia" (Ferguson 1959) and may usefully be placed under the generic term "disemia" (Herzfeld 1987:114).

4. At that time, government grain subsidies coupled with massive emigration to West Germany and elsewhere created a sharp increase in the specialization of subsistence activities.

5. I have given this textual segment in Greek (rendered in a modified phonemic transcription), as well as in English, in order to give a sense of the original idiom. My interventions in the conversation are in standard script placed between square brackets ([]).

6. This aspect curiously appears to be absent from Goody's (1978) otherwise fundamentally Austinian theoretical framework for the analysis of questions.

7. Once men reach a certain age (usually in their late 60s) and are presumed to be relatively near death, villagers joke that they become more concerned about the care of their souls and the anticipation of the afterlife. This makes them more cautious socially and more observant in religious practice, leading them closer to the stereotypical ideal of female comportment.

8. Campbell (1964) treats the Sarakatsani as a moral community, which is in some sense a microcosm of larger entities such as the Greek nation and the Christian *oikoumene*. In more general terms, it fits the segmentary concept of *dhiki mas* (lit. ' our own [people]').

9. House animals may be kept by women, and there is at least one obscene *mandinadha* (rhyming or assonant couplet), that jokes about widows' presumed buggery with a house sheep. On attitudes to widows' sexuality, see also du Boulay 1974:123.

10. The formulation is that of Ferguson (1959): the H-register is formal, the L-register vernacular. These terms are based on a high-low distinction, but it is important to avoid the evaluative or judgmental implications of that terminology.

11. Although the relationship between *filia* 'friendship' and other kinds of social ties varies enormously among Greek communities, my own sense from fieldwork on Rhodes and Crete is that it is rarely if ever applied to relationships between close kin, among whom the appropriate kinship term would be thought to be more honorific and more exclusive of outsiders. On instrumentality in *filia*, see especially Loizos 1975:91.

12. The point here is that farmers (agriculturalists) are said to be effeminate in comparison to shepherds, and also that farmers should not steal because they have no flock animals that their foes could raid reciprocally. The wife's intervention as protector of her husband thus crushingly deflates his attempt to gain a more masculine status by raiding a real shepherd.

13. Cf. the proverbial phrase *o,ti ghrafi dhe kseghrafi* 'what it [i.e., fate] writes it does not unwrite'.

Works Cited

Abu-Lughod, Lila. 1986. *Veiled sentiments: honor and poetry in a Bedouin society.* Berkeley: University of California Press.
Ardener, Edwin. 1975. The "problem" revisited. *Perceiving Women,* ed. Shirley Ardener, pp. 19–27. London: J. M. Dent.
Austin, J. L. 1971 (1956–57). A plea for excuses. *Philosophy and Linguistics,* ed. Colin Lyas, pp. 79–101. London: Macmillan.
Bourdieu, Pierre. 1977. *Outline of a theory of practice,* translated by Richard Nice. Cambridge: Cambridge University Press.
Briggs, Charles L. 1986. *Learning how to ask: A sociolinguistic appraisal of the role of the interview in social science research.* Cambridge: Cambridge University Press.
Campbell, J. K. 1964. *Honour, family, and patronage: A study of institutions and moral values in a Greek mountain community.* Oxford: Clarendon.
Douglas, Mary. 1966. *Purity and danger: An analysis of concepts of pollution and taboo.* London: Routledge & Kegan Paul.
————. 1975. *Implicit meanings: essays in anthropology.* London: Routledge & Kegan Paul.
du Boulay, Juliet. 1974. *Portrait of a Greek mountain village.* Oxford: Clarendon.
Ferguson, Charles A. 1959. Diglossia. *Word* 15:325–40.
Goffman, Erving. 1959. *The presentation of self in everyday life.* New York: Doubleday.
Goody, Esther N. 1978. Towards a theory of questions. In *Questions and politeness: Strategies in social interaction,* ed. Esther N. Goody, pp. 17–43. Cambridge: Cambridge University Press.
Herzfeld, Michael. 1985a. *The poetics of manhood: Contest and identity in a Cretan mountain village.* Princeton, NJ: Princeton University Press.
————. 1985b. Gender pragmatics: Agency, speech, and bride-theft in a Cretan mountain village. *Anthropology* 9:25–44.
————. 1987. *Anthropology through the looking-glass: Critical ethnography in the margins of Europe.* Cambridge: Cambridge University Press.
————. 1988. Rhetoric and the constitution of social relations. In *Working papers and proceedings,* no. 22. Chicago: Center for Psychosocial Studies.
————. 1990. Pride and perjury: time and the oath in the mountain villages of Crete. *Man* (n.s.) 25: 305–22.
Hobsbawm, Eric. 1959. *Primitive rebels: Studies in archaic forms of social movement in the 19th and 20th centuries.* Manchester: Manchester University Press.
Loizos, Peter. 1975. *The Greek gift: Politics in a Cypriot village.* Oxford: Blackwell.
Meeker, Michael E. 1979. *Literature and violence in North Arabia.* Cambridge: Cambridge University Press.
Mintz, Jerome R. 1982. *The anarchists of Casas Viejas.* Chicago: University of Chicago Press.
Needham, Rodney. 1972. *Belief, language, and experience.* Oxford: Blackwell.
Saulnier, Françoise. 1980. *Anoya: Un village de montagne crétois.* Paris: P. H. Stahl/ Laboratoire d'Anthropologie Sociale.

Shore, C. N. 1989. Patronage and bureaucracy in complex societies: Social rules and social relations in an Italian university. *Journal of the Anthropological Society of Oxford* 20:56–73.

Silverstein, Michael. 1976. Shifters, linguistic categories, and cultural description. In *Meaning in Anthropology*, eds. Keith H. Basso and Henry A. Selby, pp. 11–55. Albuquerque: University of New Mexico Press.

ELINOR OCHS, RUTH C. SMITH,
& CAROLYN E. TAYLOR

Detective Stories at Dinnertime
Problem Solving Through Co-Narration

In this essay, we focus on storytelling as a problem-solving discourse activity. Our concern is the interface of cognitive and social activity, as outlined in Vygotskian theory (Vygotsky 1978, 1981; Wertsch 1985; Rogoff and Lave 1984) and displayed in the context of everyday family dinnertime talk. Our research base consists of 20 white, English-speaking, American families, varying in social class, whom we visited on two evenings for several hours, video- and audio-recording them as they ate dinner, relaxed, and put their children to bed. Our data indicate how problem solving through storytelling is a socially accomplished cognitive activity, how family members articulate solutions to problems posed by narrated events and at times work together to articulate the narrative problem itself. Such joint cognizing can be seen as part of what families do—what makes a family an "activity system" (Engeström 1987). We suggest that this joint problem solving through narrative gives structure to family roles, relationships, values, and worldviews.

Dinner as an Opportunity Space

Narratives are told among family members in numerous settings, but dinnertime seems to be a preferred moment for this activity in many American families. Dinner is a time when adults and children often come together after being apart throughout the day, a somewhat unique time for many families because there is some assurance of a relatively captive audience for sounding things out. Dinnertime is thus an *opportunity space*—a temporal, spatial, and social moment that provides the possibility of joint activity among family members. Families use this opportunity space in different ways: some families talk more than others; some talk only about eating; some use the time to make plans or recount the day's events. Whatever direction the talk takes, dinnertime is a potential forum for generating both knowledge and social

95

order/disorder (e.g., in elaborating and resolving problems and conflicts) through interaction with other family members. Dinnertime thus may provide a crystallization of family processes (cf. Feiring and Lewis 1987), what activity theorists (Leontyev 1981; Wertsch 1985) might call a "genetically primary example" of family life.

Dinner Arrangements

Physical arrangements for eating dinner varied across the families in our study and within households in the course of a single evening. As illustrated in the following table, dinner arrangements can vary in terms of three dimensions: time, space, and activity focus. In terms of the *temporal* dimension, dinners may be staggered or synchronous. That is, family members may eat at different times or concurrently. In some families, children and adults eat when they are hungry and not necessarily at the same time. Families often do not eat at the same time every day. Second, dinners may vary *spatially* in that family members may be either dispersed or assembled while eating. Sometimes children eat in one room or one part of a room and one or more adults eat elsewhere. Third, dinners vary in terms of whether family members are overtly attending to different activities or share the same *activity focus*. For example, certain members may be watching television as they eat, while others are talking to one another. In other families, all members, at least on the surface, appear to be engaged in the same activity focus, either as ratified participants in the same conversation or as co-viewers of the same television program.

Dinner Arrangements			
DIMENSIONS	ARRANGEMENT TYPES		
	Decentralized		*Centralized*
Temporal	Staggered	$\longleftrightarrow$	Synchronous
Spatial	Dispersed	$\longleftrightarrow$	Assembled
Activity Focus	Diverse	$\longleftrightarrow$	Shared

Dinners characterized by features along the right side of the table (i.e., family members eating at the same time and place and sharing activity focus) are more centralized and tended in our corpus to be more formal and last longer than dinners characterized by features along the left side (i.e., family members eating at different times and places and engaging in different activities).

Dinner and Talk

The different dinner arrangements shown in the table have implications for the amount and kind of talk that takes place at dinnertime. In our corpus, the more centralized dinners promoted more extensive problem solving through talk. Family members who sat down together to eat appeared to use a wider range of problem-solving genres—not only stories, but plans and arguments as well. With respect to stories, centralized dinners tended to promote longer stories, with more audience involvement in sorting out problems, solutions, and stances. Stories in the decentralized dinners tended to fill one page or less of transcript and did not significantly involve other interlocutors in problem solving. In contrast, stories in the centralized dinners sometimes filled several pages; in one example, a narrative threads through 46 pages of a 64-page dinner transcript as family members work through unresolved aspects of a narrative situation over a 40-minute period.

In this sense, families who ate together exploited the opportunity space differently from families who decentralized dinnertime. Centralized dinners appear to provide an enduring moment in which family members can help one another sort out problematic events in their lives through co-narration. The resulting narratives, which we shall illustrate in this essay, differ markedly from narratives in which a story line is presented in an orderly fashion, that is, where settings and relevant background are fixed at the outset of the telling and events are chronologically and causally ordered.

Centralized dinner arrangements may promote more than co-narrated stories; they may also promote opportunities for adults to exert and extend power over children. Relative to decentralized dinner arrangements, the centralized dinners we observed appeared more ritualized, entailing conformity to numerous eating conventions. Many dinners involved opening and closing rituals, such as saying grace and asking permission to be excused. Further conventions included where to sit, how to sit, which utensils to use, how close the serving dish should be from the plate, how much food one should serve oneself, how to request food, how to respond to offers of food, when to speak vis-à-vis eating, the order of eating different foods, which foods must be eaten, quantity of food that must be eaten, and so on. Each of these conventions may become a locus of compliance-gaining negotiation between adults and children. In this sense, centralized dinners provide a greater opportunity space for the exertion of social control over children. In contrast, decentralized dinners seem to empower children more to organize their own dinner activities, allowing children greater freedom while potentially exposing them less fully to adult narrative styles and problem-solving approaches.[1]

Approaches to Narrative

Studies of narrative tend to be either cognitive or sociological. Cognitive studies focus on stories as problem-solving genres. Although definitions of what constitutes a story differ, most studies emphasize that stories contain one central problematic event—sometimes called an "initiating event"—that precipitates a series of actions and reactions. The presentation of the core narrative problem and its resolution or nonresolution entails several story components, including setting, initiating event, internal response, attempt, consequence, and reactions (Stein 1979; Stein and Policastro 1984; Trabasso et al 1984). In these studies, a major interest is the cause-effect relations among components and their mental representation by children and adults.

Sociological studies focus on social consequences or social production of a story. For example, Labov and others have demonstrated how narrators restructure their biographies through careful reframing of past events (Labov 1984; Fisher 1985a, 1985b; Schiffrin 1987). Other studies have emphasized the role of the audience as coauthor of the narrative (Duranti 1986; Goodwin 1986; Haviland 1986; Jefferson 1978; Lerner 1987; Mandelbaum 1987a, 1987b; Sacks 1992). These studies look at the co-construction of stories and consider the impact of the audience's (i.e., the story recipients') participation on the telling of stories. In this framework, recipients as well as tellers impact the life of a story in various ways: they may derail a story, encourage its continuation and elaboration, or change its direction.

Our approach is synthetic, recognizing the importance of both cognitive and sociological approaches to narrative and their implications for each other. In particular, cognitive approaches tend to focus on *individual* tellings and retellings of stories without attending to the fact that stories are often, if not typically, collaboratively produced, that is, *co-narrated*, by those participating in the social interaction. On the other hand, sociological approaches emphasize co-narration but do not link co-narration to *co-cognition*, specifically to the joint working out of problems. Building on such work as Wertsch and Hickmann (1987), our study will demonstrate both that narrative components are constituted, ordered, and clarified through social collaboration and that problem solving motivates co-narration. We believe, in other words, that the activity of co-narration stimulates problem solving, while the activity of problem solving stimulates co-narration.

Detective Stories

The stories in our corpus differ in the degree to which story problems are reformulated in the course of storytelling. Certain tellings involve extensive participation of other family members in a groping process to make sense of the problem underlying the narrative's initiating event. We call such narratives "detective stories" in the sense that there is missing information that is felt by some co-narrator(s) to be vital to understanding the problem that motivates actions and reactions of protagonists and others in the storytelling situation. Co-narrators return, sometimes again and again, like Lieutenant Columbo, to pieces of the narrative problem in an effort to find "truth" through cross-examination of the details, sometimes struggling for an illuminating shift in perspective.

The co-narrated detective stories in our corpus differ from stories in which a story problem is laid out by an authoritative teller, whose perspective on the problem is relatively undisputed (see Lerner 1987 and Mandelbaum 1987a, 1987b for extended discussion). In the latter case, the perspective on a story problem (i.e., the version of an initiating event presented by an authoritative teller) is more or less sustained throughout the telling. In detective stories, however, authority to define a narrative problem is not vested solely in a single knowing teller. A story problem is scrutinized in the course of the telling: other co-present participants, even those who do not have direct knowledge of the narrated events, probe for or contribute information relevant to clarifying a narrative problem. This new information may or may not lead to a reformulated perspective on a narrative problem. When family co-narrators do overtly adopt a novel perspective on a narrative problem, we see evidence of a paradigm shift. Such cognitive shifts are socially engendered and have social implications, reaffirming the family as a dynamic activity system capable of working through problems.

Besides subverting the notion of one authoritative teller, detective stories also impact the organization of story components. In detective stories, at least two versions of a narrative problem emerge. A story with a setting, an initiating event, and subsequent responses is presented and could be treated by those co-present as complete; however, the mark of the detective story is that somebody persists in examining the narrative problem beyond this point, eliciting or introducing relevant information not provided in the initial version of the story. Sometimes the ''missing'' information is presented immediately following the first version of a story, as in example (1) (see page 100). In other cases, the missing information surfaces much later and, as we shall see in example (2), may be extracted from or triggered by other stories that involve relevant characters or events. Turning two or more seemingly inconsequential stories, or bits and pieces, into one detective story requires someone who makes a commitment—someone who persists, makes connections, and draws inferences. The information that surfaces may lead to a reanalysis of the earlier story's central problem. Such information thus recontextualizes the earlier story as not *the* story but *a* story, that is, only one version of the narrated events.

We believe talk that recontextualizes earlier storytelling is storytelling as well. Our analysis of detective storytelling illustrates our more general view that storytelling in conversation is dynamic and open-ended. Stories often do not come in neat packages. Research has shown that story beginnings are socially negotiated (e.g., Lerner 1987; Mandelbaum 1987a, 1987b). In detective stories, we see that ''the end'' is also socially negotiated.

Our working hypothesis is that detective stories are typical of everyday narration. They grow out of the process of grappling with incomplete understandings of life's complexity and multiple ''truths'' and perspectives, often manifest (and in conflict) in everyday events and their telling. Initial narrators often seek the kind of co-narration that helps further their own comprehension of their stories and gives meaning to their stories and their lives.

Slow Disclosure and the "Looking Good" Constraint

The structure of detective stories in conversation parallels that of certain literary and cinematic tales. Such stories are particularly characterized by a strategy known as "slow disclosure," that is, the gradual emergence of relevant information or the "prolonged delay in giving away crucial facts in a story" (Sharff 1982:119). For film directors and writers, slow disclosure is a conscious technique for drawing audiences into some unfolding problem; its strategic use creates rhetorical and powerful effects, such as heightened tension. In the narratives we are examining, slow disclosure does not appear to be a conscious technique but rather an outcome of problem solving through co-narration. Critical elements of the narrated events are slowly disclosed through joint attention to particular parts of the narrative, especially through the probing contributions of intimates.

For example, the setting, which provides physical and psychological background to understanding the narrative problem, may be probed and subsequently elaborated or revised through further co-narration. Experiences and events critical to assessing the psychological setting—beliefs, values, and attitudes—may not even be treated by initial tellers as relevant or desirable to reveal at the outset of the narrative. Although family members can assume some of this information because of familiarity with the narrator and the narrative circumstances, they also depend on the talk itself to index parts of the psychological setting. These may prove critical to their assessments and thus to the evolution of the narrative itself. New settings present opportunities for co-narrators to recontextualize the initiating event and the responses and reactions it incurs. Thus, co-constructed, unfolding settings orient and reorient a story throughout its telling.

Slow disclosure of elements such as psychological setting may result in part from a preference of initial tellers to present narrated events in a way that portrays themselves in the most complimentary light. We refer to this preference as the "looking good" constraint on storytelling.

Example (1) is a relatively simple illustration of slow disclosure and the "looking good" constraint operating in a detective story, showing how settings unfold through co-narration.

(1) "The Detention" Story[2]

Mother
Father
Chuck (6;1)
Lucy (9;7)

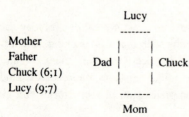

*In answer to a question from Chuck, the family has been discussing degrees
of familiarity a person can have with colleagues at work or school. Chuck has
just mentioned Mrs. Andrews, the school principal, as an example of someone
he knows very well, triggering approval from Mother and this story initiated
by Lucy.*

Lucy: Mom? =

Mother: =(and) she's a good person to know (too)

                              [

Lucy: (Just?) - I don't think Mrs um

      Andrews is being fair because um

Mother: ((*high-pitched*)) (?do you?) =

Father: = (about what)

         [

Lucy: When we were back at school um - this girl? - she pulled um - Vicky's

      dress ((*puts hand to knee*)) up t' here ((*gestures with hand high on chest*))

      in front of the boys

Mother: mhm?

Lucy: She only - all she did was get a <u>day</u> in de<u>ten</u>tion

Mother: mhm? - <u>You</u> think she should have gotten suspended?

      (0.6)

Lucy: at <u>LEAST</u> - That's

      (0.4)

Mother: mhm?

      [

Lucy: (it's) not allowed in scho?ol. =

      = ((*Father clears throat*))

      (1.8)

Father: ((*to Mother*)) <u>hm</u> - Fortunately capital punishment is still =

Chuck: = Was it a <u>girl</u>? Lucy? that did it? or a boy.

                      [

Father: (beyond the pur? - view) of elementary school principals

      (1.0)

Chuck: that did that?

          [

Mother: (Vicky/Lucy) (was so embarrassed huh Lucy)

Chuck: hm?

Mother: (cuz Lucy) was <u>really</u> embarrassed ((*nodding yes, talking while eating*))

      (1.6)

Mother: (I mean you/Lucy really) would have liked to kill the - the girl - huh?

Lucy: ((*nods yes slowly, as she chews, fork in mouth*))

      [

Mother: (cuz) you were upset with her - ((*speaking very fast*)) But you were held

      back because you (thought) your school was goin' to do it and the school

      didn't do it and you feel up<u>set</u>

      (2.6)

Chuck: I think? she should - be: in there for a h- whole MONTH? or so =
??:   = (well maybe)
           (0.6)
Chuck: each day she('d) hafta go there - each day each day each day even if? - (the-)
           [
Lucy: If you go to detention more than three times - then you get suspended
Father: ((head leaning forward)) More than how many times?
Lucy: three ((raises hand as if to show three fingers))
Father: ((nods yes))
           (0.4)
Chuck: Lucy? - you only ever went to it once - right? =
Father: = ((clears throat))
           (1.0) ((Lucy arches her back, eyes open wide, looks shocked, starts
           shaking her head no once; Father looking at her))
Mother: (You've been in it/You can tell us can't you?)
                     [
Father: (I'm lis?tening)
Lucy: ((low to Chuck, glaring?)) (thanks)
           (0.4)
Lucy: ((louder)) yeah (that was   )
                       [
Mother: (She was in it) once?
           (0.6)
Lucy: Once.
Mother: (It was) in (Mr Dolby)'s year
           (1.4)
Chuck: only once - that's all
           [
Mother: (for fighting on the playground)?
Chuck: ((with conviction, building speed to a crescendo)) (Lucy/only if you) get (it)
           a second and (a) third and the fourth? that means you're out right?
Mother: Well? no honey not every year. - You're allowed to start new every year.
           (1.4)
Father: ((looking to Mom, grinning)) like the statute of limitations hh
           (1.8)
Mother: ((to Chuck)) Things run out after a while

In this narrative, the information that Lucy, the initial narrator, was once punished by Mrs. Andrews, the principal of her school, is a critical aspect of the setting,
because it illuminates Lucy's psychological stance toward the same principal's
punishment of another student's misdemeanor. Lucy at first does not present her
own past misdemeanor as part of the setting but simply situates the initiating event in
a physical setting ("When we were back in school . . ."). In line with the "looking good" constraint, Lucy would probably never have disclosed this personally
damaging critical background information.

Prior to this disclosure, family members had only Lucy's version of the narrated problem as data for interpreting her reactions. In this light, Lucy presumably felt the way she did only because of the morally offensive nature of the misdemeanor. This is the interpretation her mother promotes, co-constructing the telling of her daughter's internal responses and emotional reactions. A joint sense of moral indignation stimulates increasingly drastic proposals for punishment—from "suspension" to "at LEAST [suspension]" to "would have liked to kill the girl"—until Lucy's younger brother elicits the crucial background information by asking his sister, "Lucy? - you only ever went to it [detention] once - right?" Lucy starts to shake her head no but eventually acknowledges having gone to detention.

This new coauthored setting recontextualizes both the narrative problem and Lucy's reactions: Now the principal is not fair because the principal gave the same punishment—one day's detention—to both Lucy and the horrid girl who committed a far more serious transgression than Lucy presumably had. Thus we see how co-participants in the telling of a story "assist" one another in bringing a narrative problem into focus. Such assistance, however, is not always welcome: it may subvert the initial narrator's attempt to look good. In this case, the narrative seems to have backfired on Lucy and left her damaged by the account, further indexed by her sudden inarticulateness after the revelation.

Paradigm-Shifting Detective Stories

In the case of "The Detention" narrative, there is no overt evidence that the family has, in fact, used the newly disclosed setting to reanalyze the problem embedded in the initiating event. That is, they do not overtly use the knowledge of Lucy's own misdemeanor and her day of detention to reframe the morally untenable misdemeanor (the pulling up of the dress) in a new context—as being *more* serious than the wrongdoing committed by Lucy in the past. The family's doubletake does lead to a softening of response toward transgressors, now that Lucy is included in this category, but then the topic is abruptly dropped.

In other narratives, however, co-tellers display through talk their realization that there is a problem with earlier framings of the problem. Attending to the unfolding disclosures, co-narrators negotiate and in some cases adopt an entirely new perspective, or even a new paradigm, for considering a narrated problem. The adoption of a new paradigm is akin to scientific paradigm shifts of the sort described by Kuhn (1962, 1977).

Such paradigm shifting through co-narration is illustrated in example (2), a very complex detective story extending over 40 minutes of dinnertime talk and still going on during cleanup. The initial narrator of this story is Marie, the mother in the family being recorded and director of a day-care center in their home. Her story grows out of an incident that occurred just prior to dinner, when Bev, the mother of one of the day-care children, presented Marie with $320. The evolving issue that drives the narrative concerns the meaning of this act—the definition of the narrative problem. Is it payment for one month's child care? Or is it a penalty fee for pulling the child out of day care without two weeks' notice? As Marie first reports the incident in (2a), only the first of these considerations arises between Marie and Bev:

(2a) Bev Story (introductory excerpt)

Mother (Marie)
Father (Jon)   Dick Janie
Evan (3;7)   ----------   Evan
Janie (5;11)   Dad | | Mom
Dick (8;7)   ----------

Food has been served, Jon has said grace, and a friend has just left.

Marie:	Bev walked up? and handed me three twenty?
Jon:	mhm
	(0.6) ((*Marie holding corn, looking at Jon as she talks*))
Marie:	And I <u>thought</u> she only owed me eighty. - and she said she didn't want a receipt - and I went in and got the: receipt book n: she only owed me ((*nodding yes*)) eighty =
Jon:	= hmmhm.
	(0.4) ((*Marie keeps nodding yes*))
Marie:	n she was real happy about that
	(1.0) ((*Marie starts to eat corn, then stops*))
Marie:	She says "No no no no no:: I don't need a receipt."
	(0.8)
Dick:	<u>Mom</u> Did Bev - (tch)
	[
Marie:	and just hands me three twenty
	(2.0) ((*sounds of eating corn of the cob*))
Marie:	I - took my <u>book</u> out though - cuz she hardly <u>ever</u> - makes mista:h:kes ((*laughing*)) - I thought maybe I wrote it wrong but I went back and got three receipts
Dick:	(N:ah::) ((*to the cat*))
	[
Marie:	and they all were
Jon:	mhm =
Marie:	= in - you know - What do you call that?
Dick:	Daddy? (is - the) cat's still hungry.
	[[
Jon:	consecutive order?
Marie:	Yeah mhm
	(0.6)
Jon:	(Cat) Are you hungry? - Has he been fed today?
Marie:	mmhm? - Twice. . . .

In this initial version, Marie views the narrative problem as whether or not Bev was in arrears. Her reported internal response was one of self-doubt, grounded in the belief that Bev hardly ever makes mistakes. In keeping with the looking good constraint, this version reveals Marie as an honest businessperson. The telling thus far provokes minimal involvement from Marie's husband, Jon.

After a considerable interval—15 minutes of attention to eating and other narrations—alternate reformulations of the Bev-narrative problem emerge in piecemeal fashion. The reformulations grow out of a second narrative about Bev, introduced by Marie, in which Bev is characterized as opportunistic. At this point, Jon is drawn in as an active co-narrator.

(2b) Bev Narrative (second excerpt, 15 minutes later)
Jon has picked up on another narrative involving Bev and is equating Bev's receiving unwarranted insurance benefits after an accident with the behavior of a customer who gets excessive change back from a grocery clerk.

Jon: . . . you're supposed to think "Hey: that's great" and walk out the
      ((*laughing*)) sto?:re n "She gave me back - .h twenty dollars too much? cuz
      she must've thought I gave her a fifty"

Marie: mhm

Jon: you know .h and you're not supposed to consider yer- consider=
                                                              [

Marie: ((*looking away and down toward table*))   mm

Jon: = whether or not that comes out of her pay if the drawer doesn't balance=
                                                                       [

Marie: (I know)

Jon: = at the end of the night .h or whether it's the ethic - right thing to do is to
      say "Hey lady you - you: - gave me too much money" .h
                                                        [

Marie: ((*looking up at Jon, extends arm on table*))   Well: you know what=
      ((*Marie is pointing index finger at him*))

Jon: That's not in anymore It's gone to even to the extreme?
      =[

Marie: You know what thou:gh I started questioning was the fact she gave me -
      no - notice
      [
      ((*Marie raises left hand, wagging index finger at Jon*))

Marie: She just called up? after the accident and said.

Jon: Yeah "I'm not comin anymore"
      [

Marie: "That's it" - no - no two weeks' pay - not=
                                        [   ]

Jon: Marie?

Marie: = no: consideration - (whether I had to find-)

                     [

Jon: ((*wiping mouth*))   She did a:ll that when she paid you the three hundred and twenty dollars She didn't do that by mistake

        (0.2) ((*Marie with hand to mouth, reflective; Janie goes to kitchen*))

Jon: She wanted to see how you felt about it n she felt she owed you

                                                    [

Marie: No: wa:y -

        ((*shaking head & hand no*)) no: nonono - no

                            [

Jon: Oh no? - You don't think so?

Marie: No She thought she had not paid me for the month =

        [

Jon: (hoh?) ((*lightly*))

Marie: = of June. and she was paying me fro:m =

Jon: = yeah =

Marie: = the first week of Ju:ne

            [

Jon: I would rea:d it- Oh - (yeah/mm)

                           [

Marie: to:: - the? - the ending - the third of

                                   [   ]

Dick?:   ((*to Dad*))   (   )

                                         [

Jon: You had said that she never made a mistake in the past? though didn't you? She was always very - good about that.

        [

Dick: hhh ((*heaving a sigh and backing away a bit from Dad*))

Marie: No - She- She's made ((*extending index finger*)) one mistake in the past =

Jon: = oh oh huhuh ((*slight nod yes?*))

        [

Marie: but her record i:s - very few mistakes? ((*as she speaks, Marie's raised finger moves horizontally to indicate Bev's record over time*))

Jon: hmhm (okay) ((*nodding yes*))

In the height of portraying Bev as opportunistic, in (2b) Marie suddenly brings up "new" information that is relevant to Bev's handing over $320 to Marie. Marie recalls Bev's failure to give two weeks' notice before pulling her daughter out of child care. Jon and Marie now attribute to Bev different intentions concerning the $320 in light of Bev's knowledge of the two weeks' notice requirement. Their discussion prefaces a reconceptualization in (2c) of the problem embedded in Bev's offering of the money.

(2c) Bev Narrative (third excerpt, 5 minutes later)

The kids have just remembered that Dad had promised them ice cream if they ate a good dinner, and Marie has encouraged them to chant "Haagen Dazs" over and over until Jon submits to taking them to the ice cream store. In the throes of these negotiations, Marie abruptly returns again to the unresolved narrative problem:

Marie: You know - Jon I verbally did tell Bev two weeks' notice Do you think I
          shouldov stuck to that? or just done what I did?
          (0.8) ((*kids standing by table between Mom & Dad*))

Jon: When I say something I stick to it. unless she: - s-brings it up. If I set a
          policy - and a- - and - they accept that policy. unless they have reason to =
                                                         [

Dick: Let's go outside and play

Jon: = change it and and say something? I do not change it - I don't automatically
          assume .h "We:ll it's not the right thing to do" If I were to do that e- I would be
          saying in the first place I should never have mentioned it I should never have set
          the policy if I didn't believe in it If I thought it was - a hardship on people I
          shouldn'a brought it up? - shoulda kept my mouth shut .h If I: say there's two
          weeks' notice required - .h I automatically charge em for two weeks' notice
          without thinking twice? about it I say and i - "If you- you need - Your pay will
          include till such and such a date because of the two neek-weeks' notice that's
          required." - I:f THE:Y feel hardship it's on thei:r part - it's - THEIRS to say .h
          "Marie I really? - you know - I didn't expect this to happen 'n I'm ((*softly*))
          sorry I didn't give you two weeks' notice but it was really un - avoidable" -
          a:nd you can say "We:ll - okay I'll split the difference with you - it's har- - a
          one week's notice" - and then = they s- then if they push it
          [

Marie: See? you know in one way wi- in one (instance) ((*pointing to Jon*)) she
          owed me that money - but I just didn't feel right? taking it on that =
                                            [

Jon: well you're - you

Marie: = pretense because she (wanted) - she thought she was paying it for
          something ((*twirling her corn cob*)) that (she didn't)
                                  [

Jon: You: give her the money and then
          you let it bother you then - you - get all ups-set You'll be upset for weeks
                      [

Marie: No no no - I'm not upset - it's just =

Dick: = Janie? Go get Spot out ((*from outside?, re dog*))
          (0.4) ((*Marie plops corn cob down, raps knuckles on table*))

Janie: ((*from living room?*)) Why::?

Marie: I guess I just wish I would have s:aid -

                 [

Dick: ((*from outside*)) (   )

Marie: I'm not upset with what happened - I just wanted- I think I - would feel better if I
            had said (something)

In (2c), Marie and Jon take the reanalysis of the problem one step further, a step which we propose constitutes a paradigm shift. The paradigm shift is a result of problem solving enriched through co-narration. Jon and Marie's earlier dispute over Bev and the two weeks' notice sets in motion a shift in perspective. The issue of the two weeks' notice has continued to haunt Marie, as indicated by her abrupt re-introduction of the topic. Here Marie emphatically confirms that she did indeed make the two-week rule very explicit to Bev prior to the initiating event. Marie uses this new piece of the setting to reformulate the narrative problem in terms of a new dilemma—namely, whether she should have insisted that Bev give her the $320 to compensate for the lack of a two-week notice or should have kept quiet. This reformulation evidences, for us, a paradigm shift, wherein the $320 is now seen as rightfully Marie's and not Bev's (Marie: "In one instance she owed me that money . . ."; Jon: "You: give her the money. . ."). The reformulation casts Marie's way of responding to Bev's handing her $320 in a new light. Whereas Marie's action of taking out the receipt book and proving that Bev was not in arrears successfully resolved the first formulation of the narrated problem, the newly formulated definition of the problem makes that action seem inadequate. This inadequacy is articulated by both Jon ("If I: say there's a two weeks' notice required - I automatically charge em for two weeks' notice without thinking twice") and Marie ("I think I - would feel better if I had said something") and leads to Jon's further chiding Marie for feeling upset.

A critical factor in determining whether or not a detective story takes on the dimensions of a paradigm shift is the uptake of listeners and their willingness to actively enter the narrating process. Our data demonstrate that important missing information surfaces in the throes of collaborative narration. For example, Marie's rather sudden recall of the two-week notice in (2b) overlaps with Jon's active involvement in assessing Bev's insurance dealings, as if inspired by the energy and support of the collaboration. When a new paradigm is internalized by a narrator, as Marie seems to have internalized the reconstituted problem, we suggest an exemplar of the Vygotskian passage from interpersonal to intrapersonal knowledge through co-narration. The presence of familiar others as co-narrators, apparently facilitated in more centralized family dinners around a common table, may inspire or otherwise contribute to socially accomplished problem solving and transport narrative co-construction into the arena of joint and individual cognition.

Social Consequences of Narrative Practices

It is widely recognized that narratives strengthen social relationships and a general sense of co-membership by providing a medium for illustrating common beliefs, values, and attitudes of tellers and audiences. Research on *co*-narration demonstrates further that beliefs, values, and attitudes are not so much transmitted from teller to audience as they are *collectively* and *dialogically* engendered (see Holquist 1983). Audiences are coauthors and as such co-owners of the narratives and the moral and other premises that these narratives illustrate. They co-own the narrative as an interactional product and more importantly share control over cognitive and verbal tools fundamental to problem solving itself. Co-ownership is not a relationship that one enters into lightly, given that it involves sharing control as well as a commitment, however temporary, both to the activities of co-narration and collaborative problem solving and to the product, that is, the story. In function of these constraints, interlocutors vary the extent and type of their narrative involvement.

Detective stories, particularly paradigm-shifting ones, display considerable cognitive, affective, and linguistic involvement from interlocutors. Such extensive involvement structures and restructures social relationships among co-narrators and impacts the balance of power in the social unit. Interlocutors co-own the story in the sense that they participate in re-perspectivizing the fundamental narrative problem. As such, they take on shared responsibility for the story as a product, with or without the invitation of the initial teller. Entitlement to tell a story is thus not the exclusive right of an initial teller (Lerner 1987; Mandelbaum 1987a, 1987b). Even those who have not directly experienced the narrative events can acquire entitlement through expanding, querying, correcting, or challenging existing formulations of the narrative problem.

This sharing of narrative "rights" is evidence of a sharing of power. At the same time, such sharing makes participants' perceptions of the world vulnerable to coauthored change. In detective stories, the sharing of narrative rights empowers co-present interlocutors to coauthor one another's biographies, that is, to construct collectively one party's past experience through co-narration. Such reconstruction (or deconstruction) potentially threatens tellers' drive to look good. It is our hypothesis that this vulnerability serves as a constraint on full-fledged participation in detective storytelling. Whether participants undertake extended "detecting" appears to be a function of the participants' willingness to commit time and energy and of an initial teller's willingness to risk vulnerability. And that is where the prolonged, centralized dinner may be a special opportunity space for familial coauthorship. In the activity of coauthoring detective stories, family members share perspectives within a framework of shared family values that are reconstituted through the activity. Such exercise of their narrative rights results in a unique type of shared construction and shared ownership—and reconstitutes family relationships and the family itself as an activity system.

Collaboration in the form of detective storytelling is akin to scaffolding and joint problem-solving practices characteristic of American middle-class caregiver-child interactions (Ochs and Schieffelin 1984). Such practices empower intimates to influence each other's perceptions of the world and, in so doing, to socialize one another. In our view, the co-narrated detective story is not only a *vehicle* for the socialization of family values and the family's sense of order/disorder in the world; it is also an *object* itself of socialization. Children and others participating in such co-narration are being socialized into ways of articulating and solving problems through social construction of a genre. Families who sit together for the duration of a meal have a potentially unique opportunity space for socializing this mode of problem solving—and some families do just that, exploiting narratives to co-construct new paradigms that order and reorder their everyday lives.

Notes

This essay is the result of the equal work of the three authors. It was presented at the Symposium on Narrative Resources for the Creation of Order and Disorder, during the American Ethnological Society Annual Meeting, St. Louis, Missouri, March 25, 1988, and was originally published in 1989 in *Cultural Dynamics*, vol. 2. It is reproduced here with permission from E. J. Brill Publishers and with relatively minor revisions. The research was funded from 1986 to 1990 by NICHD (grant no. 1 ROH HD 20992-01A1, "Discourse Processes in American Families"). Members of the research team included principal investigators Elinor Ochs and Tom Weisner, and research assistants Maurine Bernstein, Dina Rudolph, Ruth Smith, and Carolyn Taylor. We thank Mary Walstrom for her help on final editing.

1. Although the problem-solving narrative practices described in this essay were observed at dinnertime and notably in centralized dinners, we recognize that families vary considerably in where and how they do their problem solving and that families may engage in the detective-story type of narrative described here in settings other than centralized dinners. However, when dinners bring together a maximum number of family members, they may be especially conducive to the detective-story processes we characterize here.

2. All family names are pseudonyms. Ages of children are shown in years and months (e.g., 6;1 means 6 years, 1 month). Transcription procedures are essentially those established by Gail Jefferson (see Atkinson and Heritage, 1984, pp. ix–xvi), to wit:

[a left-hand bracket indicates the onset of overlapping, simultaneous utterances

= two equals signs (latches) link utterances either by two different speakers where the second jumps in on the end of the first, without any interval, or by the same speaker when lengthy overlap by another speaker requires that a continuous utterance be interrupted on the transcript to show simultaneity with another utterance or action

(0.4) a number in parentheses indicates length of pause within and between ut-
       terances, timed in tenths of a second
a - a a hyphen with spaces before and after indicates a short pause, less than
       0.2 seconds
sa-   a hyphen immediately following a letter indicates an abrupt cutoff in
       speaking
(( )) double parentheses enclose nonverbal and other descriptive information
( )   single parentheses enclose words that are not clearly audible (i.e., best
       guesses)
/   a slash (inside single parentheses) separates alternate hearings of what
       was said or alternate best guesses
       underlining indicates stress on a syllable or word(s)
CAPS   upper case indicates louder or shouted talk
:   a colon indicates a lengthening of a sound (the more colons, the longer
       the sound)
.   a period indicates falling intonation
,   a comma indicates a continuing intonation
?   a question mark indicates a rising intonation as a syllable or word ends
       Note: bounding question marks (e.g., ''Did you go to the ?animal hospi-
       tal?'') are used (instead of rising arrows) to indicate a higher pitch for
       enclosed word(s)
h   an ''h'' indicates an exhalation (the more h's, the longer the exhalation)
.h   an ''h'' with a period before it indicates an inhalation (the more h's, the
       longer the inhalation)

Works Cited

Atkinson, J. Maxwell, and John Heritage, eds. 1984. *Structures of social action: Studies in conversation analysis.* Cambridge: Cambridge University Press.

Duranti, Alessandro. 1986. The audience as co-author: An introduction. *Text* 6:239–47.

Engeström, Yrjö. 1987. *Learning by expanding: An activity-theoretical approach to developmental research.* Helsinki: Orienta-Konsultit Oy.

Feiring, Candice, and Michael Lewis. 1987. The ecology of some middle class families at dinner. *International Journal of Behavorial Development* 10:377–90.

Fisher, Walter. 1985a. The narrative paradigm: In the beginning. *Journal of Communication* 35:75–89.

———. 1985b. The narrative paradigm: An elaboration. *Communication Monographs* 52:347–67.

Goodwin, Charles. 1984. Notes on story structure and the organization of participation. In *Structures of social action: Studies in conversation analysis,* ed. J. M. Atkinson and J. Heritage, pp. 225–46. Cambridge: Cambridge University Press.

———. 1986. Audience diversity, participation, and interpretation. *Text* 6:283–316.

Haviland, John B. 1986. ''Con buenos chiles'': Talk, targets and teasing in Zinacantan. *Text* 6:249–82.

Holquist, Michael. 1983. The politics of representation. *The Quarterly Newsletter of the Laboratory of Comparative Human Cognition* 5:2–9.

Jefferson, Gail. 1978. Sequential aspects of storytelling in conversation. In *Studies in the organization of conversational interaction,* ed. J. Schenkein, pp. 219–48. New York: Academic Press.

Kuhn, Thomas S. 1962. *The structure of scientific revolutions.* Chicago: University of Chicago Press.

———. 1977. *The essential tension.* Chicago: University of Chicago Press.

Labov, William. 1984. Intensity. In *Meaning, form, and use in context: Linguistic applications,* ed. Deborah Schiffrin, pp. 43–70. Washington, DC: Georgetown University Press.

Leontyev, A. N. 1981. *Problems of the development of the mind.* Moscow: Progress Publishers.

Lerner, Gene H. 1987. "Collaborative turn sequences: Sentence construction and social action." Doctoral dissertation, University of California at Irvine.

Mandelbaum, Jennifer S. 1987a. Couples sharing stories. *Communication Quarterly* 35:144–70.

———. 1987b. *Recipient-driven storytelling in conversation.* Doctoral dissertation, University of Texas at Austin.

Ochs, Elinor, and Bambi B. Schieffelin. 1984. Language acquisition and socialization: Three developmental stories and their implications. In *Culture theory: Essays on mind, self, and emotion,* ed. R. Shweder and R. LeVine, pp. 276–320. New York: Cambridge University Press.

Rogoff, Barbara, and Jean Lave, eds. 1984. *Everyday cognition: Its development in social context.* Cambridge, MA: Harvard University Press.

Sacks, Harvey. 1992. *Lectures on conversation,* vols 1 and 2, ed. Gail Jefferson. Oxford: Blackwell.

Schiffrin, Deborah. 1987. *Discourse markers.* Cambridge: Cambridge University Press.

Sharff, Stefan. 1982. *The elements of cinema: Toward a theory of cinesthetic impact.* New York: Columbia University Press.

Stein, Nancy L. 1979. How children understand stories: A developmental analysis. In *Current topics in early childhood education,* vol. 2, ed. L. Katz, pp. 261–90. Norwood, NJ: Ablex.

Stein, Nancy L., and Margaret Policastro. 1984. The concept of a story: A comparison between children's and teachers' viewpoints. In *Learning and comprehension of text,* ed. H. Mandl, N. Stein, and T. Trabasso, pp. 113–55. Hillsdale, NJ: Erlbaum.

Trabasso, T., T. Secco, and P. Van Den Broek. 1984. Causal cohesion and story coherence. In *Learning and comprehension of text,* ed. H. Mandl, N. Stein, and T. Trabasso, pp. 83–112. Hillsdale, NJ: Erlbaum.

Vygotsky, Lev S. 1978. *Mind in society: The development of higher psychological processes,* ed. M. Cole, V. John-Steiner, S. Scribner, and E. Souberman. Cambridge, MA: Harvard University Press.

———. 1981. The genesis of higher mental functions. In *The concept of activity in Soviet psychology,* ed. J. Wertsch, pp. 144–88. Armonk, NY: M. E. Sharpe.

Wertsch, James V. 1985. *Vygotsky and the social formation of mind.* Cambridge, MA: Harvard University Press.

Wertsch, James V., and Maya Hickmann. 1987. Problem solving in social interaction: A microgenetic analysis. In *Social and functional approaches to language and thought,* ed. M. Hickmann, pp. 251–66. Orlando, FL: Academic Press.

WILLIAM M. O'BARR & JOHN M. CONLEY

Ideological Dissonance in the American Legal System

In this essay, we present the results of a study of lay ideologies of law as revealed in the narratives told by small-claims litigants. Small-claims courts are the lowest civil courts in most American jurisdictions. They vary from state to state but are generally limited to hearing cases where the awards sought do not exceed a specified amount, usually $1,000 to $2,000. Litigants represent themselves in most instances, and some states actually prohibit lawyers from appearing in court. In addition, these courts do not observe the formal rules of evidence and procedure that characterize courts in which lawyers and juries are present. Therefore, a significant difference between small-claims and more formal courts is the considerable extent to which litigants actually structure and manage the presentation of the details of their cases.

As a part of a more extensive research program whose goal is the investigation of the American legal system from the perspective of laypersons,[1] we have found that litigants have two stories to tell. One is the account of the trouble that brings them to court. The other is the story that develops as a result of their experiences with the court. By combining what litigants say in court with what they say in pre- and post-trial interviews, we have the opportunity to hear both of these stories.[2] We use these stories to discover lay ideologies of law and to investigate how litigants' beliefs and expectations differ from the ideology of law as officially practiced. Our analysis reveals that lay litigants hold diverse legal ideologies, and that they devise subtle strategies for managing the dissonance that sometimes arises between their idelologies and those held by judges and other court officials.

Defining Ideology

The definition of ideology is elusive. Most definitions share the core element of ideology as a system of beliefs by which people interpret and impart meaning to events. Scholars from different disciplines tend to elaborate on this core in different ways, selecting from a range of additional attributes that have been discussed in a literature that is both broad and deep (Hunt 1985:12).

Marxist scholarship, which has been inconsistent in its use of the term, has traditionally emphasized at least three additional defining elements of ideology. First, the set of beliefs called ideology is not an attribute of the individual, but of a group or a class. In this view, ideology "expresses the essential conditions of a social class, section or group within society and in a historical situation" (Kulscar 1980:61; cf. Deutsch 1983:395–96). Second, the consciousness that comprises ideology is often false, distorting the underlying and usually repressive reality (Hunt 1985:20–21). The third and related point is that by legitimating the status quo through the perpetuation of false consciousness, ideology performs a hegemonic function (Hunt 1985:19; Merry 1986:254). Contemporary Marxist scholarship has tended to de-emphasize the issue of false consciousness and, more generally, the distinction between action and representation, and to argue instead that "the nature of the relationship between reality and its ideological representation should be seen as 'the problem', or object of analysis, without prejudgment as to the way in which the relationship can be captured or portrayed" (Hunt 1985:21; cf. Bourdieu 1977:2–4).

Anthropologists have treated ideology as an aspect of culture, emphasizing its constitutive role as a system of meaning. For purposes of our analysis, we find most useful Merry's (1986:253) effort "to join the anthropological view of ideology as an aspect of culture with the Marxist view of ideology as a way of maintaining relations of power and dominance." She argues that one must look simultaneously at the constitutive and hegemonic aspects of law, reasoning that "[t]hinking of idelolgy as culture highlights questions of harmony, integration, and consensus, while thinking of ideology in terms of power and dominance highlights questions of conflict, control, and hegemony" (1986:253–54).

We define legal ideology as a system of beliefs about the nature and purpose of law. These beliefs guide those who hold them in constructing meaning in the legal environment. We use linguistic evidence to explore such questions as the diversity and distribution of legal ideologies among laypersons, the degree of congruence or dissonance between lay ideologies and ideologies held by those who exercise power in the legal system, the way in which laypersons respond to dissonance between their own beliefs and those of legal professionals, and the role of legal ideologies in shaping relations of power and dominance.

Methods

The data we present are drawn from a comparative study of American small-claims courts in North Carolina, Colorado, and Pennsylvania. We conducted the study in three stages: Interviewing plaintiffs as they came to the courthouse to file their cases,[3] observing and tape recording trials, and interviewing many litigants, both plaintiffs and defendants, after trial. We obtained data on at least one stage of more than 100 cases.[4] The trials themselves were of varying duration. For those in which defendants appeared and presented their versions of what happened, trials ranged from as short as five to 10 minutes to as long as two hours.[5] Trials typically include a mixture of questioning by the presiding judge, opportunities for relatively uninterrupted speech by the litigants and their witnesses, and dialogue between litigants in the form of cross-examinations and rebuttals. A noteworthy feature of virtually every litigant's account is an extended monologue in which the litigant seizes an opportunity to narrate the details of the troubles that brought him or her to court. This form is such a regular feature of the trials that we have argued elsewhere that litigants appear to prefer it over the question-answer format typical of more formal courts and sometimes imposed by small-claims judges (see O'Barr and Conley 1985). Whether litigants' accounts of their troubles take the form of a self-managed account or a story told in response to questions posed by an examiner, or a combination of the two, they provide evidence about why litigants come to court and what they expect the legal system to deliver.

We interviewed litigants before and after their court experiences in order to investigate the degree to which their out-of-court accounts might differ from those told in the courtroom. We were also interested in whether the out-of-court accounts might change as a result of the litigants' experiences with the legal system. The interviews, which ranged in length from five minutes to over an hour, were open-ended. Most pre-trial interviews were conducted at the time litigants filed their cases. We asked them what their cases were about and their reasons for coming to court. With little prompting and a great deal of active listening on our part, the litigants talked about the details of their cases, often providing multiple, increasingly elaborate versions of "what happened." In addition, they talked about what they believed they had to prove in court and what they would use as evidence. They also discussed their expectations of the legal system.

In post-trial interviews, usually conducted a few weeks after the trials and in the litigants' homes, we focused on their experiences with the legal system. Most litigants talked about what had happened in the trial, why they believed they had won or lost, and what they might have done differently in hindsight.

In all interviews, we attempted to let litigants present their own accounts of their troubles and of their experiences with the legal process. Only when litigants failed to do so did we introduce specific topics of interest to the research program.

In analyzing the data, we met in two-hour workshop sessions with our research assistants and, occasionally, faculty colleagues from the social sciences of the law. With a transcript in hand, we listened repeatedly to an audiotape of an interview or trial. Each participant noted issues of particular interest to him or her, and the group then discussed each member's observations. Although we began the project with a number of general issues in mind, the method proved most productive in bringing to our attention other issues—including the one we discuss here—that were not on the original agenda. Such issues emerged as topics of interest because the litigants themselves made us aware of them through their talk. We call this method the *ethnography of discourse,* to emphasize that we are engaged in the fine-grained analysis of speech, but for the traditional ethnographic purpose of understanding how social institutions work.

Some Observations on Courtroom Discourse

The litigant narratives on which we base our analysis of ideology are also significant from a linguistic perspective. They reflect the expectation of most lay litigants that the rules of everyday speech will govern courtroom discourse. All but "professional litigants" with extensive courtroom experience (for example, landlords and collection agents) seem to believe that it is appropriate to follow the conventions of ordinary discourse in presenting a legal claim to the judge. Several specific instances illustrate this general point.

First, most litigants expect that the recipient of a narrative will interact with the teller, as is usually the case in everyday social interactions. In court, however, the judge typically invites the litigant to speak and then sits impassively until the litigant decides to stop. As a result, litigants often ask where they should begin and when they should stop (eliciting an answer such as "Wherever you want"). Litigants may also pause in mid-narrative to await or even ask for an indication that the judge is paying attention to the story and ready to hear more. Many litigants struggle with the burden of producing a narrative unilaterally, and this unexpected violation of conversational norms may put them at a serious disadvantage in presenting their case.

Relatedly, lay litigants tend to assume that the kinds of information that are typically included in everyday narratives will also be relevant to the judge. For example, everyday accounts of troubles often include information about the personal backgrounds of the actors, evaluative comments about their motives, and digressions about matters of personal concern to the narrator. Judges, however, react to such information as inappropriate and distracting, and often display considerable irritation toward narrators who offer it.

Finally, in attempting to follow everyday conventions in the courtroom, lay litigants display their ignorance of many special conventions that have long been important elements of legal discourse. For example, contrary to the assumptions of many litigants, the law treats a written document as better evidence than an oral description of its contents. Similarly, through the hearsay rule, the law states a preference (confounding to many litigants) for what a witness has seen over what a witness has heard. The law also refuses to accept corroboration from sources outside the courtroom. Thus, a suggestion such as "You can call Mr. Smith to check my story if you don't believe it," which many litigants view as appropriate, will be rejected out of hand by the judge.

The point of each of these examples is that the rules of courtroom discourse differ from those of everyday conversation in many important respects. Inexperienced litigants tend to be unaware of these differences and surprised when confronted with them. Ultimately, we suspect, their failure to respect the differences may limit their access to justice (see O'Barr and Conley 1985).

Discovering Lay Ideologies of Law

We draw inferences about lay ideologies of law from three categories of evidence: what litigants say about the law, the choices they make in structuring and presenting their cases, and their reactions to their experiences with the legal process. We have chosen two cases from different jurisdictions that illustrate these categories of evidence. As these cases demonstrate, there is no unified lay ideology of law, but a range of lay perspectives on the nature and purpose of law and the legal process. The cases also suggest the complexity of the interaction between lay ideologies and the "official" ideology as expressed by judges in individual cases. In some cases, there is ideological congruence among judge and litigants, whereas in others a variety of discrepancies are present.

Notwithstanding the complexity and variability we observe, certain general patterns do emerge from our data. Lay litigants hold beliefs about social governance that range from interpreting rights, duties, and obligations in terms of status and social relationships; to seeing society as organized according to principles that apply without reference to social or personal characteristics (see Conley and O'Barr 1990a, 1990b). We use the terms "relational" and "rule oriented" to apply, respectively, to these two approaches. The evidence we present in this essay suggests that this continuum of beliefs has an ideological component. Rule-oriented litigants tend to view the law as an institution whose purpose is to determine responsibility for events according to precise rules that are of limited applicability. Relational litigants, by contrast, see the law as a system empowered to assign rewards and punishments according to broader notions of social worth and social need. The rule-oriented conception of law is consonant with a political ideology that posits that the individual is an autonomous contracting agent, whereas for the relational litigant, the individual is more often a passive victim or beneficiary of decisions that he or she is powerless to influence.

The distinction between rule-oriented and relational litigants also manifests itself in the contrasting ways that they construct narratives. The narratives of rule-oriented litigants tend to be circumscribed, dealing only with those issues that are directly relevant to the legal claim. Consistent with the law's preferences, rule-oriented narratives emphasize documents and concrete observations and minimize conversations, personal background details, and evaluative comments. They assume no shared knowledge on the part of the hearer, proceed sequentially through events, and include precise references to dates and quantities.

Relational narratives, by contrast, are characterized by their discursive nature. Rather than proceeding sequentially, they wander unpredictably through time and space. The hearer is often presumed to share the speaker's knowledge of the relevant people and places. These narratives are typically rich in evaluation and personal details. They reflect a broad notion of relevance and thus include information from a variety of oral and written sources, much of which may be performed for dramatic effect. In all these respects, relational narratives follow the conventions of everyday discourse and violate many of the special conventions of the courtroom.

We next present data from two cases that illustrate our method of investigation and bear directly on the nature of the ideologies of law held by litigants and officials of the courts. We have selected these cases from more than 100 that we have studied. Given the amount of detail in which each case must be presented, it is not feasible to treat a greater number of cases in a single article of manageable length. The two cases are typical of many others, and the conclusions that we draw from them are supported by the other cases we have investigated.

Case 1: The Leaky Roof

The plaintiffs in Case 1 are Higgins and Andrews, two young men who are joint owners of a house. They hired Riva Roofing company to fix a leak in their roof, signed a contract, and paid a five hundred dollar deposit. According to the plaintiffs, the roofers removed the leaky segment but then simply covered the area with tar paper and aluminum siding, which made the leak worse. When Higgins and Andrews called the company to complain, they were told that the work had been done by subcontractors, and that Riva would refund only half the deposit.

After a demand letter proved unavailing, Higgins and Andrews went to small-claims court. Following the local procedure, they were interviewed by a court clerk who inquired about the case, made sure that they had the relevant documents, and then wrote out a complaint form, including a brief narrative description of their claim, for their signature. We interviewed them in the hallway as they walked out of the clerk's office.[6]

In Text 1A, taken from the beginning of our interview, Higgins responds to a request for "general comments on what brings you to court."

Text 1A.[7] Interview with Higgins and Andrews

Higgins: My—, basically a wrong has been done to me and I want it righted.

Interviewer: Yeah.

Higgins: I put out money to someone to provide a business service. The person did, first of all, a faulty job, uh, didn't come in when they were supposed to have come. The people that they subcontracted to, I've no idea.

In these opening remarks, Higgins makes two point that are striking on their own as well as by virtue of their juxtaposition. First, he begins with a forthright, powerful statement of values. He has come to court not to get his roof fixed or to collect money, but to right a wrong. If this is indeed why he has come to court, then he presumably believes that the court shares his interest in righting wrongs, and has the power to do so.[8]

Second, having expressed his expectations of the legal system, he moves directly to state his legal theory of the case. He made a contract by giving money in exchange for a promise of future services, and the other party breached the contract by failing to render the services in satisfactory fashion. Higgins also anticipates Riva's possible defense by disclaiming any knowledge of or assent to their subcontracting arrangement. In coming to this understanding of the legal elements of his case, he has undoubtedly benefited from his conversations with the clerk and, as we shall see, his brother, who is a law student.[9] What is particularly interesting is that in this short passage Higgins reveals an insider's knowledge of some of the legal technicalities of his case coexisting with an ideology of law that insiders would probably regard as naive. This combination of realism and idealism becomes a major theme as the interview continues.

In Text 1B, Higgins narrates the factual background of the case. There is no explicit statement of ideology comparable to that in Text 1A, but a number of inferences can be drawn from the way in which he selects and emphasizes particular facts.

Text 1B. Continuation of interview with Higgins and Andrews

Higgins: OK, the contractor that did come, came up, nailed, first of all, took off my barge board, nailed up some aluminum siding right to my wall—which if you don't know anything about roofing, you just don't—I mean, it just doesn't work that way. The water seal is not there, nothing. Then they proceeded to roll some, uh, asphalt tar paper down and nail that to the roof and by this time it took like an hour, OK. My roommate decides it was done 'cause I was at work—I told him to stay home, make sure the work was done—which they also went over the contract before they even started. OK. So first of all, they were two hours late when they got there. Two people came, they had no barge board in the truck which was in the contract, "new barge board." He [the roommate, Andrews] complains that, "Look, you know, aren't you supposed to put the barge board on?" The man started saying obscenities to him.

As in Text 1A, Higgins again displays considerable sophistication about the law as it actually works. Apparently aware of the legal significance of the precise terms of the contract, he notes that the parties went over it before the work began, and emphatically quotes the contractual reference to "new barge board." At the same time, however, he reports other details that reflect a concern with breaches of social convention to which the court is unlikely to attach any meaning. Higgins relates, for example, that the roofers were two hours late, and he stresses this detail with the preface "first of all"[10]; he concludes these remarks with a reference to the roofers' obscenities. Thus, his perspective is simultaneously rule oriented and relational. He is attentive to the law's agenda, even as he stresses his own social agenda. He implies, consistent with his explicit statements in Text 1A, that although he understands the "official" ideology of the law, his personal beliefs presume a legal system with a broad interest in social justice.

At the end of the interview, Higgins and Andrews describe the interaction with the legal system that has brought them to their present understanding of its objectives and limitations. In Text 1C, they respond to the question, "How did you think to come to small claims?"

Text 1C. End of interview with Higgins and Andrews

Higgins: Uh, well, first of all, just from common knowledge. Second of all, my brother's a law student. Oh, OK. He's a, a interna-, uh, insurance lawyer for a multinational insurance company.

Interviewer: Uh-huh.

Higgins: OK. And, and he basically guided me as to the steps that were necessary to do, like send the cer-, send in the letter, send in the certified letter. . . .

Andrews: Which is very difficult for the average citizen who's never done it before.

Higgins: Exactly.

Interviewer: Yeah.

Andrews: We've been here [to the clerk's office], we were here three times before we got it correct.

Interviewer: Oh, OK.

Andrews: We came the first time, the guy said, "Well, you need this. . . ."

Higgins: Three, three copies of everything.

Andrews: So we went back and we got. . . .

Higgins: So we got three copies of everything.

Andrews: Then we came back and they said, "Oh. . . ."

Higgins: "You don't have specific. . . ."

Andrews: ". . . you really should get that organized." So we got that, and today they almost said the same thing to us.

Higgins: Luckily, we have the original.

Andrews: She [another clerk] pulled out another piece of paper that we didn't know about last time. So it's difficult for the lay person to deal with.

Because of their discussion with Higgins' brother, the law student, Higgins and Andrews came to the legal system considerably better prepared then "the average citizen who's never done it before." In particular, they were forewarned about the law's concern with such details as certified letters. Nonetheless, even they had to show extraordinary persistence to find their way through the procedural maze of the small-claims court. Their belief in the law as an agency for righting wrongs seems to have been challenged at every turn. They repeatedly encountered an institution whose apparent purpose was to preserve the status quo by granting access only to those with an unusual combination of technical knowledge and perseverance. What is remarkable is that their faith in the system survived this experience, such that they still saw themselves as invoking the law to right a wrong.

It is interesting to consider the way in which Higgins and Andrews manage the dissonance between the beliefs they brought to the system and the beliefs that they found to be guiding the operation of the system. Rather than abandoning their naive idealism about the law, they draw a distinction between the law as a symbolic abstraction and the law as an everyday reality. Their comments suggest that they retain their belief in the abstract law as a force for righting wrongs, while developing cynicism about the day-to-day practices of legal administators. Instead of challenging the fundamental legitimacy of the law, Higgins and Andrews direct their frustration at those who administer it. Ultimately, they modify their behavior to meet the administrators' needs. The result is that they are able simultaneously to espouse one ideology while doing business with another.

When the case went to trial, the evidence was essentially as Higgins had predicted. Higgins and Andrews stressed the terms of the written contract and Riva's failure to live up to its obligations. Riva acknowledged that there were problems, but blamed them on the subcontractor. The judge took the position that Riva was responsible for the actions of the subcontractor. She found for Higgins and Andrews and awarded them $425.

In a post-trial interview, Higgins virtually repeated the principal points that he had made in the initial interview. He said that after the trial, he "felt vindicated and righted by law." He found the judge to be fair and "very objective." He would "most certainly" go to small-claims court again in the event of a similar problem.

Despite this overall satisfaction with the outcome and the process, a number of things troubled Higgins. As in the pre-trial interview, he was particularly concerned that "the average person" would be unable to fight his way through the procedural morass that the system presents.[11] He continued to resolve the dissonance between the images of law as an instrument of vindication and an instrument of limitation by distinguishing between the abstraction of law and the reality of its daily practice. As he had in the earlier interview, he strongly criticized the clerks and other functionaries, calling them "bimbos . . . who couldn't give a shit." His device of personalizing the shortcomings in the system was so effective that his faith in the system as a whole was not only undiminished, but had been strengthened.

Case 2: The Super Fixer-Upper

Case 2 provides a different perspective on the discrepancy between lay beliefs about the law and the functioning of the legal system. Analysis of the interaction between the judge and the litigants during the trial demonstrates the process of constructing, manipulating, and managing meaning in court, as well as the difficulties that emerge when litigants and the court approach the case from different ideological perspectives.[12]

The plaintiffs, Mr. and Mrs. Sutter, express a relational outlook on society and a belief in the law as an institution that actively seeks out and corrects social iniquities. The defendants, Mr. and Mrs. Ross, have a rule-oriented social perspective and view the law as passive and oriented exclusively toward rights and obligations created by mutual consent. The judge shares the Rosses' beliefs, with the result that those things that are of greatest concern to the Sutters have little impact on the development of the case. In a post-trial interview, Mrs. Sutter recognizes and attempts to resolve this dissonance.

Mr. and Mrs. Sutter rented a somewhat dilapidated house—they termed it a "super fixer-upper"—from Mr. and Mrs. Ross. The Sutters had an option to buy the house in six months if they could get a mortgage. They anticipated doing considerable work on the house to bring it up to local building code standards before they would be able to get a mortgage. Their legal claim is that the Rosses misled them about the extent of the work that needed to be done, and that after they had spent more than $1,000 on repairs they concluded that they would never be able to afford all the work that would be necessary to meet the requirements of the building code. They seek $1,500 in damages (the limit of the court's jurisdiction), consisting of a full refund of their $500 security deposit and $1,000 in partial reimbursement for improvements they made. The Rosses' position is that they owe the Sutters nothing because their so-called repairs were so poorly done that they caused more than $1,500 damage to the house. From the court's perspective, the critical legal issue is whether the Rosses concealed or misrepresented the problems with the house, or whether the Sutters had an adequate opportunity to inspect the house and discover the problems for themselves.

Text 2A is Mr. Sutter's initial narrative before the court. Notice that he begins with a number of personal factors: the Sutters' need for a house and a home, their desire to establish and maintain social relationships, and his wife's need to maintain her animals (she works for the local animal protection society and often keeps strays). Then he addresses several problems with the house, including the amount of insulation, the cost of heat, and the condition of the foundation. Two things are significant about this portion of his testimony. First, even though this is his first statement to the court, he says little of an affirmative nature, but largely limits himself to responding to things the Rosses have said in correspondence before trial or earlier in the trial itself.[13] Second, on each point Mr. Sutter does not directly dispute what the Rosses have said. He admits that he has no personal knowledge of what was said about insulation and that he was told that the Rosses had moved into a single room because of heating problems, and he acknowledges that the holes in the foundation are small, as the Rosses have contended.

Text 2A. Mr. Sutter's initial narrative before the court

> *Mr. Sutter:* . . . Um basically, um what the situation is here is that we needed a home, a house to live in. It looked like a good opportunity for one; I wanted to be close to town, so that we could be close to our friends and neighbors. Nan needed a large yard for her

animals. Uh, this is why we looked at the Rosses' home. OK, now, um, as for insulation, I have no—I was not told anything about the insulation. I noticed that they had high ceilings. I heard that they put in the new windows. I realize that they said it would cost about $150 a month to heat the house in the winter time, but they had one bill that, um, was at worth—exceeded $300 for one month during winter time. They had mentioned that they had at one time blocked off the rooms and lived in one room of the house, OK. That's—now what I had heard or what I had understood from the situation was that they were working to complete, to fix up the house so it wouldn't cost so much to heat. They put in these double windows. My wife and sister-in-law both say that the house was presented to them as being fully insulated. When we walked around to the outside of the house and I did indeed, did indeed notice the holes in the foundation. They are small holes basically where Mr. Ross needed to get under or to cut holes to see what he was doing to put in the electrical work. OK, I assume that was done before we moved in the house in the winter time. So that was not a problem in heating the home. The pictures my wife showed you of the foundation here—this one for instance—now I don't know that the Rosses were the ones who put on this uh. . . .

The fact that Mr. Sutter begins his testimony with several personal details suggests two things: first, that these details are important to him, and second, that he believes that they will be important to the court as well. The implication is that he sees the law as an institution that will take an interest in the personal needs of litigants, and perhaps be inclined to help those whose actions are motivated by sound values. The factual presentation that follows is subject to a similar interpretation. From a normative legal perspective, a plaintiff in a misrepresentation action does not help himself by listing things that the defendants did not misrepresent to him. His approach is understandable, however, if viewed from the perspective of one who sees the law as oriented toward solving human problems in human terms. By acknowledging that he cannot challenge the defendants' position on several important issues, he presents himself as an honest and forthright person, willing—indeed, going out of his way—to sacrifice strategic advantage for principle. His factual presentation harmonizes with the personal details, since a forthright acknowledgment is just what would be expected from a person who values home life, friends, neighbors, and kindness to animals. If our inferences about Mr. Sutter's understanding of the law are correct, then his testimony may reflect a well-conceived strategy[14] rather than a naive blunder.

It is clear from other portions of the trial that the presiding judge does not share this understanding of the law's interests. In Text 2B, for example, Mrs. Sutter is showing the judge a series of photographs that illustrate the condition of the house.

Text 2B. Mrs. Sutter and judge

Mrs. Sutter: This is here a picture of the backyard and the fence, showing that none of the drains or anything has ever been attached. This is one of the chimney, showing that both the chinmey foundation and the house is falling away from the house and is falling apart. The part. . . .

Judge [interrupting]: Did you not have a chance to inspect the property before you bought it?

Mrs. Sutter: Uh, we didn't really know what we were looking for at the time. We had never, you know. . . .

Judge [interrupting]: If it is so obvious from these photographs, I wonder how you didn't catch it?

Mrs. Sutter: Well, we weren't looking for it. But when we moved into the house, we were in a predicament at the time. We had formerly been renting a house in the country. The lady that we were renting from had been living in Florida, and she moved back to our place instead of, uh, moved back to [unintelligible]. And so we were in a bind. We had only one month to find another house to move our . . . [Mrs. Sutter stops talking and waits for the judge, who examines the photographs at length, to speak].

Text 2B portrays succinctly the contrasting ways in which the lay plaintiffs and the judge assign meaning to events.[15] For the Sutters, events take on meaning in the context of their human impact. In their testimony, both Mr. and Mrs. Sutter suggest their belief, or at least their hope, that the judge will share their values. With just two questions, however, the judge confounds this expectation. For her, the law is not concerned with predicaments, friendship, and neighborliness. In her view, the law operates in a context of competent, autonomous, and economically self-interested individuals who make informed judgments and commit them to written contracts. Those who seek relief from the terms of their contracts thus bear a heavy burden of demonstrating the reasonableness of their conduct. Accordingly, she focuses on the single issue of what was visible at the time of the inspection, putting aside such factors as the personal situations of the litigants.

The Rosses' presentation is much more closely oriented to the agenda of the court. Their exclusive focus is on what was disclosed, what the Sutters had an opportunity to inspect, and the terms of the parties' written contract. They ignore the human and social considerations that are so important to the Sutters. The Rosses' approach to the case is epitomized by the excerpts in Text 2C, which are drawn from their cross-examination of the Sutters.[16]

Text 2C. The Rosses' cross-examination of Mrs. Sutter

Mrs. Ross: Did you not, excuse me, did you not state that you wasn't worried about the heat, because you was going to heat with a wooden stove?

Mrs. Sutter: Yes, I did. I stated that to her also.

Mrs. Ross: O.K. So you wasn't worried about the heat to begin with?

Mrs. Sutter: That's right.

. . .

Mr. Ross: When you, when y'all come up to look at the house, did you not know the reason why the holes was in the foundation?

Mrs. Sutter: I didn't. My husband is shaking his head yes, but I didn't know the holes, why the holes were in the foundation.

Mr. Ross: Did we not state why?

Mrs. Sutter: Not to my knowledge. Again, maybe when my husband gets up—he's nodding yes, but, uh, to my knowledge, no, I don't recall that.

. . .

Mrs. Ross: Uh, did you not state to me that you noticed the chimney's being ready to fall in at the time, that you was getting the one outside the bedroom, the master bedroom?

Mrs. Sutter: I probably did. Uh, yes. We weren't . . .

Mrs. Ross: OK.

Mrs. Sutter: . . . going to use it at all. You told me that was closed off, and that it was unusable, correct?

Mrs. Ross: Yes, ma'am. Did we not state to you that neither fireplace was in satisfactory condition to use—that they was, it was an old house and the fire inspector refused to let it be used?

Mrs. Sutter: Yes, you did. And that's why the furnaces weren't attached to the fireplaces.

Mrs. Ross: That's all.

In rendering judgment at the end of the case (Text 2D), the judge confirms that the outcome has turned on the inspection issue. At the start of Text 2D, she turns the "predicament" argument on its head, suggesting that the plaintiffs should be grateful that their predicament is no worse than it is. She then focuses on the provision in the lease that all repairs are to be done at the tenant's expense, suggests that the Sutters can avoid its effect only by proving "gross misrepresentation," and concludes that this is an impossible task, given the opportunity for inspection. Finally, she declines to order the return of the security deposit, apparently agreeing with the Rosses that the Sutters' repair efforts did more than $500 damage to the house.

Text 2D. Judge renders verdict

Judge: I listened long and carefully to all the testimony. This is an interesting situation. I'm, I am sure that the plaintiffs in this action are thankful that they did not buy the property for $15,000, that they first rented it for six months with the option to purchase, because you found these things that caused you to decide so your losses are minimized to some extent by reason, uh, by virtue of the fact that you did not actually close the deal on the very day that you signed this lease agreement. You could have been paying her $15,000 and you would have been stuck with what you have here. Uh, on the other hand, on examination of the lease, there is a section in it—Section D—"The lessee shall use the demised premises for residential purposes. Lessee shall keep the premises, including but not limited to the plumbing fixtures, in a clean, safe, sanitary, and presentable condition. The lessee shall be responsible for mowing of the grass, watering the plants as needed. The lessee shall make all repairs that are required to the premises at his own cost and expense and all repairs shall be made in a good, workmanlike manner." I cannot see, um, gross misrepresentation here. I believe that you as tenants had a chance to inspect the property but there were some visible flaws, that you expected to get a really good deal and if it had worked out for you, it would have been a very good deal. Uh, it is the burden of the plaintiff to prove to the court that you're entitled to the amount that you are suing for. I don't feel that the plaintiff has carried this burden in this action, therefore the case is dismissed. You each have suffered the losses far above, um, the $500 security deposit. You're gonna have to get work done on the house to bring it up to standard, um, they put the chain-link fence up, which is to your advantage, but your losses are large and I think one more or less cancels the other out. That is the judgment of this court. Case dismissed.

It is interesting to imagine how this case might have been handled by a judge with an ideology more consistent with that of the Sutters. This judge would have started from a view of society which stressed interdependency rather than individual autonomy, with the written contract the exception rather than the rule in the structuring of relationships. Such a judge might have identified as relevant other legal principles in addition to those of contract and misrepresentation (e.g., unjust enrichment). Similarly, our hypothetical judge might have taken a broader view of the relevant facts, perhaps paying more attention to the Sutters' predicament in evaluating the reasonableness of their failure to notice the defects in the house. With respect to the specific legal issue of the meaning of the lease, it would have been possible to construe the phrase "all repairs that are required to the premises" as referring only to ordinary maintenance, and not to major structural repairs.[17]

The result in the case is not inevitable. Legal results such as this do not flow ineluctably from raw facts, but are strongly influenced by the way in which the judge and the parties weave a fabric of meaning out of the strands of the events that led to the dispute. There is little or no connection between the Sutters' approach to the construction of meaning and that of the judge. As a result of this ideological dissonance, the plaintiffs and the judge talk past each other, each framing events in terms that are of little interest or meaning to the other.

In an interview several weeks after the trial, Mrs. Sutter offered a remarkably incisive analysis of the "meaning gap" that developed between the judge and her husband and herself. Her remarks in Text 2E are in response to a question about what she wished she had done differently at the trial. Her general point is that the "damage" the judge attributed to the Sutters involved items that the Rosses would have had to repair anyway to meet the building code.

Text 2E. Post-trial interview with Sutters

Mrs. Sutter: Yeah, after we left the courtroom and stuff and on the way home, we were thinking, "well, we should have said it this way, or we should have been more clear here, or clear there, or something."

Interviewer: Where do you think those areas were? I mean, any specific ones that you can remember?

Mrs. Sutter Sister: I don't think we come right out. . . .

Mrs. Sutter: Well, we didn't.

Mrs. Sutter Sister: . . . and told the judge, you know, this stuff. . . .

Mrs. Sutter: . . . had to be done anyways.

Notice Mrs. Sutter's emphasis on their failure to state the problem explicitly. She recognizes the facts are not self-evident, but acquire meaning through a process of negotiation between speaker and listener. As the interview continues, she also displays grudging admiration for the Rosses' ability to package the facts in a way that was seductive to herself and appealing to the court.

Text 2F. Continuation of post-trial interview with Sutters

Mrs. Sutter: Um, and so they seem, they portrayed a big Christian family, you know, um, just uh, you know, dainty and particular and, "We would never do this."

Interviewer: Right.

Mrs. Sutter: And so I guess I, it suckered me in. I just assumed what they said was gospel and . . .

Interviewer: Uh-huh.

Mrs. Sutter: . . . let it go at that. And then they come to court with these half pictures of these different things . . .

Interviewer: Right.

Mrs. Sutter: . . . and these half, different, uh, just the whole thing is, was—totally mislead from anybody that had ever seen the house or would see the house . . .

Interviewer: Uh-huh.

Mrs. Sutter: . . . wouldn't know. So I was mad at them for that, but what could I do?

Interviewer: Yeah.

Mrs. Sutter: You know?

Interviewer: Yeah.

Mrs. Sutter: I can't say, uh, "Well, this picture is not what it is," OK, you know . . .

Interviewer: Right.

Mrs. Sutter: "It shows a nail there, yeah, but—the nail, yeah, we did put the nail there, but this is why." "Well, let me see the picture to prove it."

Ultimately, she shifts some of the responsibility for this communication failure from herself to the judge.

Text 2G. Continuation of post-trial interview with Sutters

Interviewer: What did you feel about the judge? Um, do you think she was fair, or . . . ?

Mrs. Sutter: Well, the more I thought about it as the fact, I, I didn't think so, because. . . .

Interviewer: Uh huh.

Mrs. Sutter: I, I guess I thought that she is a judge. She should have a lot of common sense and she should have thought of those things even if we forgot them at the time.

In other words, Mrs. Sutter concludes, it is the duty of a judge to understand the perspectives and experiences of litigants, and to be able to bridge the gap between lay and legal systems of meaning. Simply put, her view seems to be that judges should conform more closely to her expectations about how the legal system should operate. As Mrs. Sutter put it a few lines later, "Somebody in that position should have been around the block a few times and thought of some things."

Interestingly, Mrs. Sutter claims to have noticed the communication gap between the judge and herself even as it was developing. Near the end of the interview, she remarked, "I was so confident, you know; I had everything planned. And so I knew in my mind when I was saying this one, that it wasn't coming out like I was thinking it or wanting it to, but, on the same hand I wasn't sure how to change it. . . . And it just, it just sort of, uh, you know, unraveled a little once it got into court."

The informal court litigants and judges we have studied show a fundamental division between those who consider the law to be an enabling mechanism and those who believe it to be an instrument of limitation. Among litigants, those with a legal ideology of enablement tend to be those with a philosophy of social governance that we have previously characterized as relational (Conley and O'Barr 1990a, 1990b). In speaking about their cases in and out of court, these litigants emphasize status and relationships rather than contracts, documents, and legal principles. Their accounts of events are filled with background details that are presumably relevant to them, but not necessarily to the court. They seek to apportion rights and responsibilities according to need and adherence to social conventions rather than rules of law.

These differences in ideological beliefs about law have important parallels in the linguistic behavior of litigants. For example, relational litigants who are typically inexperienced in courtroom discourse conventions bring their everyday conventions about narration to the courtroom. Most important, they expect the recipient of their account—the judge who hears their case—to play a supportive part in the same way as everyday audiences who help coproduce accounts. As with Higgins in Case 1, these litigants see the law as a force for the righting of wrongs. Like Mrs. Sutter in Case 2, they expect the law's agents to pursue this objective aggressively. They expect judges to "have been around the block a few times and thought of some things," and thus to be willing and able to recognize social rectitude when they see it and to use the law to ensure that it is appropriately rewarded.[18] In stressing social issues to the court, these litigants suggest that they expect that their own ideology of enablement will be the dominant ideology of the legal system.

Often, but by no means always, relational litigants see their faith confounded. Some, like Higgins, encounter procedural mechanisms that function to limit access to the system. Higgins manages to emerge from this encounter with his ideology intact. It is as if he sees "the law" as an entity separable from those who carry it out. Court clerks and law students may present a picture of the law as an institution that thwarts those seeking justice by the erection of procedural barriers, but Higgins looks past them and continues to see the "real" law as receptive to those seeking to right wrongs.

Mr. and Mrs. Sutter experience a subtler kind of ideological dissonance. There is no direct effort to deny them access to the enabling potential of the law. They are frustrated, rather, by the court's passivity. In the post-trial interview, Mrs. Sutter acknowledges her own failure to construct meaning in a way that would have articulated with the court's agenda, but at the same time decries the failure of the judge to come forward and do the necessary reformulation of the raw materials she provided. It is unclear whether this experience has affected her ideology of law in any fundamental way. Mrs. Sutter's recognition of the reasons for her failure in court, and her rueful admiration of the Rosses' ability to manipulate symbols and meaning,[19] suggest that she, at least, has forsaken her ideology of enablement in favor of a more cynical view of the law. However, her post-trial comments reflect disappointment not in the law itself, but in the judge as an unworthy representative of the law. It is possible that Mrs. Sutter, like Higgins, sees the ideology of limitation that she encountered not as the dominant ideology of the law, but as a heresy espoused by an errant functionary. Under this interpretation, her ideology of enablement may survive, perhaps to be tested another day against the behavior of those who carry out the law.

Not all litigants manage dissonance in this manner. On rare occasions, a litigant may openly challenge the legitimacy of the court. In one case that we studied, a litigant accused the court of collusion with a large corporation in the oppression of poor people. The judge dismissed the litigant's grievance on technical evidentiary grounds, and the litigant dropped the argument. In the out-of-court interviews we conducted, litigants occasionally raised similar fundamental questions about the legitimacy of the system. However, these comments tended to have the quality of offhand complaints and none of these other litigants provoked a direct confrontation in the courtroom.

Our observations also prompt a number of inferences about issues that transcend the problems of individual litigants. The first of these issues is the distribution of legal ideologies in American society. We believe that the ideology of enablement is a naive one, but we hesitate to describe it solely as a class-based phenomenon (cf. Merry 1986). In our sample of civil litigants, it is undoubtedly more common among working-class people than the ideology of limitation. However, we have observed both ideologies among people of varied social, economic, and educational status. In particular, wealth and social position do not seem to correlate directly with rule orientedness and espousal of the ideology of limitation. Rather, these attitudes appear to derive specifically from experience with the culture of law and business. This experience is differentially distributed among the population, of course, but our limited sample suggests that the distribution does not follow clear class lines. Moreover, the obvious parallels to Gilligan's (1982) comparison of male and female moral reasoning suggest that gender may influence the distribution of the two ideologies, as well as the rule-oriented and relational perspectives of which they are a part.

Our findings also have implications for understanding the hegemonic function of legal ideology. In our study of informal justice in America, we have rarely seen the conscious manipulation of ideology to deny rights, stifle change, or defuse discontent. Instead, as we noted above, we see a subtle process whereby litigants rationalize their experiences by separating the ideal of the law from the reality of its implementation. Their future legal behavior may be shaped by the ideology of limitation, but they retain a belief in the law as an instrument of enablement. The more sophisticated become competent players in the game of law and business, achieving enough satisfaction in small victories to distract them from the larger issues that originally brought them to the legal system. The officials of the legal system rarely play an active role in this process; rather, they provide the evidence that persuades many naive litigants of the existence and power of the ideology of limitation. Nonetheless, it is hard to imagine a more effective mechanism for maintaining the status quo.

From a methodological perspective, these findings argue for the importance of detailed ethnographic research in the study of ideology. Broad theoretical statements about the nature, distribution, and function of ideology can take on new meaning when read against the background of the day-to-day behavior of the law's practitioners and consumers. Ideology is most clearly revealed when analyzed simultaneously from above, as a theoretical construct, and from below, as an inference drawn from the observation of many particular instances of human behavior.

Finally, we note that the ethnography of discourse also yields understanding of how linguistic ideologies may differ among litigants and officials of the legal system. Just as they rationalize the dissonance between their expectations about the nature of law and their experiences with the legal system, litigants also explain away the discrepancies between their expectations about discourse and their linguistic experiences in the courtroom. As a result, neither ideological nor linguistic dissonance undercuts the prevailing belief in American law as an ideal system of justice.

Notes

The research reported here is a joint project. The authors alternate priority of authorship in their publications. The research was supported by Grants SES 85–21528 and 85–21574 from the Law and Social Science program of the National Science Foundation, and by a grant from the University of North Carolina Law Center Foundation. We acknowledge with appreciation the assistance of the officials of the small-claims courts in Colorado, North Carolina, and Pennsylvania; of the persons (identified in this paper by pseudonyms) whose cases we studied; and of our research assistants, Mark Bielawski, Mark Childress, Amy Thomas, and Rebecca Schaller.

1. In previous papers reporting results of the study, we have discussed the structure of litigants' courtroom accounts (O'Barr and Conley 1985), the reasoning processes they employ (Conley and O'Barr 1990a, 1990b), their expectations of the legal system (O'Barr and Conley 1988), and the role played by informal court judges (Conley and O'Barr 1988). These reports of research findings, along with those contained in the present paper, are incorporated in our book, *Rules Versus Relationships: The Ethnography of Legal Discourse,* published by The University of Chicago Press in 1990.

2. It is not our finding that there is a "real" story to be heard and that the right circumstances will capture it. Stories simply do not exist outside their telling, but are context- and audience-specific. We base this study on the stories that we have been told under the circumstances we describe.

3. Despite an equal interest in defendants, we had limited success in interviewing them before trial. Very few informal court defendants come to the courthouse before the trial date. Almost all of those we contacted at their homes or places of employment declined to be interviewed. We suspect that this is largely because of their unhappiness in being named as defendants.

4. Primarily because of high rates of default and settlement, as well as the mobility of the litigants, we were able to obtain complete, three-stage data on only 19 cases.

5. In instances when defendants did not appear in court to respond to the charges against them, the typical outcome was a default judgment. In such cases, plaintiffs usually were asked to give only a brief outline of the story they would present if called upon to do so.

6. The degree of litigant contact with clerks differs across jurisdictions. Most jurisdictions do not require lengthy, detailed interviews conducted by members of the clerk's staff.

7. To make the texts accessible to a wide audience, we have not used special transcribing conventions such as those used by linguists and conversation analysts. We believe, following Ochs (1979), that the act of transcribing is a statement about the theoretical significance of the data. Because we are focusing on the sociolegal issues involved and not on the interaction patterns per se, we believe we are justified in electing to use a straightforward set of conventions that do not bring in issues that we do not intend to discuss. Moreover, as anyone who has worked with transcripts knows, there is never a totally complete transcript. There are always other issues to be noticed, such as prosody, rate, pauses, overlapping, accent, and even nonverbal features when videotapes as opposed to audiotapes are available.

8. One might well question whether Higgins's statement of values is disingenuous. However, he has just spent 15 minutes with a clerk responding to detailed questions about the nuts and bolts of his case, in a conversation where values and beliefs had no place. We think it significant that in his first statement to the first person he saw after coming out of the clerk's office, Higgins put aside the mundane content of the prior conversation and took up the abstract question of justice.

9. For a useful comparison, see Sarat and Felstiner's (1986) discussion of divorce lawyers' transformation of their clients' stories.

10. A delay constitutes a breach of contract only when the contract specifically provides that "time is of the essence." It is inconceivable that a court would find this delay to be of any legal significance.

11. He also noted that the judge had reduced his damages by about 20%. He said that his brother had prepared him for this, and told him to "hit for more, they'll come back for

compromise.'' He was concerned again about "the average person" without access to inside information who "would have been terribly disappointed" with this result.

12. Because of logistical problems in the jurisdiction where this case was tried, we were not able to interview the litigants before trial. Our analysis of the case thus begins with the trial.

13. Mrs. Sutter and her sister testified before Mr. Sutter. Mr. and Mrs. Ross cross-examined each of them, frequently injecting statements of their own position. The issues that Mr. Sutter discusses were among those raised by the previous witnesses and the Rosses.

14. We mean "well-conceived" in the sense of designed to play to the concerns of his audience, as he sees it.

15. Plaintiffs in misrepresentation cases must prove that they reasonably relied on the defendants' misrepresentations. Courts are reluctant to find reasonable reliance where the allegedly misrepresented condition is plainly visible.

16. The judge who heard Case 2 is one of the few in our sample who regularly invited lay litigants to cross-examine their adversaries. Most litigants have difficulty framing questions and end up arguing with the other party or trying to make a statement. From a tactical standpoint, the Rosses' cross-examination of the Sutters is by far the most effective we have observed.

17. In an article on judicial decision making in informal courts (Conley and O'Barr 1988), we demonstrate that judges' conceptions of the law and the judicial role in the legal process influence how they deal with particular cases. For example, the "mediator" judge that we describe might have reacted to this case by moving the parties toward a negotiated settlement based more on social considerations than legal formalities.

18. For another perspective on litigant expectations of the legal system, see O'Barr and Conley (1988, 1990b).

19. Recall Mrs. Sutter's comments in Text 2F on the Rosses' ability to present themselves as "a big Christian family," and their skillful use of photographs.

Works Cited

Bourdieu, Pierre. 1977. *Outline of a theory of practice.* Translated by Richard Nice. Cambridge: Cambridge University Press.

Conley, John M., and William M. O'Barr. 1988. Fundamentals of jurisprudence: An ethnography of judicial decision making in informal courts. *North Carolina Law Review* 66:467–507.

———. 1990a. Rules versus relationships in small claims disputes. In *Conflict talk: Sociolinguistic investigations of arguments in conversations,* ed. Allen Grimshaw, pp. 178–96. Cambridge: University Press.

———. 1990b. *Rules versus relationships: The ethnography of legal discourse.* Chicago: University of Chicago Press.

Deutsch, Jan G. 1983. Corporate law as the ideology of capitalism. *Yale Law Journal* 93:395.

Gilligan, Carol. 1982. *In a different voice: Psychological theory and women's development.* Cambridge: Harvard University Press.

Hunt, Alan. 1985. The ideology of law: Advances and problems in recent applications of the concept of ideology to the analysis of law. *Law and Society Review* 19:11–37.

Kulscar, Kalman. 1980. Ideological changes and the legal structure: A discussion of socialist experience. *International Journal of the Sociology of Law* 8:61–81.

Merry, Sally Engle. 1986. Everyday understandings of the law in working-class America. *American Ethnologist* 13:253–70.

O'Barr, William M., and John M. Conley. 1985. Litigant satisfaction versus legal adequacy in small claims court narratives. *Law and Society Review* 19:661–701.

———. 1988. Lay expectations of the civil justice system. *Law and Society Review* 22:137–61.

Ochs, Elinor. 1979. Transcription as theory. In *Developmental pragmatics*, ed. Elinor Ochs and Bambi Schieffeln. New York: Academic Press.

Sarat, Austin, and William L. F. Felstiner. 1986. Law and strategy in the divorce lawyer's office. *Law and Society Review* 20:93–134.

Consensus and Dissent in
U.S. Legal Opinions
Narrative Structure and Social Voices

One of the ways in which disputes are settled in this country is through the decisions of appellate courts. These decisions, which often take the form of written texts composed of a majority opinion and one or more dissents or concurrences, represent one of our legal system's answers to situations of conflict. This paper examines the U.S. Supreme Court's infamous decision in *Plessy v. Ferguson*, contrasting it with *Brown v. Board of Education*, the case that overruled *Plessy*. This juxtaposition of texts is invited not only by the language of *Brown* in particular, but also by a broader narrative convention that is central to the semiotics of U.S. legal doctrine. Authors of legal textbooks, opinions, and law review articles commonly treat cases from diverse times and courts together if they are understood as developments in a single "doctrine" (see Gunther 1985:633–41). By juxtaposing *Plessy* and *Brown*, we can begin to understand the semiotic features of this narrative convention, analyzing the way in which these authoritative narratives attempt to restore order to conflictual situations.

This paper takes the position that legal opinions may be fruitfully approached as narratives.[1] There is some room for debate on this point, and in one sense it makes little difference to much of this analysis whether we view opinions as narratives or as texts containing some narrative features. At first glance, it might seem tempting to attach the label "narrative" only to those portions of legal opinions that "tell the story" of the underlying events producing conflict, distinguishing these passages from those that recite legal arguments or pronounce legal conclusions. This approach, however, would divert our attention from the way in which an opinion as a whole is the carefully—and often quite self-consciously—constructed story of a social conflict and its legal resolution.[2] We would also fail to see the ways in which the description of events and the discussion of legal issues and conclusions are integrally intertwined, shaping and framing one another. When we treat the opinion as a narrative, we can also bring to bear aspects of literary theory that focus on authors and audiences, a fascinating perspective from which to examine signed and per curiam legal opinions. This essay will accordingly treat the majority and dissenting opinions at issue as narratives. (Because the majority and dissent are generally clearly distinguished as the products of two different authors, it probably makes sense to treat them as distinct, albeit closely related, narratives—although, here again, there is room for argument.)

U.S. Legal Opinions: Textual and Contextual Structures

Any analysis focusing on Supreme Court opinions should begin with an important caveat. Law school professors routinely warn their students that appellate opinions are atypical outcomes of American disputes; many cases are never appealed, and still more never get to court in the first place. The Supreme Court opinions that I will be discussing are indeed unusual; they are high-profile cases that are viewed as watersheds, as changing the course of American law. Although they may be atypical, these cases are nonetheless important to our formal system of dispute resolution—not only because they dictate the terms on which countless subsequent cases will be decided by other courts, but also because these key cases play a symbolic role within U.S. political and legal culture. The paradigm-changing cases are often ones in which the individual disputants represent more widespread and highly charged splits within American society, whether over racial desegregation, abortion, or protective economic measures. When the Court issues decisions in such cases, it is often reaching beyond the particular parties in the case to attempt to resolve a divisive social issue, an issue that has threatened social harmony and consensus. It is not surprising, then, that Supreme Court decisions, to a far greater extent than those of other courts, receive regular media coverage and attract widespread attention beyond the legal community. The Court often acts symbolically as the arbiter of serious social disputes dividing large portions of the community.

If these narratives represent an attempt to resolve broad *social* conflicts, they also try to restore *legal* order in several ways. First, cases that reach the Supreme Court often raise issues upon which lower courts are divided—a situation commonly referred to as a "split in the circuits." The division is not only one between members of the community, but is also a conceptual disruption within the legal doctrine in question, that is, either it has been found to be internally inconsistent, or it is inconsistent with other legal principles (often constitutional). The Court's decision, then, at once seeks to restore order to the practices of the legal community (i.e., so that cases that are purportedly alike will be treated in ways that are thought to be similar) and to the semiotic system of supposedly coherent legal doctrine.

U.S. Supreme Court opinions are generally composed of a majority opinion and one or more concurrences or dissents. The majority opinion, which is usually thought to be the most authoritative part of the text, expresses the decision of the

Court, as determined by a majority of the Justices who voted. Members of that majority may also write concurrences, to stress grounds for the decision not emphasized in the majority opinion, or to reiterate support for the Court's decision. Justices who disagree with the majority's decision express their disagreement in dissents. Lawyers often dismiss dissenting opinions as unimportant—"not worth the paper they're written on," a common saying goes. For the practicing attorney this may be true, because basing an argument on a Supreme Court dissent is unlikely to win a case. However, dissents may nonetheless have a role to play in the dispute-resolution process.

Social Utility and Semiotic Structure: The Power and the Limits of Narrative Analysis

In exploring what that role might be, I want to distinguish between social utilitarian explanations and more semiotic approaches. Although narrative control may be both socially useful and symbolically powerful, this essay will only address the semiotic significance of narrative structure in legal opinions. In making this distinction, I do not advocate a return to the old dichotomy between meaning and social structure, for semiotic effects are themselves social and certainly affect legal praxis; similarly, socially useful approaches are also meaningful.

This is also not an argument for downplaying the social power of language. However, I am stressing that the mutual embeddedness of text and context cannot be assumed to be iconic; the mediations are more complex and must be analyzed and worked out carefully. This is essentially to raise a warning at the methodological level—that we cannot jump from "voices heard" to social function; we cannot simply read text into context without any accompanying social analysis. I will briefly discuss the particular importance of distinguishing between semiotic and social effects in the legal context.

There are a number of recent studies suggesting in various ways that there is a relationship between participants' satisfaction and control of narrativity—that is, that people who are allowed to tell their own stories, construct their own narratives with minimal interruption, or at least hear their story told in an authoritative text feel better about the legal procedure or political structure in which they have participated.

In their study of small-claims court narratives, for example, O'Barr and Conley (1985) demonstrate that litigants in small-claims courts use everyday storytelling practices that would not be permissible under the rules of evidence employed in more formal courts. This freedom comes at some cost, because everyday storytelling does not tend to produce legally adequate narratives designed to win cases. However, O'Barr and Conley note that even losing litigants who had been allowed to tell their stories with relative freedom seemed fairly satisfied with the process. Thus, one losing defendant commented that he felt better, and a losing plaintiff even found the process therapeutic. These findings are compatible with earlier observations by Yngvesson and Hennessey (1974) that participants were more willing to compromise if given more opportunities to express themselves.

Employing somewhat different methodologies, psychologist Tom Tyler (1988) has found that citizens tend to be more concerned with procedural justice than with outcomes, so that litigants who win may still be unsatisfied if they feel they have been treated unfairly. Similarly, litigants who lose will be more satisfied with the result if they feel that they were treated fairly. Included in Tyler's conception of "procedural justice" are "inferences that the authorities are trying to be fair, judgments of honesty, opportunities for correcting errors, and interpersonal issues such as being treated politely." Some of these procedural notions implicitly involve relative control of the discourse—for example, whether an authority who makes mistaken assessments maintains authoritarian control of the exchange, never allowing the litigant an opportunity to correct errors—or whether a litigant is interrupted incessantly rather than treated "politely" when telling his or her story.[3] This link between uninterrupted narration and "polite" treatment is unsurprising given the importance of deference to "informational authority" in American folk theories of language (see Sweetser 1987).[4] Tyler's larger conclusion is that citizens are more likely to follow laws which in their opinion are enforced in a procedurally fair manner. In another study, Tyler, Rasinski, and Spodick (1985) found that citizens who had more of a "voice" about how decisions should be made were more satisfied with the resulting decision, even when their increased input into the decision-making process was not matched by any increased control over the result. This finding leads to a somewhat troubling conclusion: "The support for the value-expressive hypothesis reported here lends credence to the fears expressed by Edelman . . . and others that citizens might be beguiled by authorities who publicly present "myths of the state," myths that misleadingly imply that citizen expressions of preference are an important input into public policy dicisions, although in reality citizens have voice without decision control" (Tyler, Rasinski, and Spodick 1985:80). Thus, these studies appear to support the perspective of political scientists who view enhanced procedural opportunities for expression as a ruse diverting citizens' attention from their lack of actual control over political outcomes (see Edelman 1985; Reich 1966; Scheingold 1974).

Although she reaches similar conclusions about the effect of giving citizens increased "voice," Glendon (1987:40) has a quite different evaluation of the merits of this outcome. In her study of abortion law in Europe and the United States, Glendon suggests that the reaction against liberalized abortion laws in Europe was less violent than in the United States because the anti-abortion segment of the community in Europe felt that its voice was heard to a greater degree and its concerns accorded more weight in the more gradual legal transition there. Glendon's controversial conclusion is that Western Europe's restrictive approaches to abortion law are preferable to the laissez-faire solution found in the United States, because the

European approaches evolved through the "conversation" of legislative struggle and compromise. (For discussions of the problematic character of Glendon's normative assumptions, see Ashe 1988; Cohen 1989; Fineman 1988; Francis 1988.)

It would be possible to analyze the dissent in a similar way, that is, as performing an important social function, allowing the portion of the community that lost to feel that its voice has been heard, its concerns noted. The reference within the texts of many opinions of majority opinion to dissent, dissent to majority, indexes an exchange in which multiple points of view have been acknowledged. The dissents not only express alternative views, but often force the hegemonic voice of the majority opinion to explicitly recognize and respond to these alternative views. In doing so, the dissents give expression to the grievances and concerns not only of the losing litigant, but also of the larger social groups for whom the decision is a defeat. And, as the cases I will analyze demonstrate, dissenting voices may become majority opinions years later. The division in the rhetorical structure of appellate opinions into majority and dissent is a reflection (or, in Peircean terms, an icon[5]) of the division in the community.

This iconic reflection at once mirrors a disruption in society and creates a semiotic restoration of order, a narrative in which strongly held clashing views are recounted within the same text, and in which a final decision is reached. Should we go further, however, as Glendon did, and argue that when a group's voice is heard, they will be more likely to accept a contrary result? Should we expand the insights of the "micro" level studies of litigant satisfaction to the "macro" level of social groups? I would argue against taking the semiotic insight as an indication of social utility. That rhetorical structure may effect a semiotic transformation of social conflict does not mean that it is necessarily socially effective or useful in assuring social harmony; that a group's voice has been heard does not mean that it will thereafter be silent.[6]

Indeed, even at the "micro" level it may be important to examine the effects of narrative control in different kinds of situations. In Sarat and Felstiner's (1988) discussions of talk in divorce lawyer's offices, there is an indication that giving clients unlimited narrative control may actually reduce their willingness to accept less than optimal settlements. In no-fault divorces, Sarat and Felstiner note, lawyers often listen silently to a client's narrative about a spouse's behavior and character (1988:764). Because it contrasts with the critical questions employed by lawyers to check their clients' information on legally salient points, this silence may seem to indicate affirmation or acquiescence in the client's account. When a story that paints the spouse as the sole villain goes unchallenged, a client may be less likely to enter negotiations prepared to moderate his or her demands (1988:765–66).

At the "macro" level, we can similarly see that allowing a social group to be heard need not result in greater satisfaction with adverse decisions. It may, indeed, have quite the opposite effect, as when minorities and women were further inspired to continue their struggle the more their voices were heard (see Brown, et al 1971;

Cover 1975:163–66; Miller 1966:259–62, 398–400; Tushnet 1987). As in the Sarat and Felstiner example, permitting someone's story to be told helped to legitimate the story's fundamental claim.

Thus, gaining narrative control may well leave participants "feeling better," but feeling better about having been heard may not lead to the conclusion that the process was just and the end result fair. Instead, it may lead participants to conclude that the story was a good one, one which deserved to win out, and that further struggle is called for in order to achieve a more just result. Of course, to refuse to acquiesce in a result is not to refuse any participation in the system that produced the result. At that level, allowing a voice to be heard may be socially effective even though it does not produce satisified litigants. This is a point that First Amendment theorists have noted as they have attempted to generate philosophical rationales for providing free speech protection: permitting dissenting voices to be heard is necessary to keep dissenters within society's structure.[7] It is possible in the abstract to construct quite a number of conflicting stories about what will happen when social groups are given some sort of voice or opportunity for expression. Careful attention to the role and cultural salience of particular kinds of speech at specific sociohistorical moments is probably more valuable than generalizations about the utility or function of free expression in the abstract.

Many aspects of the context may affect the social outcomes of this semiotic process. To name just a few, one might consider (1) the stakes (e.g., reimbursement for a burned overcoat in small-claims court would seem to carry quite different significance than vindication in a divorce battle); (2) the social setting (e.g., relative social power, whether a particular outcome is possible given current social conditions); (3) who is telling the story (e.g., producing one's own narrative in small-claims court versus having the story told by a legislature or court); and (4) third-party reactions (e.g., silence, encouraging comments, or rephrasing the story in a dissent [see Brenneis 1987 on the role of audience]).

Indeed, one of the most obvious differences between litigant satisfaction studies involving individuals and studies focusing on social groups is in the very character of the "voice" or "narrative control" at issue. The voice in the case of the individual litigant is that of the individual, and narrative control means that the individual has had the opportunity to tell her or his story with minimal constraint or structuring by legal authorities. But where the focus is on social groups gaining a voice in legal outcomes, the "speaker" is generally a court or legislature, through whose case law or statutory language a group's voice is translated. As we shall see, even where a group's political views or legal positions are adopted in a court's opinion, there remains a serious question as to whether we are hearing the group's voice or that of the court. A very different kind of narrative control is implicated here, for the social groups are clearly not "telling their own stories." Rather, they are seeking to hear their story acknowledged in authoritative legal texts; they gain control not by writing the texts themselves, but by exerting some sort of influence over the narratives produced by others. To attain a fuller understanding of the dynamic we will need to be sensitive to this "translation" issue. How great an impact narrative "control" has on participant satisfaction (and on participant acquiescence in the results of particular cases) must surely depend on these and other dimensions.

A narrative analysis of the sort undertaken here, however, does not focus on social-efficacy questions; in that sense it is quite different from Glendon's approach to social "voices."[8] Here the focus is on the semiotic order produced by the narratives of legal opinions, an order that is grounded in the social conflict it attempts to address. To further understand its social impact would require that we move beyond strictly textual or rhetorical analysis, or else fall into a semiotic determinism unlikely to render a useful reading of social texts (see Mertz 1985:16).

Consensus and Dissent

The following are excerpts from the majority opinions in *Plessy v. Ferguson* and *Brown v. Board of Education:*

> The information filed in the criminal District Court charged in substance that Plessy, being a passenger between two stations within the State of Louisiana, was assigned by officers of the company to the coach used for the race to which he belonged, but he insisted upon going into a coach used by the race to which he did not belong. Neither in the information nor plea was his particular race or color averred. . . .
>
> It is claimed by the plaintiff in error that, in any mixed community, the reputation of belonging to the dominant race, in this instance the white race, is *property,* in the same sense that a right of action, or of inheritance, is property. Conceding this to be so, for the purposes of this case, we are unable to see how this statute deprives him of, or in any way affects his right to, such property. [*Plessy v. Ferguson,* 163 U.S. at 541, 549; emphasis in original]

> In each of the cases, minors of the Negro race, through their legal representatives, seek the aid of the courts in obtaining admission to the public schools of their community on a nonsegregated basis. In each instance, they had been denied admission to schools attended by white children under laws requiring or permitting segregation according to race. This segregation was alleged to deprive the plaintiffs of the equal protection of the laws under the Fourteenth Amendment. [*Brown v. Board of Education,* 347 U.S. at 488]

These two cases were important turning points in the legal treatment of racial segregation in the United States. Although the texts of these opinions were produced in very different times by different authors, I will treat them together. In doing so, I am employing the convention for approaching legal texts used in law school case-books and in the parts of briefs or court opinions that summarize doctrinal development. Law students are commonly trained to approach texts in this way, taking opinions that address the same problem out of their historical contexts and juxtaposing them to create a continuing story about the development of legal doctrine (see Mertz n.d.; see Bauman and Briggs 1990 on recontextualization). Indeed, the second case I will analyze affords an example of this approach to text, forging narrative continuity with the first case, which was decided 86 years earlier. A close analysis of these stories reveals the way in which narrative resources are marshaled to form a semiotic order across time and across social divisions, creating a self-referencing textual tradition that contains a continuing conversation about fundamental social values.[9] In order to explore that tradition, this essay examines two key cases on desegregation from different time periods. Here, I will be exploring the tradition from "within" in order to examine the semiotic results that follow from the textual convention; further analysis of each opinion within its social and discursive setting would also shed light on the role of legal narratives.

At issue here, then, is the way in which these narratives can be viewed as systems of signs that, by virtue of their relations with one another and with their contexts of production and use, convey and crystallize meaning. Much has been written about the role of linguistic signs as a key medium through which human social interaction is accomplished (see traditions discussed in Mertz and Parmentier 1985). When U.S. legal narratives perform this kind of "semiotic mediation," they mediate symbolic divisions as well as social schisms. This analysis will focus on a number of linguistic features: agency, metalinguistic framing, active and passive constructions, authorial voice, the deictic structuring of the texts, thematic and rhetorical construction, and the narrative representation of social events, social actors, and legal texts.[10] In the intersection of many complex, sometimes subtle features of these legal narratives we can see how narrative resources are mustered to address social conflict in three ways: (1) how the narrative represents[11] and indexes the conflict it seeks to resolve; (2) how the narrative represents and indexes the role of the legal system, and thus its own production and source of authority; and (3) how *in* representing social conflict and legal resolution, legal narratives function in a performative fashion to accomplish the semiotic mediation of social divisions.

The first case, *Plessy v. Ferguson* (163 U.S. 537), provided a key decision upholding the notion that separate could be equal, that is, that segregation could be constitutional. Decided in 1896, the case centered upon a Louisiana statute that mandated separate accommodations for white and black passengers on railway cars. The majority opinion, authored by Justice Brown, upheld the statute. There was one dissent, written by Justice Harlan. The second case, *Brown v. Board of Education* (347 U.S. 483), was a unanimous opinion authored in 1953 by Chief Justice Warren. Warren's opinion effectively overruled *Plessy*, holding that segregated schools were "inherently unequal."

The Narrative Appropriation of Social Conflict

How do these two opinions represent the conflict over racial segregation that they are seeking to resolve? To answer that question, we will examine the way in which each opinion presents the parties and issues involved in each case, as well as the presentation of the wider social context within which this particular legal conflict emerged.

The majority opinion in *Plessy* is primarily framed as a response to the arguments of the plaintiff, Plessy, first rephrasing his arguments, then attempting to refute them. No direct response is made to the arguments of the dissent. As is often the case in opinions of this kind, the Court at times merges Plessy's voice with that of his attorney, sometimes attributing technical legal arguments directly to Plessy and often shifting between "the plaintiff in error" and "the learned counsel for the plaintiff" as if the two were a single speaker.[12] Although the more technical legal arguments are fairly clearly not Plessy's there are times when the source of the claim being argued against is thoroughly ambiguous: "We consider the underlying fallacy of the plaintiff's argument to consist in the assumption that the enforced separation of the two races stamps the colored race with a badge of inferiority" (163 U.S. at 551). This sort of translated argument is the closest we come to hearing Plessy's "voice" in the opinion.

The opinion begins by introducing the Louisiana statute under attack, the "facts" of the case, and the legal grounds upon which the statute was attacked—that it violated the Thirteenth and Fourteenth Amendments. These paragraphs are almost entirely composed of reported language, either the written text of the statute or excerpts from written documents submitted to a court by the prosecutor or Plessy's attorney. The statute is directly quoted, with framing verbs such as "enacts" and "provides." These framing verbs are metapragmatic in that they index, at the metalevel, the way in which language carries socially powerful meaning by virtue of its contextual connections. Here metapragmatic framing verbs quite self-consciously point to the way in which statutory language performs a powerful social function "in the writing" (and by virtue of the way in which that writing indexes its own socially powerful context of production).

In contrast with the use of direct quotation to convey statutory language, Plessy's (and/or his attorney's) description of the events in the case is reported indirectly, and the "speaker" in the framing phrase is the document: "the petition for the writ of prohibition averred." Direct quotation "preserves" characteristics of the quoted speech (she said, "It's cold"), whereas indirect quotation alters them (she said that it was cold). As Hickmann (1985:185) has noted, direct quotations can reproduce a reported token (or instance) of speech with all its deictic anchoring and expressive quality, whereas indirect quotations present reported utterances as tokens of types of speech, adjusting deictics to the interpretive frame and reducing or obliterating modality. Bakhtin calls this the "analytical tendency" of indirect discourse, which translates "all the emotive-affective features of speech . . . from form into content" (Vološinov [Bakhtin] 1973:128). Although indirect quotation retains a clear demarcation between reported and reporting speech, it represents one step away from the sharper boundaries of direct quotation.

Bakhtin attributed particular significance to the role of boundaries between reported and reporting speech: "the basic tendency in reacting to reported speech may be to maintain its integrity and authenticity; a language may strive to forge hard and fast boundaries for reported speech. In such a case, the patterns and their modifications serve to demarcate the reported speech as clearly as possible, to screen it from penetration by the author's intonations, and to condense and enhance its individual linguistic characteristics" (Vološinov [Bakhtin] 1973:119).

In discussing judicial language and political rhetoric, Bakhtin admonishes us that "the position that a specimen of speech to be reported occupies on the social hierarchy of values must . . . be taken into account. The stronger the feeling of hierarchical eminence in another's utterance, the more sharply defined will its boundaries be, and the less accessible will it be to penetration and commenting tendencies from outside" (Vološinov [Bakhtin] 1973:123). This association of strong boundaries and iconic repetition of the original utterance with socially powerful speech is made still more explicit in Bakhtin's discussion of authoritative discourse, which "permits no play with the context framing it, no play with its borders, no gradual and flexible transitions"—indeed, which "demands" quotation marks (Bakhtin 1981:343). Parmentier (1993) has added a cautionary note, drawing our attention to the way in which direct quotation of authoritative discourse can play a creative role, in part because the quoted words are serving ends never envisioned by their original speakers. Parmentier also observes that speakers may use direct quotation strategically in efforts to gain legitimacy or authority. Of course, all of this may vary across cultures, times, and genres; iconic repetition of an utterance only carries significance of any kind by virtue of linguistic conventions that give it particular meaning. As Bakhtin himself noted, "[i]t is important to determine the specific gravity of rhetorical speech, judicial or political, in the linguistic consciousness of the given social group at a given time" (Vološinov [Bakhtin] 1973:123).

As a first step in making such a determination, it is interesting to contrast the majority's deference to the original wording of statutes with its free translation, in indirect quotation, of Plessy's petition. Plessy's legal arguments are never directly quoted, much less his own speech, so that we never hear from him in the first person. The only directly quoted language is from statutes and case law.

Indeed, Plessy rarely appears at all. The exceptions come in the initial statement of facts: "Plessy . . . was assigned by officers of the company to the coach used for the race to which he belonged, but he insisted upon going into a coach used by the race to which he did not belong." The summary of facts also quotes from Plessy's petition: "The petition . . . averred that petitioner was seven eighths Caucasian and one eighth African blood; . . . that he was entitled to every right, privilege and immunity secured to citizens of the United States of the white race; and that, upon such theory, he took possession of a vacant seat" (163 U.S. 541). The remainder of the text refers to Plessy only in occasional transitional passages when the Court is rephrasing claims of the "plaintiff in error" in order to rebut them. The bulk of the text is concerned with interpreting and discussing laws and legal cases.

Because of the Court's focus on explication of various legal texts, almost all of the agents in the narrative apart from Plessy and the railroad he sued are legal "actors." And although some are individual human agents—attorneys and judges—most of the agents in the opinion are either collective bodies (such as courts or legislatures) or documents (such as cases, statutes, constitutional amendments, and legal arguments). By contrast, the dissent, authored by Justice Harlan, introduces individual human actors—managers of the railroad, individual passengers, citizens "of the black race who . . . risked their lives for the preservation of the union."

On the other hand, Harlan's dissent never refers to Plessy by name, and alludes to him indirectly only once: "It is scarcely just to say that a colored citizen should not object to occupying a public coach assigned to his own race" (163 U.S. 561). Thus the dissent's treatment of Plessy's individual "voice" is generally as removed as that of the majority opinion. The one exception to this is a passage in which Harlan speaks indirectly for Plessy. This is the only time in any of the narratives analyzed here that a plaintiff was permitted to "speak," however indirectly: "He [Plessy] does not object, nor, perhaps, would he object to separate coaches for his race, if his rights under the law were recognized. But he objects, and ought never to cease objecting to the proposition, that citizens of the white and black races can be adjudged criminals because they sit, or claim the right to sit, in the same public coach" (163 U.S. 561). Apart from this one oblique reference, however, Plessy does not appear in Harlan's narrative. This is one source of continuity in the two narratives' treatment of the particular conflict at issue here, despite their differential weighting of legal actors.

This differential weighting leads to quite different treatments of the social problem at issue in the case. Thus, an interesting contrast emerges if we distinguish the agent of the first-level or framing language from agents within frames. (Take, for example, the passage "But I deny that any legislative body . . . may have regard to the race of citizens when the civil rights of those citizens are involved" [163 U.S. 554–55]. Here "I" would be coded as a framing agent and "legislative body" as an agent within frame.) The majority opinion first-level and framing agents were exclusively cases, statutes, Justices, Congress, the Constitution, legislatures, courts, arguments, issues, information, and questions. The dissent used a much more diverse array of first-level agents: passengers, "every true man," "friends of liberty," "everyone," "a white man and a black man," etc. To the extent that the majority opinion did refer to social actors or issues—"persons of color," the "white race," a "school committee"—it limited these occasional references to framed portions of the opinion, with one exception.

That one exception comes in the penultimate paragraph of the opinion, in which the Court faces what it views as the fundamental fallacy of the plaintiff's argument: "If the two races are to meet upon terms of social equality, it must be the result of natural affinities, a mutual appreciation of each other's merits and a voluntary consent of individuals" (163 U.S. at 551). Although this is the one example of a sentence in which the first-level agent is not a legal entity or actor, the passage is very clearly in the Court's voice. Nonetheless, this breakthrough from legal agency echoes at the level of narrative structure the semantic emphasis this paragraph receives, as the key passage in which the Court refutes the idea that separate is necessarily unequal. The refutation takes the form of flat declarative statements insisting that social equality can only be achieved voluntarily. This paragraph is also distinguished by heightened used of the first person plural, as the Court rejects Plessy's views: "We consider the underlying fallacy of the plaintiff's argument to consist in"; "We imagine that the white race . . . would not acquiesce in this assumption"; "We cannot accept this proposition."

As a result both of the paucity of references to nonlegal social actors and of the way the few references found in the opinion are structured, the majority opinion presents the social issues involved only indirectly, filtered through the framing "voice" of legal texts and courts. The focus of the discussion of segregation and racial problems is more on to what extent the law applies than on the problem itself: "The object of the amendment was undoubtedly to enforce the absolute equality of the two races before the law, but in the nature of things it could not have been intended to abolish distinctions based upon color, or to enforce social, as distinguished from political equality" (163 U.S. at 544). Here we are presented with the issue of segregation framed entirely as a question of what the goal of a constitutional amendment was; the key question, the Court seems to indicate, is the translation of this social issue in legal terms. Note also that to the extent that racial segregation is discussed, it is addressed in abstract, declarative language that assert the self-evident "nature of things."

The dissent, by contrast, describes the social situation quite directly, translating the problem into concrete social situations and actors: "If a colored maid insists upon riding in the same coach with a white woman whom she has been employed to serve, and who may need her personal attention while travelling, she is subject to be fined or imprisoned for such an exhibition of zeal in the discharge of duty" (163 U.S. 553). Harlan brings the social issue raised by this case to the fore in his dissent, writing of social actors and situations as much as of courts and statutes. On the other hand, Harlan is careful throughout his dissent to reassure white citizens that his proposed solution would not upset the current balance of power between races. This passage is one of the less objectionable examples of this rhetorical ploy, which reaches its depths at other points in the dissent (see 163 U.S. at 559).

When the *Plessy* dissent presents us with social actors and situations—with racism in action—it in one sense resembles the unanimous majority opinion in *Brown*, written by Justice Warren. Warren similarly presents us with agents who are social actors involved in a racially divided society: "Today . . . many Negroes have achieved outstanding success in the arts and sciences" (347 U.S. at 490). Although, like the majority and dissenting opinions in *Plessy*, the *Brown* opinion contains frequent references to legal "actors," primarily courts, it shares with

Harlan's dissent an attempt to break out of strictly legal frames for discussing social problems. Direct descriptions of social context—the historical development of education and the effects of segregation—are followed by the conclusion "that in the field of public education the doctrine of 'separate but equal' has no place" (347 U.S. at 495). Where Harlan's description of the social context used vignettes as hypothetical exemplars—the maid who insists upon riding with a white woman, the sheriff assigning whites to one side of the courtroom and blacks to the other—Warren paints a broad social history centered on the role of education in society, whose key pivot is the deictic contrast between "today" and the past of *Plessy* and the Fourteenth Amendment.

However, as in the other two opinions, the plaintiffs in *Brown* are never quoted directly, and make only a rare appearance of any kind. Direct quotation is reserved for language from previous legal opinions. The plaintiffs' arguments are once again translated and rephrased in indirect quotation: "The plaintiffs contend that segregated public schools are not 'equal' and cannot be made 'equal,' and that hence they are deprived of the equal protection of the laws" (347 U.S. at 488). Despite drastic changes in the way the "social" is represented, there is continuity in the way these narratives translate the speech of the protagonists.

Narrative Indexes of Legal Processes and Texts

We have seen differences among these opinions in the narrative treatment of social conflict. The opinions also differ in the way they characterize the legal system.

A striking feature of the majority opinion in *Plessy*, for example, is its heavy use of the passive voice[13] and very rare attribution of agency to humans. The most common agents in the text are constitutional amendments, cases, statutes or laws, and arguments. Courts are also agents and are frequently presented in the passive voice (as, for example, "The case was decided . . . and affirmed by this court"). Or they make only a shadowy, elliptical appearance (for example, "Similar statutes . . . were held to be constitutional [in the following cases]"). It is not uncommon for judges to distance themselves from unpleasant legal results by attributing agency to the system rather than themselves; they reach the decision because of the automatic operation of the law's logic, which goes on outside their control and dictates to them the decisions they write (see Mertz 1987, 1988; Noonan 1976).

In *Plessy* there is a similar tendency. Legal rules and precedential cases are frequently appearing agents, and are directly quoted. Individual litigants or social actors are almost never agents. Justice Brown occasionally uses first person plural to speak in the voice of the Court, but these breakthroughs are always interestingly positioned after he has settled a major substantive point in the third person. In answering most of Plessy's main arguments, Brown uses a very removed declarative voice that simply explains "how things are." He then reports cases that support his conclusion. For example, in answering Plessy's Thirteenth Amendment claim,

Brown begins, "That [the statute] does not conflict with the Thirteenth Amendment, which abolished slavery and involuntary servitude . . . is too clear for argument" (163 U.S. at 542). After citing two cases to support a narrow reading of the amendment, he concludes, "A statute which implies merely a legal distinction between the white and colored races . . . has no tendency to destroy the legal equality of the two races, or reestablish a state of involuntary servitude" (163 U.S. at 543). The Thirteenth Amendment claim is dismissed, and neither Brown nor the Court has "decided" anything nor "spoken" to us.

This pattern is repeated a number of times. For example, after an extended third-person narrative that narrows Plessy's Fourteenth Amendment claim to a question of reasonableness, Brown tells us that "So far . . . as a conflict with the Fourteenth Amendment is concerned, the case reduces itself to the question whether the statute of Louisiana is a reasonable regulation" (163 U.S. at 550)—a very modest assessment of his role as author of the opinion.

In contrast with the majority opinion, Harlan's dissent spends some time on the Thirteenth Amendment claim, demonstrating that the legal conclusion on that score is not as self-evident as Brown's rhetoric indicated. Harlan's narrative, not surprisingly, reveals the Court as an agent in legal decision-making more unambiguously. For example, he uses a series of direct quotations from previous cases to indicate both that the Court's decision in *Plessy* did not follow automatically from existing law and that the Court's words in previous cases were socially creative and powerful in effecting change. Unlike Brown, for whom constitutional interpretation involved being swept along by the surface (apparent) logic of constitutional and statutory texts, Harlan required that the reader look behind the text to its contextual origins: "every one knows that the statute in question had its origin in the purpose . . . under the guise of giving equal accommodation for whites and blacks, to compel the latter to keep to themselves while travelling in railroad passenger coaches. No one would be so wanting in candor as to assert the contrary" (163 U.S. at 557). Here Harlan has broken through to "everyday understandings," introducing shared commonsense knowledge to counter the majority's claim that the statute treated members of the two races equally. As we have seen, Harlan introduces individual human actors in his narrative—managers of the railroad, individual passengers, citizens "of the black race who . . . risked their lives for the preservation of the union." He also uses both "I" and "we" relatively liberally throughout the text, so there is a stronger organizing first person narrator. Finally, Harlan directly refers to the majority opinion: "It is, therefore to be regretted that this high tribunal, the final expositor of the fundamental law of the land, has reached [this] conclusion," and, "In my opinion, the judgment this day rendered will, in time, prove to be quite as pernicious as the decision . . . in the *Dred Scott case*" (164 U.S. at 559; emphasis in original). Harlan here presents a Court that had a choice, not one driven by a force beyond its control.

It is perhaps to be expected that a narrative that is in some ways counter-hegemonic would break through the standard third person, removed account of the majority opinion, but this is a phenomenon that needs more exploring. On one level, of course, a Supreme Court dissent is anything but counter-hegemonic; it is part of the dominant discourse, issuing from a maximally empowered social actor. As we have seen, Harlan challenges neither the authority of the Court nor the ultimate hegemony of white domination. And yet, in the same sense that we speak of a dominated fraction of a dominant class, we can see the dissenting voice here as subordinate to the fully hegemonic voice of the majority. The language of the dissent is a strong challenge to the social-legal ideology of the majority.

Taken together, the majority opinion and dissent give us both the removed, tradition-bound voice retelling a story of "how it has to be," and a more immediate, critical, personal story of "why we ought to change it." The opinion as a whole gives expression to opposing groups' concerns, while reinforcing the status quo. By the time of *Brown v. Board of Education*, however, the social situation is changing, and the Court returns to *Plessy* once more.

Unlike *Plessy*, *Brown* was a unanimous decision, without dissents or concurrences. Precisely because the decision did not seek to reinforce segregation, but attempted to change it, the Court did not want to give all sides a voice. In *Brown*, the Court officially rejects "any language in *Plessy* contrary to [its] finding" that "in the field of public education the doctrine of 'separate but equal' has no place." Like Harlan's dissent, this modern opinion conveys a strong sense of the author as agent, of the justices on the Court as powerful social actors capable of effecting social change in the writing of the opinion. In that sense, the narrative has an explicitly performative quality, as when Justice Warren writes, "We come then to the question presented: Does segregation of children in public schools solely on the basis of race . . . deprive the children of the minority group of equal educational opportunities? We believe that it does. . . . We have now announced that such segregation is a denial of the equal protection of the laws" (347 U.S. at 493). Still more than Harlan, Warren presents black citizens as social actors rather than one-dimensional legal characters. His approach to constitutional interpretation looks not only at the motives and social context of the statute in question, but also at the effects of changing social context upon the meaning of constitutional protections.

Throughout *Brown*, Warren indexes the *Plessy* decision, using deictics to locate his narrative via-à-vis the earlier opinion and vis-à-vis the Fourteenth Amendment, bridging the gap between courts, texts, and times. The indexical structure of the narrative pivots on a deictic contrast between the narrative's temporal location, "today," and earlier times: "Even in the North, the conditions of public education did not approximate those existing today" (347 U.S. at 490). And, again: "In approaching this problem, we cannot turn the clock back to 1868 when the Amendment was adopted, or even to 1896 when *Plessy v. Ferguson* was written. We must consider public education in the light of its full development and its present place in American life" (347 U.S. at 492). The story that Warren tells is of a past decision that no longer fits the time within which he now writes: "Whatever may have been the extent of psychological knowledge at the time of *Plessy v. Ferguson*, this finding [that segregation has negative psychological effects on black children] is amply supported by modern authority. Any language in *Plessy v. Ferguson* contrary to this finding is rejected" (347 U.S. at 494–95).

Much of *Brown*, then, is phrased as a response not to the claims of either party to the litigation, but to *Plessy*, which is a present interlocutor firmly located in the past. If we examine *Brown* and *Plessy* together, we can begin to see the way in which changing social circumstances are at once acknowledged and yet given narrative continuity by the textual tradition of legal opinions. At one level, *Brown* carefully distinguishes its social setting from *Plessy's* historical context, stressing that the same meanings no longer apply, emphasizing discontinuities in the extratextual contexts indexed by the two different texts. And yet the narrative convention that permits the two texts to speak to one another across such radically different social contexts sends a somewhat different message, emphasizing the power of legal co-text across these social changes. Here the power of history is acknowledged yet circumscribed by the power of legal narrative to forge links across time, providing a doctrinal structure in language for dealing with social "problems"—a structure that is somehow able to remain "the same" while admitting radical change.

Performativity and Narrative Structure

In the case of *Plessy*, social conflict is expressed in the division between majority and dissent, the majority filtering everything through the lens of the law, the dissent presenting social actors actors through third person direct description. In *Brown*, the conflict appears as a division between "now" and "then," with extensive descriptions of changed social circumstances.

There is some continuity in this approach; all three opinions mention or index the actual plaintiffs very rarely, and all reserve direct quotation for the Constitution, statutes, and cases. No reported speech, direct or indirect, gives us the "voices" of actual participants in the social conflict, apart from the rephrasing of legal arguments. Only legal actors and documents can be "speakers" in these narratives.

In terms of overall narrative structure, all three opinions begin by providing legal frameworks for the story. The *Plessy* majority begins with the Louisiana statute at issue (quoting directly in long block quotations), and the *Plessy* dissent also begins with the statute (mixing fragments of direct quotation with descriptions of the statute's consequences). *Brown* begins with a brief summary of the procedural background of the cases and moves immediately to summarize the conflict ("minors of the Negro race" have "been denied admission to schools attended by white children under laws requiring or permitting segregation according to race") and its legal frame (this is a Fourteenth Amendment question of the sort involved in *Plessy*).

Both the *Plessy* majority and dissent then move on to extended discussions of the Thirteenth and Fourteenth Amendments and attendant case law, with numerous extended block quotations from the cases. The majority's story is of a long-standing case-law distinction between "laws interfering with the political equality of the negro" (deemed unconstitutional) and laws "requiring the separation of the two races" (deemed constitutional). Honoring this distinction, the Court tells us, will give effect to the original "object of the amendment"—"to enforce the absolute equality of the two races before the law" but not "to abolish distinctions based upon color" (163 U.S. at 544–45). By contrast, Harlan's dissent paints the Thirteenth, Fourteenth, and Fifteenth Amendments as having "removed the race line from our governmental systems" (163 U.S. at 555). After a review of Supreme Court language supporting this vision, Harlan moves on to a series of hypotheticals designed to demonstrate the elusive character of any division between political and other civil rights.

Brown takes a different direction after setting up its initial legal frame. A special reargument was held on the history of the adoption of the Fourteenth Amendment, Warren tells us, and that history was inconclusive. Furthermore, the situation of public education is now so radically different that "it is not surprising that there should be so little in the history of the Fourteenth Amendment relating to its intended effect on public education" (347 U.S. at 490). The older cases cannot speak to the issue before the Court because so much has changed, and none of the recent cases has addressed a situation like the one in *Brown*. Thus, in short, simple paragraphs, Warren moves outside the narrative framework of the earlier opinions, refusing to use the history of the amendments or the case law as the key to the result. Insisting that the answer lies in the present ("we cannot turn the clock back"), Warren phrases the problem as a more or less commonsense matter to be answered based on current knowledge: "Does segregation of children in public schools solely on the basis of race, even though the physical facilities and other 'tangible' factors may be equal, deprive the children of the minority group of equal educational opportunities? We believe that it does" (347 U.S. at 493). Following this passage we find the only extended direct quotations in the opinion, primarily from the district court below, which had indicated its belief that segregation had a detrimental effect on black children. With a brief footnote to social science studies in support of the Court's position, Warren winds up his argument, reiterating in performative language ("we conclude"; "we hold that") his conclusion that segregation violates the Fourteenth Amendment.

There is one point of similarity between the ending of *Brown* and the *Plessy* opinions, for all involve passages in which the Court steps outside of legal precedent to argue "commonsense" cultural reason. The *Plessy* majority, in a most uncharacteristic passage, emerges as an agent and uses the first person plural to address Plessy's argument: "We consider the underlying fallacy of the plaintiff's argument to consist in the assumption that the enforced separation of the two races stamps the colored race with a badge of inferiority. If this be so, it is not by reason of anything found in the act, but solely because the colored race chooses to put that construction upon it. . . . If the two races are to meet upon terms of social equality, it must be the result of natural affinities, a mutual appreciation of each other's merits and a voluntary consent of individuals" (163 U.S. at 551). Harlan similarly concludes with a personal plea, although neither his use of the first person nor the tone of his appeal constitutes a very marked change from the rest of his dissent: "I am of the opinion that the statute of Louisiana is inconsistent with the personal liberty of citizens, white and black, in that State, and hostile to both the spirit and letter of the Constitution of the United States" (163 U.S. at 563). Thus, there is a curious parallel in the beginning and ending passages of these very different narratives; all begin with legal frames and end with appeals based on cultural principles derived at least in part from nonlegal reasoning. The *Plessy* opinions share a more heavy reliance on the legal past and precedent than is found in the *Brown* opinion. It is true that, in an interesting penultimate paragraph, Harlan foreshadows Warren's approach, declining to discuss precedents derived from a time before passage of the amendments: "Those decisions cannot be guides in the era introduced by the recent amendments of the supreme law, which established universal civil freedom" (164 U.S. at 563). However, much of Harlan's dissent is an argument about the amendments, their history, and the case law surrounding them. The strongest parallel between the Harlan dissent and the *Brown* opinion, then, appears to lie not in overall narrative structure, but in the narrative devices used to convey social context and conflict.

In both *Brown* and *Plessy* the social conflict is expressed but is also resolved, if only at the semiotic level of the legal "story." Despite the lingering disagreement inherent in a written dissent, the case outcome is reached. Harlan's dissent gives some voice, however attenuated, to people unhappy with the *Plessy* decision, and it does so in a way it could not have if Harlan had participated in a compromise solution. The structure of the opinion contains a sharp conflict, never directly acknowledged by the authoritative voice of the majority. In its conflictual structure the opinion mirrors and points out an enduring social conflict. The conflict is expressed as a tension between members of the Court—between a removed legal voice that doesn't acknowledge the dissent, and a more immediate dissenting voice that describes social events and argues directly against the majority at the same time that it yields to the majority's authority. The narrative structure indexes its own context of production and source of authority (or lack thereof), as it echoes the social division and reaches an authoritative conclusion. It is performative in that it functions as an authoritative semiotic expression of the conflict it describes, while it resolves the tension at one level by virtue of its decision. At another level, the tension remains; but that, too, is recognized in the structure of the opinion.

Brown translates the tension over segregation into temporal terms, a translation that is again at once a social description and a reflexive reference to the textual tradition by which it claims authority. In *Brown*, Warren simultaneously creates distance from *Plessy*, stressing differences in social contexts and overtly overruling *Plessy*'s holding, and at the same time forges a semiotic link, treating the two opinions in the same narrative space, using *Plessy* as his primary interlocutor and audience—just as Harlan uses the majority opinion as his.

Thus, both *Plessy* and *Brown* embody a divisive split as they seek to overcome it. They attempt to resolve the issue by virtue of the decision they express. At the same time, they address other legal texts as their primary audiences, taking seriously a narrative tradition in which earlier texts and current social divisions can be addressed together, re-presenting enduring social problems in a continuing legal conversation.

This essay provides only a preliminary indication of the features of U.S. legal narratives that shed light on this culture's approach to the resolution of social conflict. Some aspects of narrative structure were similar across all three of the narratives analyzed here, perhaps indicating generally shared features of this genre. However, more work is obviously required before we can delineate characteristic features of legal genres with certainty.

Although the opinions that were closest in legal ideology (*Brown* and the *Plessy* dissent) did use somewhat similar approaches in representing social conflict, these opinions were not similar in overall narrative structure. To the extent that there is any temptation to impute a necessary link between ideological view and narrative form, our conclusion here should discourage that tendency. It may be that there is a particular rhetorical effectiveness to be found in iconic pairings of ideology and linguistic form (i.e., authoritarian ideology expressed in monologic form; see Mertz 1988; White 1987). But it appears that there is no necessity to the connection, at least within this narrative tradition. Affinities between opinions with similar ideological views, if any, seem to emerge along subtler dimensions apparent in the nuances of narrative features.

One common feature of these narratives is their use of other legal texts as key interlocutors. This common thread may be one crucial way in which U.S. legal narratives accommodate change and dissent while maintaining the authority of legal language to resolve social conflict. The structuring of legal narratives around other legal narratives, and the inclusion of dissenting voices to answer that of the majority, permit the opinion to act as an indexical icon of the conflict process it embodies, encompassing continuing conflict within an ongoing story about changing discourse that is somehow the same, about semiotic resolution of conflict that nonetheless endures, about legal resolutions that are at once authoritative and yet at the mercy of the vagaries of social change.

Notes

I would like to thank Don Brenneis, Charles Briggs, Bob Nelson, Michael Silverstein, Tom Tyler, and David Van Zandt for helpful responses to earlier drafts and for discussions that contributed to the current formulation of this essay. An earlier version was presented at the Symposium on Narrative Resources for the Creation of Order and Disorder, during the American Ethnological Society Meeting in St. Louis, Missouri, March 25, 1988. I thank the session's organizer, Charles Briggs, as well as the participants and commentators, for their comments and encouragement.

1. It should be clear that I am adopting a broader approach to narrative than the more limited definition espoused by Labov and Waletzky (1967). In treating a text as a narrative, I also cannot see that other options are thereby foreclosed; narratives can perform multiple social functions and carry meaning at a number of different levels.

2. See White (1986b:241): "[The judicial opinion] is a composition in which the speaker must choose a language for telling a story and justifying a result. . . . Since the opinion must make sense as a whole, the ultimate demand is one of integration." I also rely in part here on my own recent observations as a participant in the process while clerking at a federal appellate court.

3. Notice, in contrast, that courtroom discourse is quite different in both of these respects; witnesses may not have opportunities to correct what they perceive to be misapprehensions that arise from having their testimony shaped by an attorney's examination, and they are frequently interrupted.

4. Indeed, investigations of folk theories regarding polite speech and norms for talking in our society might shed important light on legal studies of narrative control in courtrooms and law offices.

5. Charles Sanders Peirce (1974) defines icons as signs that represent their objects by virtue of a perceived structural similarity or isomorphism.

6. See White (1986a, 1987) on rhetorical structure in judicial opinions.

7. See, for example, Justice Brandeis' well-known concurrence in *Whitney v. California*, 274 U.S. 357, 375 (1927) (Brandeis, J., concurring), which espouses a "safety valve" rationale for protecting First Amendment freedoms; permitting dissenters free expression functions as a "safety valve" protecting society from the disruption that might ensue were frustrated and stifled dissenters to turn their energies to action rather than speech.

8. Like Glendon, I will examine the way in which this kind of public discourse incorporates social "voices." However, my approach has more affinity with that of Bakhtin, which does not take the normative leap made by Glendon.

9. The role of the Court in producing an ongoing reflective discussion of society's morals is discussed by Michael Perry (1988).

10. This approach takes seriously both Bakhtin's (1981) concern with "voices" and the way in which reported speech is framed, and Silverstein's (1976, 1985) focus on indexicality and pragmatics.

11. In using the term "represents," I want also to highlight the way in which events are "re-presented," in two senses: they are formulated again in the Court's terms, and they are brought back into the present as the focus of current conversation.

12. This is apparent, for example, when the opinion first notes that a claim was made "by the plaintiff" and then moves on in the following paragraph to report that another claim was "also made by the learned counsel for the plaintiff," merging the plaintiff and his attorney as speakers.

13. I note the use of passive constructions here without venturing any conclusions about how use of the passive intersects with agency or representation of issues and actors. Further work on the prevailing conventions of passive/active usage is necessary before analysis of its significance here is possible. Discourse analysts have noted that the transformation from active to passive, in reversing subject and object noun phrases and permitting deletion of the logical subject, provides "a way of distributing information differently within sentences, and of preserving . . . thematicity" (Stubbs 1983:126). Although word order may certainly indicate presuppositions about assumed knowledge of information on the part of speakers, it seems important to understand the specific salience of passive usage in this particular genre (see Vološinov [Bakhtin] 1973:123; see also Mukařovský 1964).

Works Cited

Ashe, Marie. 1988. Conversation and abortion. *Northwestern University Law Review* 82:387–402.

Bakhtin, M. M. 1981. *The dialogic imagination.* Austin: University of Texas Press.

Bauman, Richard, and Charles L. Briggs. 1990. Poetics and performance as critical persepectives on language and social life. *Annual Review of Anthropology* 19:59–88.

Brenneis, Donald. 1987. Performing passions: Aesthetics and politics in an occasionally egalitarian community. *American Ethnologist* 14:236.

Brown, Barbara, Thomas Emerson, Gail Falk, and Ann Freedman. 1971. The equal rights amendment: A constitutional basis for equal rights for women. *Yale Law Journal* 80:871.

Cohen, Jane Maslow. 1989. Comparison shopping in the market of rights. *Yale Law Journal* 98:1235–76.

Cover, Robert. 1975. *Justice accused.* New Haven, CT: Yale University Press.

Edelman, Murray. 1985. *The symbolic uses of politics.* Urbana: University of Illinois Press.

Fineman, Martha. 1988. Contexts and comparisons. *The University of Chicago Law Review* 55:1431–44.

Francis, Leslie Pickering. 1988. Virtue and the American family. *Harvard Law Review* 102:469–88.

Glendon, Mary Ann. 1987. *Abortion and divorce in Western law.* Cambridge, MA: Harvard University Press.

Gunther, Gerald. 1985. *Constitutional law.* Mineola, NY: The Foundation Press.

Hickmann, Maya. 1985. Metapragmatics in child language. In *Semiotic mediation: Socio-cultural and psychological perspectives,* ed. Elizabeth Mertz and Richard Parmentier, pp. 177–201. New York: Academic Press.

Labov, William, and Joshua Waletzky. 1967. Narrative analysis: Oral versions of personal experience. Essays on the verbal and visual arts. In *Proceedings of the 1966 annual spring meeting of the American Ethnological Society,* ed. June Helm, pp. 12–44. Seattle: American Ethnological Society.

Mertz, Elizabeth. 1985. Beyond symbolic anthropology: Introducing semiotic mediation. In *Semiotic mediation: Sociocultural and psychological perspectives,* ed. Elizabeth Mertz and Richard Parmentier, pp. 1–19. New York: Academic Press.

––––––. 1987. Realist models of judicial decision-making. In *Center for Psychosocial Studies Working Papers* 15, ed. Richard Parmentier and Greg Urban. Chicago: Center for Psychosocial Studies.

––––––. 1988. The uses of history: Language, ideology, and law in the United States and South Africa. *Law and Society Review* 22:661–85.

––––––. n.d. The socratic method: A pilot study. Senior research thesis, Northwestern University School of Law.

Mertz, Elizabeth and Richard Parmentier, eds. 1985. *Semiotic mediation: Sociocultural and psychological perspectives.* New York: Academic Press.

Miller, Loren. 1966. *The petitioners.* New York: Pantheon Books.

Mukařovský, Jan. 1964. Standard language and poetic language. In *A Prague School reader on esthetics, literary structure, and style,* ed. Paul Garvin, pp. 17–30. Washington, DC: Georgetown University Press.

Noonan, John. 1976. *Persons and masks of the law.* New York: Farrar, Straus, and Giroux.

O'Barr, William, and John Conley. 1985. Litigant satisfaction versus legal adequacy in small claims court narratives. *Law and Society Review* 19:661.

Parmentier, Richard. 1993. The political function of reported speech. In *Reflexive language: Reported speech and metapragmatics,* ed. John Lucy. Cambridge: Cambridge University Press.

Peirce, C. S. 1974. *Collected papers,* vols. I and II, eds. C. Hartshorne and C. Weiss. Cambridge, MA: Harvard University Press.

Perry, Michael. 1988. *Morality, politics, and law: A bicentennial essay.* Oxford: Oxford University Press.

Reich, Charles. 1966. The law of the planned society. *Yale Law Journal* 75:1227–70.

Sarat, Austin, and William Felstiner. 1988. Law and social relations: Vocabularies of motive in lawyer/client interaction. *Law and Society Review* 22:737–69.

Scheingold, Stuart A. 1974. *The politics of rights.* New Haven, CT: Yale University Press.

Silverstein, Michael. 1976. Shifters, verbal categories, and cultural description. In *Meaning in anthropology,* ed. Keith Basso and Henry Selby, pp. 11–55. Albuquerque: University of New Mexico Press.

––––––. 1985. Language and the culture of gender. In *Semiotic mediation: Sociocultural and psychological perspectives,* ed. Elizabeth Mertz and Richard Parmentier, pp. 219–59. New York: Academic Press.

Stubbs, Michael. 1983. *Discourse analysis.* Chicago: University of Chicago Press.

Sweetser, Eve. 1987. The definition of lie. In *Cultural models in language and thought,* ed. Dorothy Holland and Naomi Quinn, pp. 43–66. Cambridge: Cambridge University Press.

Tushnet, Mark. 1987. *The NAACP's legal strategy against segregated education.* Chapel Hill: University of North Carolina Press.

Tyler, Tom. 1988. *Why people follow the law: Procedural justice, legitimacy, and compliance*. New York: Plenum.

Tyler, Tom, Kenneth Rasinski, and Nancy Spodick. 1985. Influence of voice on satisfaction with leaders: Exploring the meaning of process control. *Journal of Personality and Social Psychology* 48:72–81.

Vološinov, V. N. [M. Bakhtin]. 1973. *Marxism and the philosophy of language*. Cambridge, MA: Harvard University Press.

White, James Boyd. 1986a. Judicial criticism. *Georgia Law Review* 20:835–70.

———. 1986b. *Heracles' bow*. Chicago: University of Chicago Press.

———. 1987. Constructing a constitution: Original intention in the slave cases. *Maryland Law Review* 47:239–70.

Yngvesson, Barbara, and Patricia Hennessey. 1974. Small claims, complex disputes: A review of the small claims literature. *Law and Society Review* 9:219–74.

Cases Cited

Brown v. Board of Education, 347 U.S. 483 (1954).

Plessy v. Ferguson, 163 U.S. 537 (1896).

Whitney v. California, 274 U.S. 357 (1927).

"We Want to Borrow Your Mouth" Tzotzil Marital Squabbles

If marriage is (social) order, then marital breakdown is disorder, and divorce a kind of reordering. "Order," in this triple metaphor, is a semiotic notion, that is, it is not a neutral description of an objective state of affairs, but a property *found* (or *sought*) in events and arrangements, *attributed* to behavior and protagonists (who may also be faulted for its absence, for "disorderliness"), and, often, *enforced* (by interpreters) on outcomes and consequences. A potent device for producing this kind of order—or for undermining or usurping it—is *talk*.

Tzotzil-speaking Zinacanteco Indians from highland Chiapas produce various sorts of discourse relating to marriages over the course of their natural histories. Some of this talk is fragmentary and ephemeral, such as snippits of gossip about a courtship or an adulterous liaison, or a shout from a squabbling household. Some of it is highly structured and formal, beginning with a petitioner's pleas to a reluctant prospective father-in-law or the ritual words addressed to a new bride and groom, and ending, sometimes, with the pronouncements of elders who preside over the division of property when a couple ends their marriage. I examine here fragments of Tzotzil talk, drawn from a range of circumstances relating to several different Zinacanteco marriages, to show how social order and disorder are cast into words and linearized into discourse.

Let me first allude to my theoretical starting point, although everything here belongs to the category of "old news." This "casting into words" is more than a process of (mere) reference; and "linearization" is not a simple reflection of facts in clauses (see, by contrast, the image of "narrative" in Labov 1972). All of what we know about discursive practices—footing and framing (Goffman 1974, 1983a, 1983b), dialogicality and addressivity (Bakhtin 1981, 1986), functional regimentation and metalanguage (Benveniste 1974; Hanks 1993; Jakobson 1980; Silverstein 1976), centering and performance (Bauman 1977, 1986), and the hegemonic effects of voicing (Bourdieu 1982a, 1982b)—is, of course, patent in Zinacanteco discourse on marriage. Goffman's "interaction order" (1983b) contrasts with the semantico-referential illusion (peculiar to Western epistemological dogma) by situating discourse in and as action: (i) indexically centered within certain participant structures, and (ii) at a higher order, also indexically, the product of the sociopolitical matrix that participants construct and project.

The notion of "order" also gives us a metaphor through which we can assess what I want to demonstrate in this paper: the *iconicity* of the discourses of marriage. The terms of this iconicity are located (i) in discursive form (which is only visible when these forms are put in counterpoint to other comparable forms), and (ii) in the *theory* of the social processes of marriage, which is not necessarily a reflection of practices or of "social structure" at some more perspicacious level (whatever the theory might be), but a clear part both of the creation and enforcement of an ideology about how married life should proceed or, at least, be considered, evaluated, or understood.

Both order and disorder emerge not simply in the *content* of nuptial exhortations or marital squabbles but also, metonymically, in three aspects of their *form* as well. My comments will start with the messages—whether the hopeful encouragement addressed *by* an elder to newlyweds, or the sour denunciations *before* an elder by a fed-up wife—but then address generic properties of the language itself, aspects of its sequential organization, and finally, the social organization of verbal performances. My conclusion will be of this form: the orderliness of the discourses of marriage parallels (and, in a sense to be described, brings about) a corresponding orderliness in the practices of marriage. Like Briggs (see pp. 204–242 in this volume) and Urban (1986), I am concerned with a relationship, analogic and iconic, between discursive form in interaction and (perhaps microscopic) social structure.

Marriage, Zinacanteco and Otherwise

There is, of course, a vast literature on marriage, an institution first endowed with unquestioned conceptual and functional universality, then dissected and relativized, then rethought, then gutted and restitched as symbolic opposition (Collier et al. 1982)—a cycle of death and resurrection familiar for ethnological concepts. The blind application of notions of "marriage" and "divorce" prods Needham to urge a characteristic remedy (in *Rethinking Kinship and Marriage*) that we abandon "conventional typological guidelines" (which he later terms a kind of "conceptual dust") and learn "to take each case as it comes, and to apprehend it as it presents itself" (1971:xx). His therapy takes as its model Borges' Funes the Memorious who suffered a fall, after which "his perception and memory had become infallible, and his apprehensions were so rich and bright as to be almost intolerable" (Needham 1971:xvii): "Una circunferencia en un pizarrón, un triángulo rectángulo, un rombo, son formas que podemos intuir plenamente; lo mismo le pasaba a Ireneo con las aborrascadas crines de un potro, con una punta de ganado en una cuchilla, con el fuego cambiante y con la innumerable ceniza, con las muchas caras de un muerto en un large velorio"[1] (Borges 1974:1488). Funes inhabited "a world in which there were nothing but details, almost contiguous details" (Needham 1971:xix), a predicament Needham likens to that of "an unusually perceptive and diligent ethnographer newly arrived in the field."

This is, I might add, a predicament shared by the student of natural discourse, burdened by ever another level of transcriptional detail, together with a commitment to a certain theory about the *interactive construction* of cultural meaning. Such an ethnographer cannot disguise (to himself or, eventually, to his readers) the discursive nature of his own access to the anthropological subject. In the work reported here, I have chosen to wallow in the situated details of spontaneous verbal interaction, rather than take (invisible) refuge behind the implicit—and unanalyzed—interviews (see Briggs 1986) and questions that populate the backstage of most ethnographies of marriage.[2]

In Zinacantán, as just about everywhere else, marriage is seen by ethnographers (Collier 1968; Laughlin 1963; Vogt 1969) as the central institution of social (re)production. Especially in Zinacantán, I might add, a Funes-like detailed eye is seemingly *invited* by the vast corpus of ethnographic research in the *municipio*. In Tzotzil, moreover, there is little problem of definition via native categories, if we start with lexical evidence. The verbs *ik'* and *ch'ak* nicely sum up the end points: 'take (marry)', and 'split (divorce)', respectively. The ratified partners (*malal* 'husband' and *ajnil* 'wife') are terminologically quite distinct from the illegitimate ones (*antz*, literally 'woman', i.e., 'man's lover'; and *ajmul*, literally 'agent of sin', i.e., 'woman's lover').

Getting married in Nabenchauk, the village I know best, was once high drama: the groom's family laid siege to the house of his intended, begging the outraged parents for the girl's hand. After much ritualized badgering, and plied with corn liquor and the layered couplets of ritual Tzotzil, the girl's father ultimately had to agree to the long process of courtship, receiving several years of gifts and service from his would-be son-in-law, until finally the costs of raising his daughter were judged repaid, and the girl could be delivered to her husband's household. There she would be grudgingly admitted into the new world of her in-laws, where the couple would live for a few years until, ultimately, they could set up a separate household, a separate corn supply, and perhaps a separate public career.

The Discourses of Zinacanteco Marriage

I will concentrate on several verbal events that punctuate the life history of marriage in Zinacantán. Within the spectrum of a Zinacanteco "ethnography of speaking," the speech events I shall describe fall at the relatively structured or "formal" end (but see Irvine 1979). They involve elders or civil authorities, who sponsor a marriage and deliver exhortation to bride, groom, and new parents-in-law, or who intercede in marital disputes, either to settle them or to declare them insoluble. The use, in these circumstances, of language that resonates with ritual tones—in this case, the characteristic parallel couplets of Mayan prayer—will turn out to be of central importance. In a seeming paradox, narrative genres, too, are permeated by these highly structured verbal forms; and narrative, ranging from ordinary amorphous gossip (Haviland 1977b) to pointed moral tales, finds it way into the discourses of marriage, both disorderly and ordered.

After the long courtship, when the church wedding is, at last, over, the marriage party returns to the groom's natal home. The two families and their entourages have an elaborate meal in the courtyard. All prepare to dance and drink away the remaining tensions between the families that are being joined. Uncomfortable in their ritual clothing and too abashed to speak, the newlyweds stand stiffly by the table, neither eating nor participating in the rounds of drinking and formal greetings, which are led centrally by the wedding *jpetom* 'embracer'.

This embracer—a kind of godfather—is chosen by the families of both bride and groom to sponsor not the wedding ceremonies but the marriage itself. Should the new husband beat his wife and cause her to run away, he will turn to the *jpetom* for help when he goes contritely to woo her back; if the new bride lazily fails to provide her husband with hot meals on time, it will be the *jpetom* who scolds her and reminds her of her wifely duties. The embracer's main virtues are possessing both the necessary influence and position in the community to guarantee a marriage, and (ideally) sufficient wealth to be a resource for a new couple as it establishes itself.

In his formal greetings to the two families, delivered in the parallel couplets of ritual Tzotzil characteristic of prayer or song in Mayan languages (Bricker 1974; Edmonson 1971; Garibay 1953; Gossen 1985; Hanks 1988), the *jpetom* employs standard "stereoscopic" images that evoke the Zinacanteco model of ideal (orderly) marriage. The language, neatly and totally arranged in matching lines,[3] is itself an icon of perfect order. As he approaches the door of the groom's house, upon returning from the church, the *jpetom* greets the ritual adviser of the groom's family with words like those of (1). (In the following transcripts explicit parallel constructions are shown with double slashes separating the paired items.)

(1) *Elicited wedding embracer prayer*, recorded in Nachij, June 1972[4]

    1 *kumpare*
      Compadre
    2 *k'usi yepal ilok' tal yo jlumal // yo kach'elal*
      How much has my earth // my mud come forth
    3 *tzobolon tal // lotolon talel*
      I have gathered here // come here side-by-side
    4 *xchi'uk jch'ul chi'iltik // jkumparetik*
      with our holy companions // our compadres

5 *xchi'uk chib kalabtik // jnich'nabtik*
  with our two children // offspring
6 *a nupiuk tal // a tz'akiuk tal*
  They have been and returned from meeting // joining
7 *ta yolon yok // ta yolon sk'ob*
  under the foot // under the hand
8 *ti Santorenso // Santorominko*
  of St. Laurence // of St. Dominic
9 *a kak' o chanib yo toj // chanib yo kantela*
  I went to give four lowly pines // four lowly candles
10 *a kik'be o xch'ulel // yanima*
  I went to carry their souls // their ghosts
11 *ti chib alabe // nich'nabe*
  Of the two children // offspring
12 *ikil to yo jbatik // ikil ta yo jsatik*
  I saw with my lowly face // I saw with my lowly eyes
13 *inupi un // itz'aki un*
  they met // they joined
14 *ti alabe // ti nich'nabe*
  the children // the offspring
15 *laj o yo jtunel uk // yo jbainel uk*
  Thereby was finished my humble service // my humble duty
16 *yayatot // ajvetik*
  Ancient father // lord.
17 *junikotik // chibikotik*
  Let us be one // let us be two.

Notice, first, that although this is formulaic prayer, it exhibits a skeletal narrative structure, not unlike that of a typical gossip story (Haviland 1977b). That is, it introduces the participants of the narrated event (the wedding), using egocentric and alterocentric kin terms, which implicitly index the participants in the current speech event. It then traces (recounts) the "events" of the wedding ceremony just completed, using standardized couplets, and concludes the "retelling" with a return to the current circumstances, a kind of ritualized "coda." The embracer begins by speaking of himself—his own body—in the deprecatory couplet 'my earth // my mud'. He goes on to address the groom's father, his 'holy companion // compadre' (lines 1,4), having taken this fictive kinship relation with all the adults of both the families of the couple. The bride and groom ('our children, our offspring'5) have been married ('met and joined' [line 6]) before the patron saints of Zinacantán (line 8). The *jpetom* speaks of his obligation (line 15), symbolized by his planting candles and carrying the souls (lines 9–10) of the newlyweds in the ceremony just completed.

Thus, the newly married couple is escorted into the first moments of social adulthood to the accompaniment of the most orderly of all Zinacanteco speech: the formal greeting. Not only does the greeting comprise formally and semantically ordered couplets, with standard imagery, but the sequential organization of the verbal performance is also stylized and supremely ordered. The *jpetom* greets the *totilme'il* 'father-mother' or ritual counselor of the groom's family. Both are experts in parallel speech, and their words roll over one another in the rapid cadences of *simultaneous* greeting and response.

(2) Embracer prayer continues

> 4 *ta x'och jlok' be yo sk'u' // spok'*
>   I'll enter to remove their shirts // their garments
>
> 5 *ti chib alabe // nich' nabe*
>   of the two children // offspring
>
> 6 *ta jchotan komel // ta jvutz' an komel*
>   I will seat // I will settle
>
> 7 *ta yo sme'anal na // ta yo sme'anal k'uleb*
>   in their poor house // their poor treasury

This greeting anticipates, in paired images, the next stage of the wedding ceremony, as, at length, the bride and groom are invited into the house. Indeed, the prayer is a kind of ''pre-narration,'' since it presages the sequence of actions that is to follow. The *jpetom* helps the newlyweds to strip down to ordinary garb by removing their wedding costumes (line 4), and he settles them in their 'poor house // poor treasury (lit. place of wealth)' (line 7). The imagery of installing the new couple includes (at line 6) the couplet *-chotan* 'seat' // *-vutz' an*, literally 'bend'—a reference to the knees of the new bride as she sits at her new hearth.

Now comes the central discursive moment of the wedding ceremony, when the *jpetom* addresses an elaborate exhortation to the young couple. The embracer instructs bride and groom in the canons of propriety for adult, married Zinacantecos. Such instruction is called *k'op//mantal* 'words' and 'orders', itself a ritual couplet that describes exhortatory words of instruction. As usual, the language provides its own metalanguage: here an element of the genre denotes, among other things, the genre of which it is a part. The embracer delivers a heavy dose of such words, while the newlyweds sit, eyes downcast, bowing and mumbling their thanks and acceptance of his wisdom.

The embracer's exhortation is itself *ideally* phrased in the couplets of ritual Tzotzil. Since the *jpetom* is recruited for the silver in his purse, however, rather than for the silver on his tongue, not all incumbents in the role can sustain the ideal. There is often extemporizing, within the limited creativity the generic materials can provide.[6] Parallel verbal form gives both an authority and a solemnity to the exhortation that clearly delineates the miniature social structure of the event.

There are two further notable features of the wedding exhortation: its content and its interactive character. Standard sentiments are unfailingly expressed in the speech, although the precise message is tailored to the circumstances. If the courtship was long and hard, marred by disputes or misbehavior on the part of the groom, he will endure a heavy sermon on obedience, faithfulness, and sobriety. If the bride's industry is suspect, or if she comes from a wealthy family, she will be lectured on the virtues of hard work, or be reminded of her changed circumstances. In either case, the *jpetom* preaches the stereotypes of Zinacanteco matrimony.

What is more, the organization of the exhortation is malleable and fluid. The *jpetom* has the responsibility for what, effectively, is exhortatory monologue, delivered in couplets. He expects no back talk, only an occasional mumbled thanks from bride and groom.

However, the exhortation, though sequentially monologic, is not necessarily univocal. Other people, particularly the embracer's "partner"—his elderly female companion who has particular responsibility for the bride—or the proud parents themselves, chime in, echoing the embracer's sentiments or adding their own, speaking simultaneously. Thus, we may have two or more concurrent monologues, all ostensibly directed at the same target, the newlyweds (compare Reisman 1974). The resulting rain of voices remains, nonetheless, highly structured, in ways to be explored.

I shall now look at exhortatory words directed to the groom, to the parents of the groom, and finally, to the bride.

First a word about the examples I present, which are transcribed in a somewhat simplified version of conversational transcript notation (Atkinson and Heritage 1984:ix–xvi).

1. Zinacanteco Tzotzil (see Aissen 1987; Haviland 1981) is written in a Spanish-based practical orthography in which the symbol ' stands for a glottal stop, and the symbol C' represents a glottalized consonant.
2. Separate numbered lines correspond roughly to extended utterances broken by pauses. Dots represent perceptible pauses within an utterance. Overlaps are marked with square brackets, and latches (lines connected with no intervening pause) with equal signs connecting latched turns. The first line of each pair shows the original Tzotzil utterance (in italics), while the second line gives a free English gloss. The spacing corresponds to the Tzotzil lines, not the the glosses.
3. Marginal arrows call attention to various sorts of parallel construction, discussed in the text, according to the following key: C = formal couplet; T = formal triplet; P = parallel construction not in formal couplet/triplet form; L = linkage between matched couplets—a higher level of parallelism; E = lexical or phraseological echoing between lines. I will exemplify these forms of parallelism in the examples that follow.

The Groom

This is the beginning of what the embracer says to young newly married Antun; the Tzotzil transcript follows in (3).

Look here Antun.
Believe me, it's really true . . .

If we obey the words // if we obey the commands
We will talk // we will speak . . .
We will see who will get a thousand on our account//
    We'll see who will earn something on our account.

This speech is delivered largely in parallel constructions, like those we met in the *jpetom*'s formal greeting. It employs, therefore, the standard images provided by this most structured of speech genres in Tzotzil. The message in turn exploits these images: pay attention to your elders, whose wise words//commands will keep you out of trouble. You must talk // speak with them, to be instructed in the proper path to success (earning a thousand [pesos?]//something [i.e., not nothing?]).

The extracted "sense" of the embracer's exhortation, however, obscures a central fact about the performance itself. The *jpetom* (shown as m in the transcript in (3)) is not the only speaker. The groom's father (shown as p) produces a simultaneous stream of speech, partly in counterpoint to the embracer, and partly following his own preoccupations. Roughly, what he has to say is the following: 'I don't know how you will turn out if you obey the embracer's advice. You don't know if perhaps you'll end up a magistrate yourself. You still don't know if you'll end up like Domingo'. Domingo is a recent municipal president and Antun's brother-in-law, being held up here as a role model for the young groom; the allusion also serves as an indirect compliment to the current *jpetom*, a minor civil official who is thus implicitly likened to this powerful political leader.

Fragment (3) shows the delicate interweaving of the two voices—the embracer's, largely in couplets, and the father's in everyday Tzotzil—in a duet of exhortation.

(3) *Exhortation to groom*, recorded at a Nabenchauk wedding, June 13, 1978

1 m; *k'elavi ali Antun*=
      Look here, Antun.

2 p;   *= ali kumpa mole*=
               My compadre here . . .

3 m; *ali vo'one, melel ka'uktik*
      As for me, it's true of course
      =[

4 p; *ilok' i kumpa mole ixch'un xa li kumpa Maryane*
      My other compadre left (the job),
        and my compadre Marian has accepted it.

5 m; *timi ta jch'untik i k'ope // mi ta jch'untik i man*=
      If we obey words // if we obey orders.

6   *tale*
      =[

7 p; *mu jna' k'u x'elan xalok' uk mi ach'un li k' op*=
      I don't know how you will come out if you obey the words

C

E

8   *= une*

9 m; *ta xik' oponaltik // ta xiti'inalotik*   ←——— C
    We'll speak // we'll talk.
    [

10 p; *mu xana' mi yech chakom (mu xana' to mi =*
     You don't know if you'll end up that way,
      you still don't know if . . .

11   *chakom k'u cha'al Romin)*   P
    . . . you'll end up like Domingo.
    =[

12 m; *ta to xkiltik ti much'u tzta jmiluk ta jtojoltike //*
    We'll still see who will gain a thousand on our behalf//
      [

13 p; *mu xana' k'u x'elan, muk' to =*
     You don't know how it will be,
      you haven't yet . . .

14   *= aviloj aba*   P
    seen yourself.

15 m; *// ta to xkiltik ti =*   C
    // We'll yet see . . .

16   *much'u tzta (??) ta jtojoltike*
    . . . who'll be able to (find something) on our behalf.

The precise orchestration here is of considerable interest, and it relates to my theme: that the *form* of marital discourse both mirrors and, in an important way, helps to create or enforce the ultimate orderliness (or disorderliness) of the social arrangements that are the explicit subject matter of the talk. First, examine the formal parallelism of the embracer's utterances (marked, as usual, with double slashes) at lines 5, 9, 12–15. In couplets (indicated by marginal arrows and the letter C), the embracer, m, enjoins the new bridegroom to be obedient and thoughtful in his words, and thereby, it is hoped, to achieve economic success. The embracer's voice is, thus, formally ordered (into couplets), structurally authoritative (since it is part of an obligatory performance by an authority figure), and also indexically distant, impersonal, and indirect—referring to Antun, the bridegroom, for example, only through first person inclusive pronominal forms.

By contrast, the interwoven anxieties of the father, p, are expressed largely in ordinary nonparallel conversational form, on a different Goffmanian footing. He addresses Antun directly, in the second person, and he displays not the standardized sentiments of the embracer's formal exhortation, but his own somewhat anarchic worries and hopes for his son, newly become a man: Will he behave properly? Will he have a political career? Nonetheless, the formal (perhaps aesthetic) flow of the exhortation is unbroken. The father does not use formal couplets, but he often repeats his sentiments in nonparallel doublets (marked with marginal P on the transcript), as at lines 10–11 and 13–14. Moreover, the father's words track closely the simultaneous imagery of the embracer's couplets, sounding not dissonance but counterpoint: *ch'un* 'believe, obey' anticipated in line 4, incorporated into a couplet (C) by m in line 5, and echoed (E) in line 6; m's reference to formal speaking in line 9, recalled in p's allusion to dispute settling in lines 10–11; and even an echo of the root *il* 'see (what the future brings)' between lines 12 and 13. There is thus a dramatic staging to the interaction that combines, in these two voices—the confident official line of the embracer, flavored by the more anxious and contingent concerns of the father—both an onstage, performed, cultural order, and a background of potential (or actual) social and biographical disorderliness.

It is important to note that the wedding from which this exhortation is drawn was the Zinacanteco equivalent of a shotgun affair: bride and groom had behaved scandalously (they had met and talked openly before being married) and had accordingly been rushed into a wedding long before the courtship had run its normal course. A tattered courtship gets a tattered wedding. As a result, there was no proper *jpetom*, and the job of delivering the instructions to the newlyweds fell by default to a young civil official, who was hastily recruited at the last minute to fill the role and to insulate the new bridegroom from any possible legal action by the girl's family.

Indeed, the subject of the unfortunate circumstances of the marriage is explicitly raised and incorporated into the matrimonial discourse, almost as if by ordering the words, the facts themselves could be partially ironed out. It is clear that, despite the ritualized form of the exhortation, there is a background text of ordinary gossip; the scandalous facts of this ramshackle courtship are known to all present and thus available to allusion. Much of the embracer's admonition to the new couple represents an indirect dance around this presupposed narrative background. In fact, many of the people present try to get into the act. Consider, in particular, the contribution of x, one of the bride's relatives, in the continuing talk. (m is the embracer, a the groom [Antun], who merely mumbles his agreement, and p the father of the groom.)

(4) *Anarchic continuation of admonition to groom* ◀— C

30	m;	*tuk' ta xkaltik ti k'ope, ti rasone*	
		. . . we correctly say the words, the reason.	
31	x;	*mu xavut (ta?) li antz une*	
		You mustn't scold the woman.	
32	m;		[*pero yok'al ali mu:k' ta=* But if you simply don't care
33		*=alel avu'un le* . . .	
		about that . . .	
		[	
34	p;	*eso .lek mantal*	
		Yes, that's good advice.	

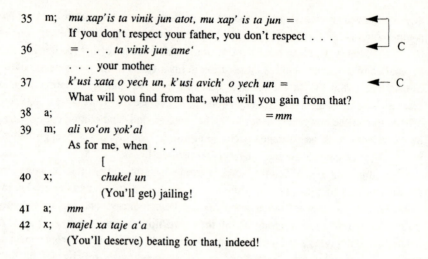

35   m;   *mu xap'is ta vinik jun atot, mu xap' is ta jun* =
          If you don't respect your father, you don't respect . . .

36   = . . . *ta vinik jun ame'*
          . . . your mother

37   *k'usi xata o yech un, k'usi avich' o yech un* =
          What will you find from that, what will you gain from that?

38   a;   = *mm*

39   m;   *ali vo'on yok'al*
          As for me, when . . .
               [
40   x;   *chukel un*
                   (You'll get) jailing!

41   a;   *mm*

42   x;   *majel xa taje a'a*
          (You'll deserve) beating for that, indeed!

It is obvious that x, a somewhat drunken and outraged prospective in-law, is still upset by the past misbehavior of the young couple, and at lines 40 and 42 he seizes on the embracer's rhetoric to announce his threats to his new classificatory son-in-law, in an insurrectionary voice.

On the other hand, m, the embracer, and p, the groom's father, continue their counterpoint in a reassuring passage.

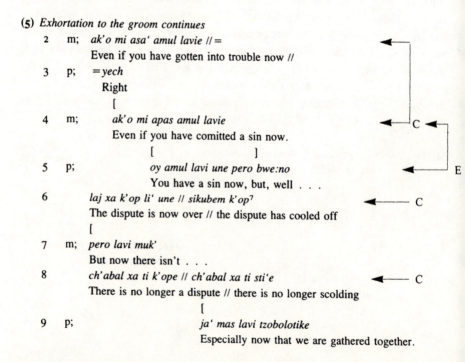

(5) *Exhortation to the groom continues*

2   m;   *ak'o mi asa' amul lavie* // =
         Even if you have gotten into trouble now //

3   p;   = *yech*
         Right
              [
4   m;   *ak'o mi apas amul lavie*
         Even if you have comitted a sin now.
              [   ]
5   p;   *oy amul lavi une pero bwe:no*
                       You have a sin now, but, well . . .

6   *laj xa k'op li' une* // *sikubem k'op*[7]
         The dispute is now over // the dispute has cooled off
              [
7   m;   *pero lavi muk'*
         But now there isn't . . .

8   *ch'abal xa ti k'ope* // *ch'abal xa ti sti'e*
         There is no longer a dispute // there is no longer scolding
              [
9   p;   *ja' mas lavi tzobolotike*
                     Especially now that we are gathered together.

Again, the precise choreography displays both the collaboration and the division of discursive labor between the two; m begins and p responds, in 2–3, and 4–5, whereupon p takes up the thread, even producing his own parallel couplet at line 6, which m now echoes in a further couplet at line 8. The message is: you may have gotten into trouble in the past, but now, with this ritual occasion (the *ordering* of marriage), these past troubles are wiped clean.

In the case of young Antun, there are, in fact, several possible causes for worry. There is first the impropriety of the courtship itself, which is smuggled into the ritual admonition as a truncated pseudonarrative. First, the embracer invokes, in "hypothetical" speech at lines 6–11 in (6), an image of a future disobedient wife.

(6) *Admonition to groom continues*

1 m; *tuk' chavich' albel yech*
        Thus are you being properly instructed.

2   *xa-xapas ta mantal avajnil*
        You will instruct your wife.

3   *xavalbe k'u xavalbe stuk un*
        You will tell her directly whatever you tell her.

4   *ora timin yu'un atimin oy mu xch'unane*
        Now if- if she doesn't obey you.

5   *ti mi ja' chas- ta stoye*
        If she- if she is rebellious.

6   *ej mu jk'an xa lapason ta mantal*
        "Eh, I no longer want you to boss me around."

7   *ej*
        "Eh . . ."

8   *ali vo'one ma'uk jkwentauk*
        "As for me, it's no business of mine."

9 x; *ali vo'one ma'uk kwenta . ta jpas mantal*
        "As for me, it's not my business. I'll give the orders."
        [

10 m; *ja' li mu onox bu nopem xka'i much'u spas=*
        "Since I am not used to having anyone . . ."

11   *ta mantal*
        ". . . boss me around."
        =[

12 x; *aje:nte ja' sna'oj lek*
        The magistrate knows what he's talking about.
        [

To counter such rhetoric, the embracer suggests, the groom need only recall (as he here retells) the facts of the couple's improper courtship.

(7) *Further admonition*

13   m;   *timi xi une*
             If that's what she says . . .
14   a;   *jmm*
          Yes.
15   m;   *mu snup*
          That isn't right.
16   *mu stak' stoyel*
          She can't act up.
17   *porke k'u yu'un ta stoye*
          Because, why should she rebel?
18   *i: ak'anoj abaik*
          . . . since you desired each other.
19   *i: ak'opon ti k'u x'elan ak'opone*
          And you spoke to her however you spoke to her.
20   *isnop i antze i anop uk*
          The woman decided, and you decided.
21   *ta parejo anopik ta cha' vo'*
          And the two of you decided equally.

Another cause for concern is Antun's drinking. The petitioner puts the issue in terms of behaving *ta muk'* 'as a grown person': having respect for oneself and acting responsibly.

(8) *Exhortation to the groom continues*

1   m;   *i tambien li vo'otuke*
         And you, too . . .
2   *tuk' xavich' aba ta muk'//*
         You must behave yourself as an adult//
3   *xavich' aba ta k'ak'aluk*   C
         You must behave yourself as mature.
4   a;   *mm*
5   m;   *mu xatambe jun (yakubel?)//*
         You mustn't set off on a (binge?)//
6   *mu xatambe jun pox*   C
         You mustn't set off on drink.

The temptation to throw one's money away on cane liquor spells ruin, in this rhetoric.

(9) *Further exhortation*

22   m;   *ora timi yu'un naka onox uch' pox//*
          On the other hand, if (it's) just drinking liquor//
23   *naka onox yakubel*
          Just drunkenness.   C

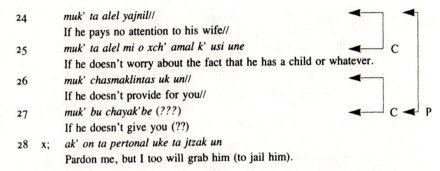

24		*muk' ta alel yajnil//*
		If he pays no attention to his wife//
25		*muk' ta alel mi o xch' amal k' usi une*
		If he doesn't worry about the fact that he has a child or whatever.
26		*muk' chasmaklintas uk un//*
		If he doesn't provide for you//
27		*muk' bu chayak'be (???)*
		If he doesn't give you (??)
28	x;	*ak' on ta pertonal uke ta jtzak un*
		Pardon me, but I too will grab him (to jail him).

The embracer's long monologue, in partly extemporized couplets, points out that drunkenness will result in suffering within a's newly formed family. Notice the footing changes: starting at line 24, the drunken husband is now spoken of in third person—he mistreats *his* wife and ignores *his* children. But at lines 26–27, the victim, in this changed footing, is still second person: he (the drunkard) doesn't provide for *you*, that is, the new bride. Here, x, a (himself drunken) relative of the bride, breaks in to assert that a's drunkenness will also attract the hostility of others: he himself promises to throw the young miscreant in jail.

The Parents

The guardians of the new order, the real adults in the new couple's home, are the groom's parents. The words addressed to them in a wedding exhortation capture—and discursively defuse—the tensions inherent in the bride's position as a newcomer to the carefully enclosed (and fenced) world of a Zinacanteco domestic compound.

Once again, the embracer raises the issues that have clouded the wedding, in this case giving the groom's father a bit of discursive space (at lines 30 and 33 of (10)) to add a bit of self-defense to the accumulating background narrative.

(10) *Embracer to the groom's father*

17	m;	*bweno k' elavi kumpa*
		Well, look, compadre.
18		*isa'li smule isa'li skolo'e*
		He sought his sin, he sought his evil.
19		*k'u ta xkutik*
		What can we do about it now?
20		*isk'upin sbaik*
		They desired one another.
21		*isk' opon sbaik*
		They spoke to each other.
22		*ni modo*
		There's no help for it.
23		*pero k'u ta jcha'letik*
		But what can we do about it now?

24	*pero timin ja' to . o k'usi k'op*
	But if eventually there should be some further trouble.
25	*mi ja' to o k'usi chutilan sbaik*
	If later on they keep fighting about something.
26	*mi mu sk'el*
	If he doesn't watch (after her)
27	*mi mu yil*
	If he doesn't see (her).
28	*mi ja' to k'u iyal ti chalbe sbaik un*
	If later on there is something they say that they are saying to one another
29	*poreso*
	for that reason
30 p;	*much'u i- ipason ta mantal*
	Who obliged them?
31 m;	*eso es pues*
	That's right
32	*ja' ta jk'eltik un yech=*
	Then we'll see . . .
33 p;	*= ma'uk ikalbe (???)*
	I wasn't the one who told them (to get married).
34 x;	(???)
35 m;	*yech'o un*
	Therefore
36	*ak'o yik' sbaik ta muk'*
	Let them marry each other with respect.
37	*ak'o yik' sbaik ta k'ux*
	Let them marry each other in seriousness.

The formal features of the exhortation to the parents are again notable. The *jpetom* continues to speak largely in couplets, although they are frequently now truncated, showing only the final paired elements of what would otherwise be wholly repeated lines, differing only in a terminal word or phrase. (Such abbreviated couplets often surface when ritually expert adults instruct one another in the proper words to use on some specific occasion, such as a ritually important errand.) His interlocutors, the groom's parents, respond directly to him, in polite but necessarily parallel speech.

There is also a possible heirarchial anomaly: the parents are likely to be older than the *jpetom*, and thus may both outrank him socially and outdistance him in terms of cultural knowledge. Nonetheless, the marriage ritual places them in the position of being, if not instructed, at most treated as collaborators in the exhortation. The following fragments come from a different wedding exhortation, which followed a relatively uneventful courtship.

Here, p is the embracer, while f and m are father and mother of the groom, respectively; p is a ritually inexperienced middle-aged man, whereas f, the father, is a reknowned ritual expert and master talked. Notice, in (11), that the embracer's parallel triplet at line (8) is foreshortened, and that he truncates an obvious potential couplet at lines (7) and (10)—perhaps because of the imbalance of expertise between speaker and interlocutor, perhaps simply because f cuts him off with his responses.

(11) *Exhortation to parents*, recorded at a different Nabenchauk wedding April 26, 1981

  7 p; *ital xa li . avalabe*
         Your child has come.
  8   *lavi tal kak' // jchotan // jvutz'ane*   ←— T
         Now I have come to offer them//to seat them//to bend them.

              [
  9 f;   *bwe:no*
              Okay.
  10 p; *te xavalbekon ya'i:=*
         There you will explain to them for me
  11 f;   *=hii*
  12 p; *k'u x'elan xave'ik//*
         how you eat//
  13   *xavuch' vo'e*   ←—┘ C
         (how) you drink water.

The standard image for the canons of domestic life is: 'how you eat // how you drink water'. The bride can be expected to be ignorant of the customs of her new house, and must thus be instructed, with patience and care.

(12) *Exhortation to groom's father continues*

  14   *komo . mu sna' to=*
         Because she still doesn't know.
  15 f;   *=mu sna' a'a*
              No, she doesn't know.
  16 p; *mu sna' komo ja'*
         She doesn't know because . . .
  17   *yech'o ja' sk'an le'e*
         therefore what one needs . . .
  18   *chavalbekon lek ti rasone//*
         (is for) you to tell her wisdom, for me//
  19   *chavalbekon ti mantale*   ←—┘ C
         (for) you to give her orders, for me.

The pronouns display the central footing: the father-in-law must help the *jpetom*—ritual guardian of the new matrimonial union—by instructing his new daughter-in-law how to behave. Such instruction will serve to head off squabbles—and separation.

In fragment (13), the embracer (p) turns his attention to the groom's mother, m, the incumbent boss in the bride's new kitchen. The canonical product of women's labor—the *panin* or corn dough from which tortillas are produced daily—serves here as metonym of the entire female domestic realm. The new bride brings her womanly skills, learned in her natal home, which must now be adjusted to the standards of her in-laws' household.

(13) *Exhortation to groom's mother*

<pre>
46 p;   melel . tzna' nan slakanel li panine
          True, perhaps she knows how to boil corn dough
47   pero ja' to ta snae pero
          But that was just at her house, but
48   lavi une chjel ya'el un
          . . . now that has changed.
49   ma'uk xa yech chk k'u cha'al ta sna une
          It is no longer the same as in her own house.
                              [
50 m;   ma'uk un
                          No, it isn't
51 p;   ma'uk yech'o xavalbekon ya'el un
          No, and therefore you will have to tell her for me.
52   k'u x'elan-
          how it is
53 m;   an yechuk kumpare =
          Why, all right, compadre.
54 p;   = xave'ik//
                    . . . you eat//
55   xavuch'ik vo'
          . . . how you drink water.
</pre>

Finally, p produces the same standard parallel image—'eat, drink water'—for household customs, but most of this exhortation is in ordinary noncouplet form, perhaps reflecting the fact that his interlocutor, the groom's mother, is not necessarily fluent in the parallel language herself, and thus can be expected to reply in minimal form (as she does, at lines 50 and 53).

The embracer ends with the plea that 'scolding // splitting up' be avoided through open and cooperative talk.

(14) *More exhortation to new mother-in-law*

<pre>
59   ja' lek mi lek ibate // ja' chopol li labal =
          It will be good if it goes well//it will be bad if they only engage in
60   = ut'ut bail//
              is scolding each other//.
61   labal . ch'akch'ak bail
          . . . just splitting up with each other.
</pre>

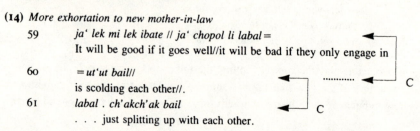

The Bride

What of the bride's place in this rhetorically ordered matrimonial universe? The *jpetom* also addresses part of his exhortation to her, the newest member of the household. Only shortly beforehand, when her bridal garments were removed, has the bride exposed her face for the first time to the gaze of her new in-laws. She now sits uttering hardly a sound as her wedding godfather instructs her in wifely virtues. At this point, he has spoken already to the groom and his parents. He feels obliged to address only a shorter speech to the bride. The performance is univocal, virtually without interruptions, as all present strain to hear how the new bride will comport herself as she is inducted into a frightening new world.

The *jpetom's* exhortation to the bride is an ethnographically acute manifesto about a Zinacanteco woman's lot—at least, from a senior man's point of view. Inspired by the thought of proper domestic economy, the embracer exploits a further symbol of female domesticity: hauling firewood for the hearth. (The parallel structure is somewhat choppy here, as the embracer appears to struggle to find his rhetorical rhythm. At lines 57–58, for example, he launches a parallel line with *ma'uk xa* 'you won't just. . .' but he completes the line by beginning a *new* couplet: 'you won't just. . . sit idly observing things // only warm yourself by the fire.')

(15) *Exhortation to bride*, recorded at the same wedding, Nabenchauk, April 26, 1981

55	*mi o bu chakuch asi'ik*
	If you have occasion to haul firewood.
56	*xabat ta si'be uk*
	You too will gather firewood.
57	*ma'uk xa li . chotol chakom ta nae*//
	You won't just stay seated at home//
58	*ma'uk xa . li' xa xak'el elav* // =
	You won't just sit idly observing things//
59	= *.yech xa nox xak'atine*
	you won't just warm yourself for nothing.
60	*bal ti chabchab chba akuchik tal k'u ora* =
	It is sufficient that you haul back two
	(pieces of firewood) whenever . . .
61	= *xaxokobike*
	. . . you have some spare time.
62	*yu'nox* . . .
	because
63	*stalel ti ta jkuchtik si'e*//
	it is normal for us to carry firewood//
64	*stalel ti ja' chive'otik o ti . x'elan kunen* =
	It is normal that we eat from our little . . .
65	= *kostumbretik vo'otik*
	. . . customs, that we have.

P

C

C

C

'Zinacantecos are not', he continues, 'like Ladinos'—non-Indians—'who don't know how to work':

(16) *More instructions to the bride*

66   *ma'uk yech chk k'u cha'al . jkaxlanetike*
It is not like the Ladinos.

67   *ja' xa ta jchantik jun xa ko'on chotolotike,*
that we can just learn to be happy sitting around

68   *i'i,*
No

69   *yu'nox chi- . chi'abtejotik jutukuk*
Because we must work a little bit.

In the following talk, which I omit here, the series of paired couplets nicely summarizes the heart of the Zinacanteco ethic of work and wealth: eating // having possessions; money // corn; arising (from bed) // waking up (decently) early.

Finally, the wedding exhortation turns to the question of central interest to the embracer: happiness and domestic tranquility, the permanence of this union.

(17) *Still more instructions to the bride*

79   *mu'nuk . ixtol ti nupunele//*
Marriage isn't a game//

80   *mu'nuk . ja' nox jun chib k'ak'al lanupunik*
You haven't gotten married for just one or two days.

81   *yu'un.*

82   *lanupunik o ta . sbatel osil // =*
Instead you have gotten married until the end of the earth//

83   *= k'u cha'al xichamotik xkaltike*
. . . until we die, as we say.

If things do not go well, says the *jpetom*, sounding a more ominous note, the elders should be brought into the affair. In consultation with them, any problems can be solved *ta lekil k'op* 'with good words'. Blame and punishment can be sorted out.

(18) *Final words to the bride*

96   *much'u ti*
which one . . .

97   *o smule // much'u ti*
is the guilty one // which one

98   *ch'iline*
. . . is the one who gets angry.

99   *bweno timin ja' . tzmul ti Chep une*
Well, if it is José's fault . . .

100   *stak' xich' stzitzel//*
he can be punished//

101   *stak' xich'.*
He can receive . . .

102   *xich' albel, jp' el // cha'p' eluk noxtok*   ⟵ C
       He can be told, a word // or two words, too.
103   *pero ta komun chka'itikotik un*
       But we'll think about it in common.

The wrong thing, the embracer goes on, would be for a wife to follow her impulse to leave the husband's home and return to her own parents. The inevitable spats and discord must be ignored.

Marital Squabbles

The words of warning in the examples given seem to foreshadow a future more disorderly than the rest of the wedding rhetoric might suggest. Marriage has always been fragile in Zinacantán—as a look at the gossip about marriages, even 30 years ago, would show (Haviland 1977b). Nowadays, however, it seems positively brittle. First, courtship is no longer the elaborate affair it once was. Often a suitor will simply pay cash for his bride—or, as jokes would have it, hand over a cow, a corn harvest, or the keys to a truck—to avoid performing the expected bride-service. Or the couple may simply elope and buy their way back into the good graces of the father-in-law, after the fait accompli. Moreover, the landscape is now littered with abandoned wives, (socially) fatherless children, and young divorced people, of both genders, who defy both the ethnographer's and the oldtimer's claims—based, no doubt, as much on normative memory as on actualities—that life in Zinacantán is for pairs, not singles.[8]

Before a year of marriage is out, any new couple is bound to experience the fragility of marriage in Zinacantán. Unmarried sisters-in-law, viewing the new bride as both incompetent and an intolerable spy in their midst—always running home to complain to her mother, not knowing how her poor husband likes his beans or his *uch'imo'* 'atol' or corn gruel—can make life unbearable for a young woman who has never before lived away from her own hearth. For the new wife, the demands of a child soon drain energy away from both domestic obligations (the food and the firewood) and girlish pastimes: weaving one's own decorative clothing, or socializing with cousins and sisters in the forest.

For many young men, on the other hand, growing independence from fathers, long periods spent away from the village in the cornfields or on the job, and the pressing need to provide for one's own hearth and larder promote wanderlust and drinking.

Occasionally, the angry shouts of a fighting couple echo through the valley of Nabenchauk, breaching the normally hermetic walls of village house compounds (Haviland and Haviland 1983). More frequently, though, the discourse of marital strife is secondhand: it surfaces in gossip, in the words of dispute settlement, and in the metacommentary of village elders who try to stitch up the seams in what some-times seems a tattered Zinacanteco social fabric.

When a girl runs home to her parents' house, after a fight or beating, the threat of separation and divorce drives one family or the other to seek the help of the *jpetom* or of other village elders to try to bring the couple together again. It is ordinarily the bride who runs away and who must be coaxed back into her husband's home. Collier gives a functionalist explanation.

> Marital disputes are a normal and indeed necessary part of Zinacanteco life, since they lead to the reordering of social relations crucial to maintaining cohesion in the developing patrilineal family. . . . It is no coincidence that the early years of marriage are the most unstable, for all the strains inherent in extended family living come to a head in this period. Young brides are unhappy at leaving home and having to work for their mothers-in-law, and young husbands may wish to break away from working with the family group but fear the wrath of the father or the risks of farming alone. Wives, always viewed as selfishly looking out for their own interests, pro-vide convenient scapegoats for husbands who wish to break away without quarrel-ing openly with their patrilineal kinsmen. Marital disputes are thus outlets for the tensions of extended family living. The fact that they are frequent, highly patterned and seldom serious makes them efficient vehicles for dissipating the hostile feelings that develop [1973:198].

Zinacantecos are aware that, sooner or later, all married couples end up squab-bling. When angry words spill violently over the edges of the domestic order, the measured words of dispute settlers, on one view, can be seen as domesticating the resulting disorder. It falls to the discourses of marriage settlement—the "words and orders" of elders—to restore domestic harmony. Another view is possible: that it is breaches of the *public* order that require *re*-domestication; and that the function of the authoritative and culturally monolithic voices of elders is to drown out bickering domestic voices, to lock them back, where they belong, *ta yut mok*—inside their own household fences.

Marital squabbles explode as angry words: a snappish remark, a sullen re-sponse; scolding, leading to shouted accusations, inspiring countercharges; and finally a full-scale dispute. The process of dispute settling, then, is necessarily *meta-linguistic:* it is, at least in part, language *about* language. We have seen that ordinary Tzotzil, and even ritual couplets, make explicit metalinguistic reference to both the codes and the circumstances of speech. A dispute about a dispute encompasses a further semiotic remove: current talk can aim not only at the content of the dispute—the "facts of the case"—but also at the processes and circumstances of the dispute (see Haviland and de León 1988). There are several discursive levels. First marriage partners quarrel partly through what they say. Second, accounts of their quar-reling—including "reported quarrels," a subvariety of "reported speech" (Banfield 1982; Hill and Irvine 1992; Lucy 1991; Vološinov 1986)—form the raw material for dispute settlement sessions, themselves comprising discursive forms. Finally, gossip and commentary about the process of settlement—a subject to which I shall turn at the end of this essay—represent metalinguistic discourse in which the original fighting words of the protagonists are at a third level of remove.

In Zinacantán, I argue, second-order discourse—dispute-settling talk about (first-order) fighting-talk—moves up the scale from disorderly to ordered by involving the disputants in a mediated encounter, in which their very words are cast into more controlled formal, sequential, and social surroundings. More than metalanguage is involved here, of course, for this second-order discourse inhabits that special social realm that Goffman (1983b) called the "interaction order": the face-to-face (or body to body) domain "in which two or more individuals are physically in one another's presence" (1983b:2). Such copresence—complicated, in miniature, by familiar issues of social identity and hierarchy, power and powerlessness (including voicelessness)—produces definite effects on the emergent order, both discursive and social, which is my theme.

Let me now return to scenes from a Zinacanteco marriage.

When Did You Stop Beating Your Wife?

Antun, the young man whose marriage exhortation we saw earlier, some years thereafter went out with friends to a cantina, got drunk, and had to be shamelessly hauled home by an obliging drinking partner. Sometime later, he beat his wife, accusing her of disobedience and disrespect. She ran home to her relatives, and was only induced to return by the promise of a mediated settlement.

Here is the scene: two village elders, Petul and Lol, have been summoned to help settle the dispute. The young man has (still) a reputation for drunkenness, and this is not the first time he has beaten his wife. The two elders are giving advice and counsel to the man, Antun (who is lying in bed with a miserable hangover and who takes scant part in the talk recounted here), and to his aggrieved wife, Loxa. There is little question of Antun's guilt, here, and he is really too sick even to try to defend himself against the elders' criticism.

However, the talk is still contentious: although the elders want Antun to mend his ways, they are also interested in preserving the marriage, and they therefore aim some of their criticism indirectly at the wife, intimating that she may have been insufficiently obedient or compliant. Not surprisingly, she defends herself, although often obliquely, and she rarely misses a chance to heap further abuse on her drunken husband's fogged head.

In elaborating their arguments, the speakers sometimes cooperate and sometimes oppose one another. Part of the process of dispute settlement in Zinacantán requires that the participants evolve a series of shared discursive understandings, along with articulated moral stances about what is being said. From disagreement and opposition, that is, they produce shared orderliness. This appearance of order, of course—like the very words from which it is constructed—may deceive: irony as well as intransigent silence may represent tactics more subversive than outright opposition. The mere suppression of *public* disorder does little to ensure domestic bliss, or to prevent seeds of discord once (perhaps discursively) sown from sprouting subsequently.[9]

Nonetheless, the *outward* ordering process is evident in both the content and the form of dispute settlement sessions. The language moves from the normal, halting, brief streams of conversational Tzotzil (which characterizes the angry speech of the disputants) to fully developed parallel constructions in the elders' final pronouncements. In a similar way, the battles for floorspace and for conversational priority consolidate, little by little, one turn at a time, the moral authority of the social order.

Talking Back

Although officially the two dispute settlers are chewing out the drunken husband, they are also trying to bring a balanced reconciliation. Their moral is from time to time pointedly directed at Loxa, the wife. Her reaction at various stages clearly shows her sensitivity to their nuances. In the following fragment, Lol admonishes Loxa (shown as Lo) about how she ought to react to her husband when he comes home drunk. Precisely at the point that Lol recommends that Loxa not talk back to her drunken husband, she begins to talk back to him.

(19) *Marital dispute settlement*, recorded December 15, 1983, Nabenchauk

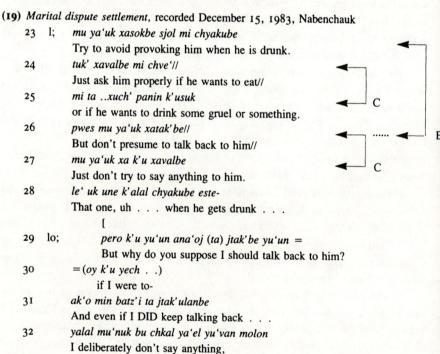

```
23   l;    mu ya'uk xasokbe sjol mi chyakube
           Try to avoid provoking him when he is drunk.
24         tuk' xavalbe mi chve'//
           Just ask him properly if he wants to eat//
25         mi ta ..xuch' panin k'usuk
           or if he wants to drink some gruel or something.
26         pwes mu ya'uk xatak'be//
           But don't presume to talk back to him//
27         mu ya'uk xa k'u xavalbe
           Just don't try to say anything to him.
28         le' uk une k'alal chyakube este-
           That one, uh . . . when he gets drunk . . .
                 [
29   lo;       pero k'u yu'un ana'oj (ta) jtak'be yu'un =
              But why do you suppose I should talk back to him?
30         =(oy k'u yech . .)
              if I were to-
31         ak'o min batz'i ta jtak'ulanbe
           And even if I DID keep talking back . . .
32         yalal mu'nuk bu chkal ya'el yu'van molon
           I deliberately don't say anything,
              do you suppose me an elder?
                 [
```

33   l;   *yu'un ali:*
          because uh . . .

34   lo; *mu jna' mi*
          I don't know if . . .

35   *mu xa xka'i jba k'u ta xkal un*
          I can't even think of anything I would say to him.

The second person verbs at line 23 are addressed directly to Loxa: 'you mustn't provoke him when he is drunk, just speak to him normally and politely, offering him food and drink'. The couplet structure gives the elder both rhetorical momentum and cultural authority.

However, Loxa breaks in at line 29, defending herself—she *doesn't* talk back, and she wouldn't know what to say to him even if she did. Is she an elder? This is ironic, and oblique, metapragmatic commentary: unlike Lol, the elder with a public, authoritative voice, she herself is mere wife—a protagonist in the first-order events—who both there and here has *nothing to say,* that is, no voice.

Lol, with Petul's rhetorical support, beats back Loxa's miniature insurrection, to regain both verbal and moral control of the floor. At line 40 of fragment (20), Loxa is apparently brought back into echoing agreement.

(20) *Marital dispute continues*

36   l;   *ali k'al chyakube, porke*
          When he gets drunk, why is that?

37   *porke mu sk'an tak'bel*
          Because he doesn't want any back talk.

38   p;   *jyakubel mu sk'an tak'bel*
          A drunkard doesn't want back talk.

          [

39   l;   *yu'un chopol sjol*
          Because he has a bad head.

          [   ]

40   lo; *mu sk'an tak'bel yu'un chopol sjol*
          He doesn't want back talk because he has a bad head.

Petul has taken up the role of Lol's interlocutor, repeating his words and hence reaffirming his sentiments starting at line 38. Ultimately, Loxa also aligns herself with this line of argument, repeating the phrase *mu sk'an tak'bel* 'he won't stand for being talked back to', and probably agreeing with heartfelt vehemence that *chopol sjol*, literally '[her husband] has a bad head', that is, one that doesn't work properly.

Again the potential irony in the wife's subaltern voice shows the ambiguity, and a possible inversion, of a piece of standard cultural logic. The elders seem to insinuate, behind their overt criticism of Antun for public scandal, that he seeks this escape—and the consequent socially defined blamelessness (or nonresponsibility) of drunkenness—in response to his wife's back talk. She, then, must take care that her domestic behavior not produce public disorder. Her reply, apparently accepting the admonition, can also be read as defying the analysis. He's not just out of his head from drunkenness: he has a *bad* head—a malevolent head—and that's why he won't stand back talk.

In the midst of such dispute settlement, narrative also has a place, as moral tales are marshalled to the disputants' purposes. However, since narrative is discursively less highly ordered than, say, the formal couplets of admonition and resolution, it also can have subversive effects. Consider how the angry wife introduces the drunken scene of the night before into the discussion. The elders offer a good example, the tale of a now sober husband, to show Antun (and his wife) how drunkards can reform themselves.

(21) *How a good wife would behave*

```
 1   p;   ali jun le' ta jote che'e
          The other (brother) there on the other side . . .
                [
 2   l;         hmm
 3   p;   iyakub li . . . jmanvele
          My son Manuel used to get drunk.
 4   l;   hmm
 5   p;   mi ch'ilin mi chut yajnil
          If he would get angry, if he would scold his wife
 6        mu xbatz'i-ba:k li antze
          The woman wouldn't make the slightest response.
 7        ja' ti mi ikux ta yok'obe
          Only when he would sober up the following day
                [
 8   l;         yech che'e
                That's right.
 9   p;   ja' to chalbe
          only then would she tell him.
                [
10   l;         ja' to u:n
                Only then.
11        ja' to chalbe un
          Only then would she tell him.
                [
12   p;        mi xana' yech tey cha(pas chk li'e) xi
               "Do you know that you behaved this way," she would say.
13        mi ja'uk mu xa stak'
          He couldn't even be able to answer her.
14        chi' o un
          He got frightened by that.
15        chikta o li pox une
          And for that he reason he gave up drinking.
16        k' exlal chava'i
          It was the shame, you see.
```

Now Loxa (shown as lo on the transcript) pounces. Here is her chance to tell the sorry tale of her besotted husband, being hauled home by his awful Chamula drinking partner.[10] (Chamulas, Tzotzil Indians from a neighboring township, are generally regarded as rural bumpkins by Zinacantecos.)

(22) *The wife's counter-tale*

21   lo;   *va'i mu kalbe li'-*
                 Listen, I didn't tell this one-

22   *k'al skuchet to le'e*
                 When he was still being hauled (home) . . .

23   *yu'un ulo'etik pe:ro tz'ukul ta o'lol*
                 . . . by the Chamulas, but he was upside down in between them

24   *bu tajmek tz'ukul une*
                 or wherever he was hanging upside down.

(. . .)

28   lo;   *manchuk xa nox li totil ulo' jna'tik*
                 If it hadn't been for the old Chamula, who knows?

To disarm the opprobrium here, the elders must first divert Loxa's story in a humorous direction. Echoing her own words, they convert the incident into a joke: the poor Chamula had only been paid for agricultural labor, but he ended up having to carry his employer home. (Note that the elder, l, indexically aligns himself with the drunken Antun, at line 33, by referring to the Chamula as *kulo'* 'my Chamula'.)

(23) *Defusing the wife's story*

33   l;   *ti manchuk li' li kulo' mole muk' bu x'eanvan*
                 If my Chamula hadn't been here, no one would have carried him.
                             [

34   p;   *kere, manchuk li'*
                       Damn, if he hadn't been here

35   *bal to*
                That was just lucky.
                [

36   lo;   *buch'u yan yu'un vo:kol iyul chcha'va'alik*
                 Who else? And the two of them had a hard time arriving here.
                       [

37   p;   *kere . bal to me stojbe=*
                       Damn! It was lucky that he paid . . .

38   *=sk'ak'al to*
                (the Chamula) for his day's work.

39   *ja'la yech*
                That's how they say it was.

40   *ja'la ulo'i'eanvan tal xi*
                They say it was the Chamula who hauled him back.

41   lo;   *pero yu' un mu jna'be (?? sjol)*
          But I just don't understand him.
             [
42   l;   *naka ulo' a'a hehh*
          Just a Chamula, indeed . . .
43   p;   *ulo' che'e batz'i toyol un*
          A Chamula, indeed; very expensive . . .
                [
44   l;   *li'- (ha ha))*
                Here– hehhh
45   p;   *ak'o ba sjak'be stojol sk'ak'al povre ulo'*
          Let him go and ask the poor Chamula how much his daily salary is.

Finally, having agreed that the whole event, though funny, was shameful, the elders seize control of the discursive floor, elaborating on the interlocked themes of drunkenness and shame. They continue with another collaborative narrative, about how l himself decided to give up drinking, ending with a parallel chorus.

(24) *"How I gave up drinking"*

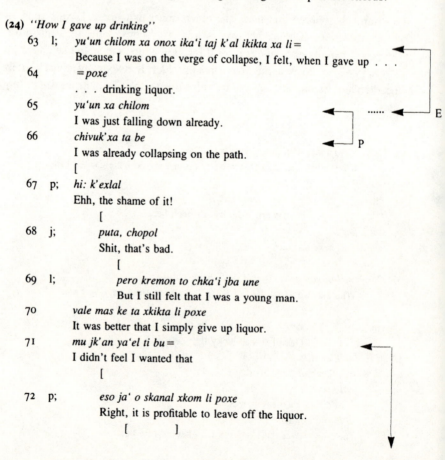

63   l;   *yu'un chilom xa onox ika'i taj k'al ikikta xa li=*
          Because I was on the verge of collapse, I felt, when I gave up . . .
64   *=poxe*
          . . . drinking liquor.
65   *yu'un xa chilom*
          I was just falling down already.
66   *chivuk'xa ta be*
          I was already collapsing on the path.
             [
67   p;   *hi: k'exlal*
          Ehh, the shame of it!
                [
68   j;   *puta, chopol*
          Shit, that's bad.
                   [
69   l;   *pero kremon to chka'i jba une*
                But I still felt that I was a young man.
70   *vale mas ke ta xkikta li poxe*
          It was better that I simply give up liquor.
71   *mu jk'an ya'el ti bu=*
          I didn't feel I wanted that
             [
72   p;   *eso ja' o skanal xkom li poxe*
                Right, it is profitable to leave off the liquor.
                   [   ]

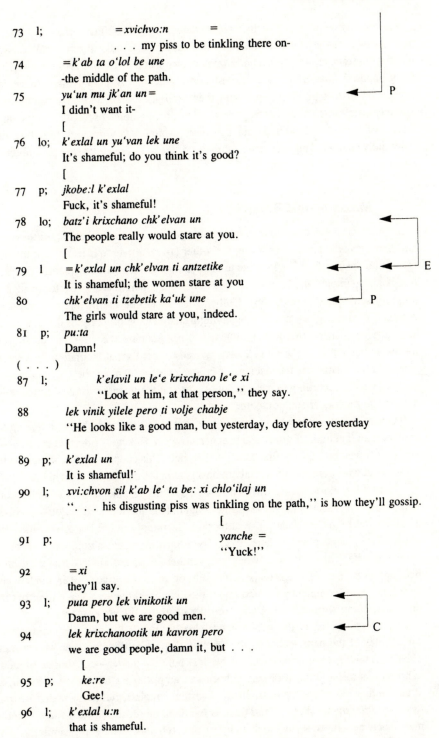

73 l;   = *xvichvo:n*   =
          . . . my piss to be tinkling there on-

74   = *k'ab ta o'lol be une*
        -the middle of the path.

75   *yu'un mu jk'an un* =
        I didn't want it-

          [

76 lo;   *k'exlal un yu'van lek une*
        It's shameful; do you think it's good?

          [

77 p;   *jkobe:l k'exlal*
        Fuck, it's shameful!

78 lo;   *batz'i krixchano chk'elvan un*
        The people really would stare at you.

          [

79 l   = *k'exlal un chk'elvan ti antzetike*
        It is shameful; the women stare at you

80   *chk'elvan ti tzebetik ka'uk une*
        The girls would stare at you, indeed.

81 p;   *pu:ta*
        Damn!

(. . .)

87 l;   *k'elavil un le'e krixchano le'e xi*
          "Look at him, at that person," they say.

88   *lek vinik yilele pero ti volje chabje*
        "He looks like a good man, but yesterday, day before yesterday

          [

89 p;   *k'exlal un*
        It is shameful!

90 l;   *xvi:chvon sil k'ab le' ta be: xi chlo'ilaj un*
        ". . . his disgusting piss was tinkling on the path," is how they'll gossip.

          [

91 p;   *yanche* =
          "Yuck!"

92   = *xi*
        they'll say.

93 l;   *puta pero lek vinikotik un*
        Damn, but we are good men.

94   *lek krixchanootik un kavron pero*
        we are good people, damn it, but . . .

          [

95 p;   *ke:re*
        Gee!

96 l;   *k'exlal u:n*
        that is shameful.

Discursive sequences like this involve the attempted resolution of a matrimonial battle, which has produced public disorderliness, which has, in turn, spilled back into the domestic realm. A dispute settlement provides a discursive forum which first frees opposed lines of private interest and argument (by giving them space for expression in this public realm), and then realigns morals and conclusions in a publicly acceptable cultural arrangement. Here, the combined social and sequential weight of the two elders' speeches conspires to limit and ultimately to defuse the potentially anarchic language and sentiments of the outraged, but also outnumbered, wife.

Mature Marital Battles

Sometimes Zinacanteco couples whose marriages have survived the first brittle years find themselves in strife. According to Collier (1973), divorce is infrequent though far from unheard of. "The Presidente always tries to reconcile a separated couple. But if all attempts fail, he will acknowledge the separation and try to arrange a property settlement" (1973:196). Collier goes on to cite the factors that seem to correlate with the wife's actually receiving a share of the property of the marriage: having been married more than four years; her keeping the children; or simply formal settlement at the town hall (as opposed to less formal mediation by village elders). Such statistical tendencies, of course, do not explain the mechanisms— some of which, according to the logic of my present argument, must be discursive— that actually engineer such outcomes.

One such case arose when a husband, jealous after observing his wife talking to another man, got himself drunk and beat her savagely.[11] Again, elders were called— not, as it turned out, for the first time—to reconcile this couple whose children were grown, and who were shortly to embark on a year in the municipal ritual hierarchy.[12]

Here the rhetoric took a different line. First, the dispute settlers talked to the wife, who complained that she could no longer stand the repeated jealous beatings administered by her husband. The authorities seemingly urged her to consider divorce. Two elders, p and r, later joined by a third, l, mount a conjoint campaign upon the wife, whose replies, when she ventures any, are always truncated and overlapped by the dispute settlers. They pile on the same argument in tandem: if your husband is completely beyond hope, then you might as well leave him; but in that case, do so without a fuss, and consider carefully the consequences.

The organization of this performance clearly mirrors the mutually reinforcing social roles of the participants: r, the primary dispute settler, together with p—an older man with greater ritual expertise but less political power—collaborate in their exhortations to the wife; p largely echoes and amplifies r's utterances, creating a structure that resembles the parallelism of formal couplets, but here created *across* turns by *different* speakers. Thus, there is overlapping repetition (and shared sentiment) between lines 5/7/9 (spoken by r) and 6/8 (spoken by p); similarly, r's

injunction to the wife simply to bid her husband goodbye, without further fighting
(lines 7/9), is interleaved with a similar move by p (lines 6/10/13).

(25) *Divorce settlement*, recorded April 26, 1981, Nabenchauk

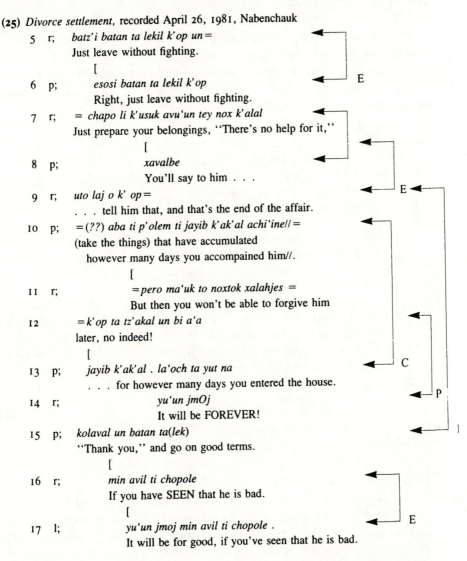

5 r;   *batz'i batan ta lekil k'op un* =
Just leave without fighting.

        [

6 p;   *esosi batan ta lekil k'op*
Right, just leave without fighting.

7 r;   = *chapo li k'usuk avu'un tey nox k'alal*
Just prepare your belongings, "There's no help for it,"

           [

8 p;   *xavalbe*
You'll say to him . . .

9 r;   *uto laj o k' op* =
. . . tell him that, and that's the end of the affair.

10 p; = (??) *aba ti p'olem ti jayib k'ak'al achi'ine//* =
(take the things) that have accumulated
however many days you accompained him//.

            [

11 r;   = *pero ma'uk to noxtok xalahjes* =
But then you won't be able to forgive him

12   = *k'op ta tz'akal un bi a'a*
later, no indeed!

    [

13 p;   *jayib k'ak'al . la'och ta yut na*
. . . for however many days you entered the house.

14 r;   *yu'un jmOj*
It will be FOREVER!

15 p; *kolaval un batan ta(lek)*
"Thank you," and go on good terms.

    [

16 r;   *min avil ti chopole*
If you have SEEN that he is bad.

    [

17 l;   *yu'un jmoj min avil ti chopole .*
It will be for good, if you've seen that he is bad.

As r points out to the wife at lines 11/12/14, after taking the drastic step of moving
out with all one's belongings, there is of course no going back. Meanwhile, p
continues with the hypothetical farewell he is suggesting the wife offer her husband
(line 15).

Finally, at lines 16 and 17, r, overlapped by the third elder l, summarizes the
somewhat sobering hypothetical case: this is what you should do if you're *certain*
that your husband is a disaster. The three elder join forces in a highly structured

moral chorus, reinforcing each other's words and sentiments. The resulting sequential verbal torrent produces unrelieved pressure on the wife to consider (and perhaps reformulate) her complaint and its consequences.

The elders then turn to the guilty husband, appealing first to a kind of male pride. How does it look, they ask, to be accompanied by an obviously battered woman? The language switches subtly from that of adomonition to that of male joking. One symptom of the switch is the lack of formally parallel structure. Notice, as well, the transitory switch, at line 4–6 to an inclusive first person pronoun, suggesting the speaker's shared perspective with the addressee.

(26) *Divorce settlement continues*

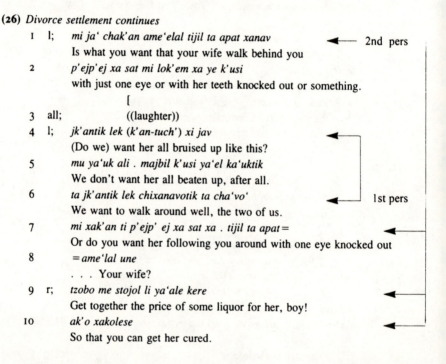

1   l;   *mi ja' chak'an ame'elal tijil ta apat xanav*   ◄——— 2nd pers
          Is what you want that your wife walk behind you
2   *p'ejp'ej xa sat mi lok'em xa ye k'usi*
          with just one eye or with her teeth knocked out or something.
                    [
3   all;   ((laughter))
4   l;   *jk'antik lek (k'an-tuch') xi jav*   ◄
          (Do we) want her all bruised up like this?
5   *mu ya'uk ali . majbil k'usi ya'el ka'uktik*
          We don't want her all beaten up, after all.
6   *ta jk'antik lek chixanavotik ta cha'vo'*   ◄—— 1st pers
          We want to walk around well, the two of us.
7   *mi xak'an ti p'ejp' ej xa sat xa . tijil ta apat=*   ◄
          Or do you want her following you around with one eye knocked out
8   *=ame'lal une*
          . . . Your wife?
9   r;   *tzobo me stojol li ya'ale kere*   ◄
          Get together the price of some liquor for her, boy!
10   *ak'o xakolese*   ◄
          So that you can get her cured.

The process of reestablishing order involves a kind of ironic transfer: the formal order of the discourse is applied to the disordered social world of the disputants. One frequent strategy emerges when the dispute settlers find a topic on which they can denounce the disputants in parallel language; they often appear to create new images extemporaneously to suit the subject, so that events are arranged in a spontaneous way into the ordered pairs of parallel couplets.

For example, the elder p "establishes" by interrogation—a rhetorical ploy, since he obviously knows in advance what the answers will be—that even the clothes on the man's back are products of the allegedly inattentive wife's labor. The husband, here, is shown as a.

(27) *More chiding in divorce case*

1   p;   *bweno lak'u' alapoj le'e*
              Well, those clothes you have on there.

2   *mi . mi manbil avak' ojbe mi ja' yabtel=*
              Did you buy them, or are they her work?

3   a;   *= i'i ma'uk une*
              No, not (bought).

4   *ja' tzjal*
              She wove them.

5   p;   *va'i un*
              So, you see!

6   *ati taj . sba avajnile*
              As for your first wife . . .

7   *mi ja' onox yech lak'u' lakom chk le'e*
              Did you always have that sort of clothes before?

                              [

8   a;   *kere . . ch'abal =*
                     Gee, no . . .

9   *=a'a tot*
              . . . indeed, father.

10   *mu xu' jnop k' op=*
              I can't tell lies.

The second-order nature of the dispute settlement is now clear, as p marshalls knowledge of previous "texts" (drawn from a's biography and having to do, for example, with his previous marriage, or with his previous episodes of jealous violence) in order to place their facts into the public discourse of this occasion, eliciting a's explicit acknowledgment.

Next, p drives the point home with some extemporaneous couplets, starting at line 14.

(28) *More divorce settlement*

12   p;   *va'i un, li=*
              So, listen, the . . .

13   *=antz une*
              woman (you have here) . . .

14   *jalom ata // j'abtel ata*   ← C
              In her you found a weaver // in her you found a worker.

15   *k'usi yan chak'an ya'el ell*   ←
              What more do you want, then?//

16   *k'usi xa li palta tajmek*   ← C
              What seems to be the big problem?

17   *batz'i lok'el xa xa'ilin // xakap un*   ← C
               You're always getting angry // getting mad.

When the elders come to the end of a topic that they have tried to resolve, they also routinely deliver their final words in a largely parallel section, drawing on the ordered couplets of ritual Tzotzil to put their admonition in an authoritative form. In particular, the issue of a ritual office, which the quarreling couple are scheduled to enter soon, gives p, in the following passage, a context in which to invoke standard paired images.

Notice at lines 5 and 6, that the parallel form involves a triplet, the first two parts of which repeat an image—*abtel // patan*—from the previous couplet (see Haviland 1987, 1994).

(29) *Admonishment to divorcing couple*

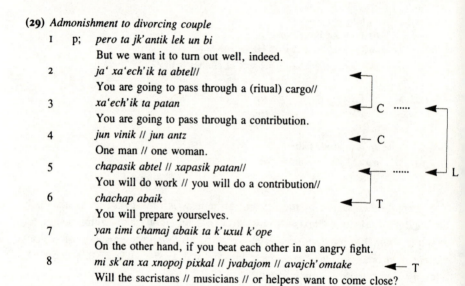

1   p;   *pero ta jk'antik lek un bi*
         But we want it to turn out well, indeed.
2   *ja' xa'ech'ik ta abtel//*
         You are going to pass through a (ritual) cargo//
3   *xa'ech'ik ta patan*
         You are going to pass through a contribution.
4   *jun vinik // jun antz*
         One man // one woman.
5   *chapasik abtel // xapasik patan//*
         You will do work // you will do a contribution//
6   *chachap abaik*
         You will prepare yourselves.
7   *yan timi chamaj abaik ta k'uxul k'ope*
         On the other hand, if you beat each other in an angry fight.
8   *mi sk'an xa xnopoj pixkal // jvabajom // avajch'omtake*
         Will the sacristans // musicians // or helpers want to come close?

Carrying through with a year in ritual office (Cancian 1965) requires the help and support of a small army of auxiliary personnel: church officials, musicians, and helpers of all kinds. Such people will not, the argument continues, find the disputatious ambience of jealous words congenial.

When an elder takes control of the discourse in this way, he exerts multiple forms of hegemonic control. By taking over the floor (partly through the momentum of his parallel words, partly through his social and interactive position), he *instantiates* authority. His words, drawn from the marked repertoire of ritual genres, drip with cultural power. Their form, as well, is a perfect icon of orderliness, control, sobriety, and proper public demeanor. Even in the final, self-deprecatory, and explicitly metalinguistic characterization of his own words of advice, the elder inserts a parallel construction, indexically assimilating himself to orderliness and absolving himself of further responsibility.

(30) *Final words in divorce settlement*

31   *yech 'o un*
      Therefore . . .

32   *mas lek yech chakalbe chk taje*
      It's better that I tell you this way.

33   *yuleso ta ajolik; vo'one*
      Remember it; as for me . . .

34   *yiyil mi xach'une // yiyil mu xach'une*   ◀——— C
      never mind if you obey me // never mind if you don't obey me

35   *yal ti chkal ya'ele*
      Now that I have said it. . . .

Recountings of Zinacanteco Marital Squabbles

I have shown that when fighting couples bring their disputes—which may have surfaced in first-order fighting words, if not directly in blows, broken crockery, and tearful fleeings—to settlement, before village elders, a second-order discourse emerges. Whereas fights throw order to the winds, settlement—what Zinacantecos call, appropriately, *meltzanej k'op* 'the fixing (i.e., repairing) of words'—begins to reintroduce order. It redomesticates passions, smooths the pointed edges of angry words—a least those that have emerged onto a public stage—and rephrases and realigns the terms of dispute. Contention is reformulated as agreement, and oppositions are converted to parallel couplets. This is, of course, a characteristic ideological trick: the elders want to reinstitute a public order, whether or not the bickering husband and wife find contentment and happiness by the domestic hearth. The idiom available for construing the dispute is limited by the procedures and personnel of settlement, as are the voices and postures of the protagonists.

Consider, finally, third-order commentary on marital squabbles: talk (e.g., gossip) about dispute settlement itself, re-presentations of re-presentations.[13] There is here a still *further* metalinguistic remove, as the discourse of disputes and their retellings in settlement are crystalized onto the discourse of the *narratable* event. If, as I have argued, the orderly *form* of discourse about disputes imposes an order (if only an idealized, public order) on the social events and relations themselves, we may predict that commentary on dispute settlement will invest it with an even more highly idealized discursive order.

Zinacanteco narrative abounds with recreated dialogue, and Zinacanteco storytellers are masters at portraying characters through their reported conversations rather than through explicit characterizations. Thus, to show how angry or upset a protagonist is, Zinacantecos put *angry words* into his or her mouth.

Such a rhetorical device—using angry-sounding words as a sign of a narrated protagonist's anger—is a somewhat more direct exploitation of what Bakhtin (1986) calls "primary genres" inside "secondary genres" than the common device in literary language of explicit performative framing of reported speech through "verbs of saying" (Silverstein 1985).[14] In the case of reported speech, however, a skilled narrator imports the evocative power of a speaking style, investing his characters with emotional states and tones by demonstration rather than by description.

In the last fragments, t, the narrator—a prominent dispute settler's wife—is telling her father, p, about an especially salient marriage dispute. It concerns a man who is currently involved in a different sort of dispute with p, who accordingly is interested in hearing about his opponent's misfortunes. Indeed, p seems to *elicit* the story, precisely by mentioning that he has forgotten it (a useful discursive device for getting someone *else* to do the telling).

(31) *Gossip session*, recorded in Nabenchauk, April 12, 1981

```
1    t;    nopbil i smul xi ka'i noxtok ali ch'akbil =
           Someone also blamed him for something else
           [              [    ]
2    p;    yu'un xchi'uk i Romine
           . . . that was with Domingo . . .
3                            k'usi ti xi une
                             . . . or they were saying
                             something like that . . .
4    t;    stzeb Maryan Xantise =
           Marian Sanchez's daughter (wanted to split up with him)
           = [
5    p;    ch'ay xa xka'i un
           I forget now . . .
6                = a:an o me yantik ika'i me a'a
           Why, yes I heard some other stories like that . . .
```

The daughter, t, goes on to *recount* a highly emotional scene in which a beaten wife sought help from her husband; t recounts, that is, the recounting of a marital squabble and its attempted settlement. The crucial episodes (Bauman 1986) of the narrative are themselves scenes of speech. The narrator conveys her protagonist's distraught state by couching her speech in the marked form of ritual couplets, appropriate to righteous denunciation. (At this third-order level, the question whether the original wife, speaking to the dispute settler, "actually" used such parallel constructions or not does not arise.) The discursive transformation, by which this performance is created from the details of one couple's squabbling, and the subsequent reconstructed discourse of settlement, displays the narrative orderliness even in the seemingly most disordered of events, the cries of a desperate woman, battered by her husband and searching for refuge. It is this dramatized wife who reportedly cries to the village authority, "We want to borrow your mouth!"

(32) *Reported wife's complaint, in narrative*

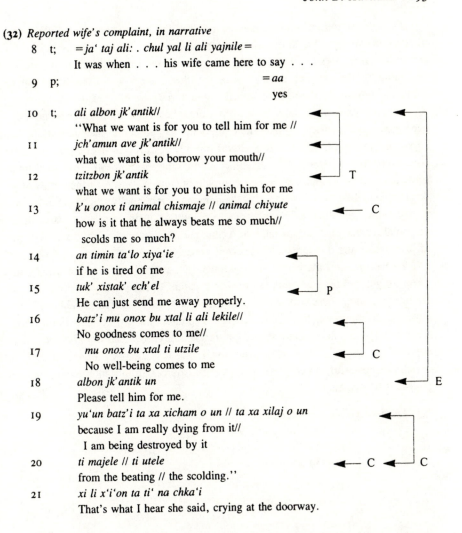

```
 8  t;    =ja' taj ali: . chul yal li ali yajnile=
          It was when . . . his wife came here to say . . .

 9  p;                                          =aa
                                                yes

10  t;    ali albon jk'antik//
          "What we want is for you to tell him for me //

11        jch'amun ave jk'antik//
          what we want is to borrow your mouth//

12        tzitzbon jk'antik
          what we want is for you to punish him for me

13        k'u onox ti animal chismaje // animal chiyute
          how is it that he always beats me so much//
            scolds me so much?

14        an timin ta'lo xiya'ie
          if he is tired of me

15        tuk' xistak' ech'el
          He can just send me away properly.

16        batz'i mu onox bu xtal li ali lekile//
          No goodness comes to me//

17          mu onox bu xtal ti utzile
            No well-being comes to me

18        albon jk'antik un
          Please tell him for me.

19        yu'un batz'i ta xa xicham o un // ta xa xilaj o un
          because I am really dying from it//
            I am being destroyed by it

20        ti majele // ti utele
          from the beating // the scolding."

21        xi li x'i'on ta ti' na chka'i
          That's what I hear she said, crying at the doorway.
```

In (32), it is the structure of double, and sometimes triple, parallel lines (augmented by a striking intonation that makes the words sound like a high-pitched, rhythmic wail) that helps convey the tone of distress, helplessness, and desperation that the beaten woman is depicted as bringing to her plea. We first met these couplets in the standard images of wedding greetings. We saw them reemerge in the pronouncements of dispute settlers, taking seeming authority from the standardized cultural logic embedded in stereoscopic imagery. Here, in third-order discourse, the parallel style is a powerful stylistic device that allows t to *portray* her protagonist's state. She makes the beaten wife sound *ritually* angry, giving her performance a tone both insistent and pathetic, as she bemoans her fate and ill treatment in a style that, for a Tzotzil audience, recalls the wailing entreaties in a cave or a shrine that a sick person might address to the ancestors or to the Lord of the Earth (Vogt 1969, 1976).

Though previous examples illustrate men's use of formal verbal parallelism as a trapping of power and authority, here a female protagonist, through the voice of a female narrator, uses ritual forms to convey *emotional* power. Women, of course, also employ the couplet genres, although there are fewer sanctioned public contexts—outside of shamanistic curing—where they are obliged to do so.[15]

This *representation* of the aggrieved woman's speech to the elder is, notably, even *more* highly structured than the complaints lodged before dispute settlers that appear in previous fragments. It is almost entirely constructed in complex parallelism. Moreover, it represents a sustained monologue that, in transcripts of dispute settlement, seems uncharacteristic of complaining wives. Whatever the events of an original squabble, the discourse of settlement is interactionally staged, so as to lead to a certain sort of culturally acceptable resolution.[16] In turn, this fictionalized portrayal further casts the speech into formal parallelism, perhaps as a stylized way of laying bare the protagonist's perceived underlying state of mind.

To recapitulate, the complaining woman has, as t tells p, come to the dispute settler to get him to speak with her husband; t finishes her portrayal, at line 21, by explicitly framing these portrayed words with the verb *x'i'on* 'crying, babbling'. She continues by exhibiting the dispute settler's responses, thereby not only dramatizing the woman's complaint, but also, by contrast, parodying the seemingly inarticulate reply of the dispute settler. Here, she inverts the hegemony of a cultural logic in which the powerful, notably the men, are the sources from which eloquence and parallelism emanate.

(33) *Further reported wife's lament*

22   t;   *xi li x'i'on ta ti' na chka'i ja' ba 'ik' le'e*
          That's what she said, crying at the doorway, when she
                went to get him.

                                                    [

23   p;   *i . i yajnil Pat 'Osile* =
                                                 the . . . the wife of Pat 'Osil?

24   t;   = *hi* =
          yes

25   p;   = *aa*

26   t;   *a: xi, a: xi*
          "Oh," he said, "oh," he said.

27   *te chkalbe xi*
          "I'll tell him," he said.

28   *'oy 'onox chkile te chkalbe te chkalbe k'uxi x- xut chka'i* =
          "I'll be seeing him, I'll tell him, I'll tell him," I heard him tell her.

At lines 26–28, t has the dispute settler saying only "yes, yes" repeatedly, as if, subjected to the unceasing stream of complaint and woe, he was unable to get a word in edgewise. (Notice, correspondingly, that p, who is hearing t's story, has not himself interrupted the long turn in which t reproduces the complaining wife's speech; it is only at this point, at lines 23 and 25, that he resumes his normal cooperative and clarifying back channel.)

The narrative shifts swiftly from one verbal scene to the next.

(34) *Narrative transition*

  1   t;   *albon che'e xi=*
             "You tell him, then", she said.

  2   p;   =i
  3   t;   *isn- isk' opon la un=*
             Evidently he did speak to him.

  4   p;   =mm=
  5   t;   =*(mu jna') mi ta muk'ta be li' ta olon bu sk' opon=*
             I'm not sure if it was down below here on the highway
               that he spoke to him.

When the dispute settler protagonist finally confronts the offending husband (who himself has a civil position at the town hall), he begins with a man-to-man interrogation.

(35) *Dispute settler meets wife-beater*

  8   t;   *an k'u onox mi batz'i layakub xut la=*
             "Well, what happened, did you get really drunk?" he said to him.

  9   p;   =mm
 10   t;   *liyakub a'a xi la=*
             "Yes, I did get drunk," he said, evidently.

 11   p;   =mm
 12   t;   *mi ali . . ana'oj to aba va'i cha'ilin une xut la=*
             "Did . . . uh . . . you still know what was going on, since
               you got angry," he evidently said to him.

 13   p;   =mm
 14   t;   *ana: mu jna' mujna' chka'i xi la*
             "Well, I wasn't conscious, I didn't know," he said evidently.

The narrated dispute settler goes on, in t's representation, to chide the miscreant in couplets as well, in an artfully constructed dance between (t, the narrator's portrayal of) his presentation of the wife's voice, and his own.

(36) *Continued reported chiding of husband*

 44   t;   *"yu'un nan `a yal avajnile*
             "because your wife has been to tell about it,

 45   *"k'un la me ti `animal chamajvan // `animal cha`iline*   ◄——— C
             "why, she asks, do you beat her so much // get so angry?

 46   *"`an ta la me chaxchuk lavajnil `une //*
             "your wife says she's going to jail you//

 47   *"ja` la me jayibuk k'ak'al chaxchuk `une//*
             "Indeed, she says she'll jail you a few days.//

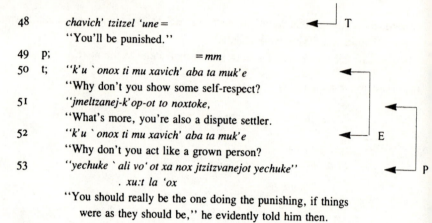

48   *chavich' tzitzel 'une =*   T
          "You'll be punished."
49   p;   *= mm*
50   t;   *"k'u `onox ti mu xavich' aba ta muk'e*
          "Why don't you show some self-respect?
51   *"jmeltzanej-k' op-ot to noxtoke,*
          "What's more, you're also a dispute settler.
52   *"k'u `onox ti mu xavich' aba ta muk'e*   E
          "Why don't you act like a grown person?
53   *"yechuke `ali vo' ot xa nox jtzitzvanejot yechuke"*   P
          . *xu:t la 'ox*
          "You should really be the one doing the punishing, if things
              were as they should be," he evidently told him then.

Here, t has conjured a picture of the dispute settler showering the guilty husband
with hard words, threatening him with jail and punishment, and admonishing him
for not behaving himself, all the while preventing him from offering excuses or
protestations. In Bakhtinian terms, there is a complex and shifting implied *addressivity* built into this speech: t puts into the magistrate's mouth a parallel couplet (at
line 45); a somewhat hesitant couplet that starts with plain repetition (line 47 recy-
cles line 46) and builds to a parallel construction ("your wife is goint to jail you,
she'll jail you a few days, you'll be punished"). He repeats the same words ("why
don't you show some self-respect?") at lines 50 and 52—perhaps once in the wife's
voice, and then in his own. In both cases, he continues with a reminder that the
narrated addressee is himself supposed to be a dispute settler (*jmeltzanej-k' op* 'fixer
of disputes' //*jtzitzvanej* 'punisher, scolder').

Thus, even in narrative about disputes, the disputatious language is so arranged
as to index iconically both (narrated) social disorder and, at least in this case, an
emerging order.

Dimensions of Order in the Rhetoric of Matrimony

Here we reach the ultimate "casting into words" and "linearization into discourse"
that I promised at the outset of this essay. No longer can it be imagined that textual
"presentation" of "events" is a matter merely of finding the correct words to go
with referents, or of lining up clauses in temporal or developmental sequences. From
the first words addressed to bride and groom in the embracer's exhortation, to the
last represented words about other people's words about marriage, in gossip, the
discourses of marriage have tried to bring "events" *into* order, casting a selective
eye over details and trying to extract what one might call a textually coherent
account.

The ethnographic distillate of this excursion into marital discourse in Zinacantán is, therefore, far from unexpected. It constitutes a cultural theory that inheres in

possible discourse. Whereas marriage joins celebrants (and their families) in a 'meeting // a union,' in their 'house // treasury,' it does so by 'seating // bending the knee of the bride,' who must thus accommodate herself to the strangeness and potential hostility of her husband's household. The responsible woman's lot centers on the hearth: the firewood that fuels it, and the tortillas it produces. The responsible man's lot is his work, at home or abroad, and a measure of self-restraint, neither squandering the 'corn // the money' of their communal wealth, nor demanding the impossible of his partner. Orderly social life thus depends partly on the bride and groom themselves, who must "measure themselves" as men // women, but also on the one word // two words and wisdom of the elders. Departures from this orderly image of life represent insurrections and indulgences that must be suppressed.

Jane Collier, following Barkun (1968), depicts law, in Zinacantán and elsewhere, as a kind of language, a "system of manipulable symbols that function as a representation, as a model, of social structure" (Collier 1973:257). The model, in turn, is used for "conceptualizing and managing the social environment," partly through the decisions people make about what parts of it to marshall, what language to employ, in formulating the terms of disputes.

Notice, however, that the semiotic processes in the discourses of marriage (which surface as well in the legal discourse of the Zinacanteco *cabildo* 'courthouse') inevitably involve more than mere "representation." Just as culturally *ratified* discourse in Zinacantán provides only certain "representational" vocabulary, within which the images of parallel couplets have special privilege and authority, so, too, does it enable only certain voices. Bourdieu's critical move from "linguistic competence" to "linguistic capital," from "symbolic interaction" to "relations of symbolic power," rests on the analytical fact of what he calls "censorship." Whereas "the linguist regards the *conditions for the establishment of communication* as already secured . . . in real situations, that is the essential question. . . . Among the most radical, surest, and best hidden censorships are those which exclude certain individuals [or, we might add, by extension, certain *voices*] from communication. . . " (1982b:648). Moreover, suppression of voices can take radically different forms. The hegemony of marital rhetoric surfaces in other sorts of silence, as when a powerful political figure's own marital scandal simply never finds its way into the courthouse (although it does surface in furtive gossip).

Bourdieu goes on to suggest that there is a direct connection between the general conditions of "linguistic production"—centrally including censorship—and linguistic form.

> The particular form of the linguistic production relationship governs the particular content and form of the expression, whether "colloquial" or "correct," "public" or "formal," imposes moderation, euphemism and prudence (*e.g.* the use of stereotyped formulae to avoid the risk of improvisation), and distributes speaking times and therefore the rhythm and range of discourse. . . . In other words, the

form and content of discourse depend on the capacity to express the expressive interests attached to a position within the limits of the constraints of the censorship that is imposed on the occupant of that position, *i.e.* with the required *formality*. (Bourdieu 1982b:656–57)

I am now in a position to summarize the iconic relationship I have argued to obtain between Zinacanteco marital order—a culturally construed social formation—and aspects of discursive form. There are at least three aspects to this iconicity.

1. First, there is a continuum of order in what I may call *code form*. The rhetoric of marriage transforms the disorderly, extemporaneous, perhaps halting speech of ordinary conversation or of argument—with ordinary words and everyday connotations—first into the measured, parallelistic constructions of careful, sober talk, and ultimately, into the pristine couplet imagery of ritual language, the quintessential order of Tzotzil as code. Another applicable metaphorical dimension, analogous to order, is "distance." The words of marital squabbles are drawn from a conceptual field close to the raw experience of domestic discord; the paired doublets and triplets of ritual language, on the other hand, even when applied to matrimonial matters, exhibit both cultural generality and conceptual abstraction. Observe the movement, on both the dimensions of order and of distance, between, say, the complaint 'He yelled at me and blackened my eye' and the denunciation 'I am victim of his scolding // I am victim of his beating'.

2. Similarly, there is a dimension of *sequential form*, that is, what conversation analysts call "sequential organization." The disordered shouting, the anarchic interruption, the uncontrolled overlap of fights and arguments, give way over the course of a marital squabble first to the orderly dialogic of normally responsive Tzotzil conversation (Haviland 1988b), which leads ultimately to the flowing, perhaps simultaneous and multiple, monologic streams of ritual language. As in prayer and greeting, the ritual style even in dispute settlement promotes a highly ordered sequential rhythm: if there are multiple participants, their speech is synchronized, their overlaps managed, and their contributions sequentially coordinated.

3. Finally, the evolving discourses of marriage produce order in *social form*. The social organization of talk, in and about marriage, produces a range of *voices*, ordered, contextualized, differentially evaluated, and differentially *effective*. A dispute, for instance, may begin with the subversive back talk of an angry wife, or the defensive excuses of a guilty husband. Such clamoring personal, or private, voices are gradually suppressed behind the unanimity and authority of certain *public* voices: dispute settlers, parents, and elders. In fact, this third dimension of order necessarily encompasses the previous two. It invokes code form because the morally authoritative voice is, by definition, the voice that controls the authoritative style: the legislating images of couplets and ritual, where the aesthetically and culturally valorized genres have ipso facto moral weight. The social dimension of order also encompasses sequential form, through the imposition of silence; the authoritative voices of public dispute

settlers drown out the personal voices of disputants. (Or they serve as the only sustaining thread around which alternate, offstage, whispered, possibly subversive, voices can weave themselves—as in the case of the father, talking in counterpoint to the embracer's wedding exhortation, or the beaten wife sliding her barbed comments in between the words of elders.) In the end, private individuals may be analysed to have no voice at all. Accordingly, the ultimate order appears in the univocality of ritual specialists: those whose words capture the world as it is supposed to be and whose mouths, therefore, we borrow.

Notes

Material analyzed here formed part of a seminar presented to the Department of Anthropology, University of California, Los Angeles, in March 1988; a paper delivered in the session organized by Charles Briggs, Narrative Resources for the Creation of Order and Disorder, at the American Ethnological Society Meeting, St. Louis, March 25, 1988; and an Anthropology Department Colloquium, Harvard University, March 6, 1989. I am indebted to Carlitos Briggs, Sally McLendon, and to an anonymous reader for suggestions. I am also grateful for a grant from the Harry Frank Guggenheim Foundation and a fellowship from the Center for Advanced Study in the Behavioral Sciences in 1985–1986, which provided the opportunity to work on Tzotzil argument. As usual, my greatest debt is to my *compadres*, friends, and neighbors of Nabenchauk for being faithful, patient teachers, and especially to Professor Evon Z. Vogt, to whom I should like to dedicate this essay.

1. 'A circle on a blackboard, a right triangle, a rhombus: these are shapes that we can fully intuit; the same thing was true for Ireneo with the windblown mane of a foal, with a herd of cattle in a narrow pass, with the changing fire and the countless ash, with the many faces of a corpse in a long wake' (my translation).
2. My favorite example of this mix of explicit and implicit discursive evidence is the following passage about the Trio.

It has been noted that divorce frequently occurs when a man takes a second wife, and this is the reason which women normally give for leaving a man. However, on the other side of the coin, a man often takes a second wife because of the inadequacies of the first. Inadequacy is either barrenness or failure, of either spouse, to fulfil their duties in the economic partnership of marriage.

Tasi (252) said that she had left her husband Tepepuru (245) because he had taken a second wife. Tepepuru, on the other hand, said that she is lazy. I can vouch for this from my own experience, and add that she is a slut and that her bread is repulsive. (Rivière 1969:166–67)

Students of marriage in other disciplines share with many anthropologists a proclivity for trying to extract *facts* about marriage (or divorce) from situated discourse whose own nature is often unexamined. See, for example, the use of counseling interviews by classic family therapists (Mowrer 1928), or the relatively more sophisticated use of "divorce documents" (i.e., family law records) by social historians (Griswold 1982; Phillips 1980).

3. For a non–Meso-American example of the work on parallelism spawned by Jakobsonian poetics (Jakobson 1985), see, for example, Fox 1977.

4. In 1972, when I was preparing to be a *jpetom* myself, I sought special instruction (from the late Chep Nuj of Nachij) in the proper prayers for a wedding, from which these fragments are drawn.

5. The words *alab // nich'nab* (in lines 5/11/14) are archaic roots for children, not used in nonritual contexts in Zinacanteco Tzotzil.

6. See Haviland (1987, 1994) for a more detailed treatment of the creative possibilities of "ritual language" in apparently "nonritual" circumstances.

7. Notice that the word *k'op* 'word, language', also has the meaning 'fight, dispute', or, indeed, in general, 'affair'.

8. In fact, research by both Collier (1968, 1973:199) and Leslie Devereaux (1987) suggests that many women, especially widows and divorcées, *prefer* to live alone in Zinacantán, eking out an impoverished but unencumbered existence.

9. Thus, the "dangerous words" in the title of Brenneis and Meyers 1984 may be designed to shake up political, or even ritual, affairs, whatever the official appearance of orderliness.

10. For a somewhat different treatment of this passage, see Haviland (1989).

11. This is an almost canonical case, in Zinacantán, where drunkenness seems a *necessary* prerequisite to beating. Drunkenness is offered as a standard excuse for misbehavior in Zinacantán (Bricker 1973; Collier 1973; Haviland 1977a). The standard Tzotzil idiom suggests that someone can *ch'ay*, that is, 'lose (awareness)', a state in which one may walk and talk as well as perform other, more sinister, movements, about which no memory will remain. Structurally, then, drunkenness can be seen as a blanket response to various private aggravations—a wife who talks back, a neighbor who slights one or steals—which, in turn, enables an equally outrageous public act: beating the wife, publicly upbraiding the neighbor, and so on, while inebriated.

12. Many Zinacantec men exchange wealth for prestige by embarking on a series of *cargos*, years during which they care for saint images and perform other ritual duties, usually at considerable personal expense. Only married men can hold such ritual office. See Cancian (1965).

13. And, of course, there can be deeper levels of embedded speech, or higher orders of discourse. See, for example, the multiple layers of Kuna reported speech detailed by Sherzer (1983).

14. Tzotzil has its fair share of such verbs, including some with affective and metapragmatic tinges: not just *-chi* and *-al* 'say', or *-ut* 'tell' (also 'shout, scold'), but also these in combination with appropriate forms based on such explicit onomatopoeic roots as *'ov* 'shout', *'i'* 'babble, stutter, wail, cry', and *'a'* 'sigh, say "ah"', mumble to self', etcetera. More concrete metaphors (striking people verbal blows, peeling their skin with insults, or sticking them with accusations) are also available.

15. One drunken New Year's Eve, I helped put two elderly siblings to bed after a lengthy ritual in Zinacantán. One, the man, had been serving as ritual adviser to a religious official, a post that required him to display, publicly, his skills at formal prayer. His aged sister—neither curer nor officeholder, but drunk on the liquor she had consumed serving as cook for special ritual foods—mocked her brother for his drunkenness, saying: "You think

only *you* know how to talk; but I, too, know one or two words.'' She thereafter fell asleep, giggling, and pouring out a torrent of fluent ritual couplets.

16. There are similarities here to the restrictive, legally circumscribed nature of legal representation—or the canons of "evidence"—in Western legal systems. See Berk-Seligson (1988), Conley and O'Barr (1988), and O'Barr (1982); Haviland (1988a) discusses the consequences of this discursive manipulation in a criminal trial.

Works Cited

Aissen, Judith. 1987. *Tzotzil clause structure*. Dordrecht: Reidel.

Atkinson, J. M., and John Heritage. 1984. *Structures of social action*. Cambridge: Cambridge University Press.

Bakhtin, Mikahil. 1981. *The dialogic imagination: Four essays*. Austin: University of Texas Press.

———. 1986. *Speech genres and other late essays*. Austin: University of Texas Press.

Banfield, Ann. 1982. *Unspeakable sentences: Narration and representation in the language of fiction*. Boston: Routledge and Kegan Paul.

Barkun, Michael. 1968. *Law without sanctions: Order in primitive societies and the world community*. New Haven, CT: Yale University Press.

Bauman, Richard. 1977. *Verbal art as performance*. Prospect Heights, IL: Waveland Press.

———. 1986. *Story, performance and event: Contextual studies of oral narrative*. Cambridge: Cambridge University Press.

Benveniste, Emile. 1974. *Problemes de linguistique generale*. Paris: Editions Gallimard.

Berk-Seligson, Susan. 1988. The impact of politeness in witness testimony: The influence of the court interpreter. *Multilingua* 7:411–40.

Borges, Jorge Luis. 1974. *Obras completas*. Buenos Aires: Emece Editoriales.

Bourdieu, Pierre. 1982a. *Ce que parler veut dire*. Paris: Fayard.

———. 1982b [1974]. The economics of linguistic exchanges. *Social Science Information* 16:645–58.

Brenneis, Donald, and Fred Meyers, eds. 1984. *Dangerous words: Language and politics in the Pacific*. New York: New York University Press.

Bricker, Victoria R. 1973. *Ritual humor in Highland Chiapas*. Austin: University of Texas Press.

———. 1974. The ethnographic context of some traditional Mayan speech genres. In *Explorations in the ethnography of speaking*, ed. Richard Bauman and Joel Sherzer, pp. 368–88. Cambridge: Cambridge University Press.

Briggs, Charles L. 1986. *Learning how to ask: A sociolinguistic appraisal of the role of the interview in social science research*. Cambridge: Cambridge University Press.

Cancian, Frank. 1965. *Economics and prestige in a Maya community: The religious cargo system in Zinacantan*. Stanford, CA: Stanford University Press.

Collier, Jane F. 1968. Courtship and marriage in Zinacantan. *Middle American Research Institute Publication* 25:139–201.

———. 1973. *Law and social change in Zinacantan*. Stanford, CA: Stanford University Press.

Collier, Jane F., Michelle Rosaldo, and Sylvia Yanagisako. 1982. Is there a family? New anthropological views. In *Rethinking the family: Some feminist questions*, ed. Barrie Thorne and Marilyn Yalom, pp. 25–39. New York: Longman.

Conley, John M., and William M. O'Barr. 1988. Fundamentals of jurisprudence: An ethnography of judicial decision making in informal courts. *The North Carolina Law Review* 66:467–507.

Devereaux, Leslie. 1987. Gender difference and the relations of inequality in Zinacantan. In *Dealing with inequality*, ed. Marilyn Strathern, pp. 89–111. Cambridge: Cambridge University Press.

Edmonson, Munroe S. 1971. *The book of counsel: The Popol Vuh of the Quiche Maya of Guatemala*. New Orleans: Middle American Research Institute.

Fox, James J. 1977. Roman Jakobson and the comparative study of parallelism. In *Roman Jakobson: Echoes of his scholarship*, ed. D. Armstrong and C. H. van Schooneveld, pp. 59–90. Lisse, The Netherlands: Peter de Ridder.

Garibay K., Angel Maria. 1953. *Historia de la literatura Náhuatl*. Mexico City: Porrua.

Goffman, Erving. 1974. *Frame analysis: An essay on the organization of experience*. New York: Harper Colophon Books.

———. 1983a. *Forms of talk*. Philadelphia: University of Pennsylvania Press.

———. 1983b. The interaction order. *American Sociological Review* 48:1–17.

Gossen, Gary H. 1985. Tzotzil literature. In *Supplement to the Handbook of Middle American Indians*, vol 3, ed. Victoria R. Bricker and Munro Edmonson, pp. 65–106. Austin: University of Texas Press.

Griswold, Robert L. 1982. *Family and divorce in California, 1850–1890*. Albany: State University of New York Press.

Hanks, William. 1988. Grammar, style and meaning in a Maya manuscript. *International Journal of American Linguistics* 54:331–64.

———. 1993. Metalanguage and pragmatics of deixis. In *Reflexive language: Reported speech and metapragmatics*, ed. John Lucy, pp. 127–58. Cambridge: Cambridge University Press.

Haviland, John B. 1977a. Gossip as competition in Zinacantan. *Journal of Communication* 27:186–91.

———. 1977b. *Gossip, reputation and knowledge in Zinacantan*. Chicago: University of Chicago Press.

———. 1981. Sk'op Sotz'leb: *El Tzotzil de San Lorenzo Zinacantán*. Mexico City: Universidad Nacional Autónoma de México.

———. 1988a. Minimal maxims: Cooperation and natural conversation in Zinacantan. *Estudios Mexicanos/Mexican Studies* 4:79–114.

———. 1988b. A father-mother talks back: The micro-creation of context in Tzotzil. Paper presented at the Workshop on Contextualization of Language, Konstänz, Germany, October 1988.

———. 1989. Sure, sure: Evidence and affect. *Text* 9:27–68.

———. 1994. Lenguaje ritual sin ritual. *Estudios de Cultura Maya* 19:427–42.

Haviland, John B., and Lourdes de León. 1988. "Me tengo que tragar mis broncas (I have to swallow my problems)." Paper presented at the Annual Meeting of the American Anthropological Association, Phoenix, Arizona, November 1988.

Haviland, Leslie K., and John B. Haviland. 1983. Privacy in a Mexican village. In *Public and private in social life*, ed. Stanley I. Benn and Gerald F. Gauss, pp. 341–61. London: Croom Helm.

Hill, Jane, and Judith T. Irvine, eds. 1992. *Responsibility and evidence in oral discourse*. Cambridge: Cambridge University Press.

Irvine, Judith T. 1979. Formality and informality in communicative events. *American Anthropologist* 81(4):773–99.

Jakobson, Roman. 1980 [1956]. Metalanguage as a linguistic problem. In *The framework of language*, pp. 81–92. Ann Arbor: University of Michigan Press.

———. 1985 [1980]. *Verbal art, verbal sign, verbal time*, ed. K. Pomorska and S. Rudy. Minneapolis: University of Minnesota Press.

Labov, William. 1972. *Language in the inner city*. Philadelphia: University of Pennsylvania Press.

Laughlin, Robert M. 1963. *Through the looking glass: Reflections on Zinacantan courtship and marriage*. Doctoral dissertation, Harvard University.

Lucy, John, ed. 1993. *Reflexive language: Reported speech and metapragmatics*. Cambridge: Cambridge University Press.

Mowrer, Ernest R. 1928. *Domestic discord: Its analysis and treatment*. Chicago: University of Chicago Press.

Needham, Rodney, ed. 1971. *Rethinking kinship and marriage*. London: Tavistock.

O'Barr, William M. 1982. *Linguistic evidence: Language, power, and strategy in the courtroom*. New York: Academic Press.

Phillips, Roderick. 1980. *Family breakdown in late eighteenth-century France. Divorces in Rouen 1792–1803*. Oxford: Clarendon.

Reisman, Karl. 1974. Contrapuntal conversation in an Antiguan village. In *Explorations in the ethnography of speaking*, ed. Richard Bauman and Joel Sherzer, pp. 110–24. Cambridge: Cambridge University Press.

Rivière, Peter. 1969. *Marriage among the Trio: A principle of social organisation*. Oxford: Clarendon.

Sherzer, Joel. 1983. *Kuna ways of speaking: An ethnographic perspective*. Austin: University of Texas Press.

Silverstein, Michael. 1976. Shifters, linguistic categories, and cultural description. In *Meaning in anthropology*, ed. Keith H. Basso and Henry A. Selby, pp. 11–56. Albuquerque: University of New Mexico Press.

———. 1985. The culture of language in Chinookan narrative texts; or, on saying that . . . in Chinook. In *Grammar inside and outside the clause: Some approaches from the field*, ed. Johanna Nichols and Anthony Woodbury, pp. 132–74. New York: Cambridge University Press.

Urban, Greg. 1986. Ceremonial dialogues in South America. *American Anthropologist* 88:371–86.

Vogt, Evon Z. 1969. *Zinacantan: A Maya community in the Highlands of Chiapas*. Cambridge, MA: Harvard University Press.

———. 1976. *Tortillas for the gods: A symbolic analysis of Zinacanteco rituals*. Cambridge, MA: Harvard University Press.

Vološinov, V. N. 1986. *Marxism and the philosophy of language*, translated by L. Matejka and I. R. Titinuk. Cambridge, MA: Harvard University Press.

Conflict, Language Ideologies, and Privileged Arenas of Discursive Authority in Warao Dispute Mediation

This essay reflects on a series of puzzles posed by a particular convergence of conflict and narrative. It focuses on some angry conversations and actions that marked the breakup of a marriage and their transformation into a dispute mediation that involved an entire community. Why would community officials focus so much attention on a particular conflict, particularly since the relationship had already been severed? Why do collective senses of the fragility of social order become so closely associated with representations of particular social interactions? To ask this question in a different way, how do specific interactional features become powerful synecdoches of broader relations of social inequality?

My focus is on meetings called to mediate conflict in indigenous communities in the Delta Amacuro of eastern Venezuela, but the issues they raise are not restricted to Warao dispute mediation. Some specific disputes that have emerged in recent years—such as the Thomas–Hill Senate confirmation hearings, the trials of four Los Angeles Police Department officers for the beating of Rodney King, and the murder trial of O. J. Simpson—have catalyzed new imaginations of race, gender, and class in the United States; as images of these events were circulated globally via television and the print media, their influence was felt transnationally.

I thus begin with a few words about the ethnographic case and the general questions I feel emerge from it. In eastern Venezuela, at the mouth of the Orinoco River, live some 21,000 people who speak an indigenous language called Warao; many speak Spanish as well, while others speak English. They generally refer to themselves as *indígenas* 'indigenous persons', and specifically as Warao. In their communities, conflicts often give rise to meetings known as *monikata nome anaka*, which can be glossed simply as dispute mediations. In this case and others like it, I find the subtle and complex dynamics of authority, power, and gender to be particularly compelling. *Monikata nome anaka* are about as egalitarian a discourse event as I have seen in Warao communities in that all parties to the conflict are accorded the right to tell their side of the story. The competing narratives that emerge focus a great deal on talk, recounting who said what to whom at which point, and on the way that what was said created conflict. Some ways that people talk and conceptualize discourse are judged to be 'good' and 'truly Warao', while the 'bad' varieties purportedly spark disputes. The differential distribution of these different ways of using language afford certain individuals much greater access to the most authoritative ways of talking than is enjoyed by other participants; here women are at a distinct disadvantage vis-à-vis men, particularly senior men. I am interested both in the way this differential access to discourse forms undercuts the ideal equality of disputants in mediation as well as some of the ways that women seek to overcome these limitations.

The attention that is directed in *monikata nome anaka* to the way that discursive concepts and practices relate to the social fabric reflects as much on the officials who stage them as on the disputants. Indeed, the prestige and authority of local leaders is on the line in these events; if conflicts are not successfully mediated in this fashion, people may start thinking about placing new individuals in charge. So here we have a privileged and precarious arena for discursive interaction. Language, authority, and notions of social order are not simply given, stable properties of "speech communities" and "social structures"; contestation surrounds not just questions as to which individuals are going to occupy dominant positions but the ways that dominance and subordination are constructed. How are persons who exercise authority able to construct this particular discursive sphere as a model of order—and of language use? How are they able to control the way that conflicts are represented in this privileged sphere and then use their success as a means of regulating the relationship among discourse, order, and conflict in society generally? Finally, what are the political limits of such control?

Similar issues have been raised through examination of the creation of a privileged sphere of discourse within civil society—the public sphere. Jürgen Habermas (1989 [1962]) argued that the emergence of a new social formation, the bourgeoisie, was tied to the construction of a discursive arena that favored disinterested, rational, public speech. A number of critics have suggested that public spheres are constituted as much by the way they *exclude* particular social groups, discursive forms, and issues as by their imagined openness and equality; it has also been suggested that we should think in terms of multiple, competing public spheres rather than one monolithic and homogenous arena (Calhoun 1992; Hansen 1993; Landes 1988; Lee 1993; Negt and Kluge 1993). As is the case with Anderson's (1991 [1983]) work on nationalism, Pierre Bourdieu's (1991) discussion of the linguistic marketplace, and Antonio Gramsci's (1971) conceptualization cultural hegemony, both Habermas's initial framework and critical reformulations have focused a great deal of scholarly attention on the co-construction of social formations (classes, nations, ethnic groups, and the like), privileged discursive arenas, and dominant forms of discourse.

A recent collection of essays by linguistic anthropologists points to the need to document the role of historical and sociocultural contexts and everyday practices in the creation of publics and political authority (Gal and Woolard 1995). The contribution of linguistic anthropologists to discussions of public spheres draws upon research that focuses on ideologies of language. Silverstein (1979, 1981, 1985) argued that the views that speakers hold of their language(s) and how they are used—no matter how naive or wrongheaded they may seem to linguistic professionals—have important effects on linguistic structure and usage. A number of researchers have suggested that scholars, including linguists, also rely on linguistic ideologies and that these ideologies are interested, that is, are shaped by historically and socially situated agendas (see Joseph and Talbot 1990; Kroskrity, Schieffelin, and Woolard 1992). Some researchers have conceptualized ideologies of language in terms of modernist notions of culture, namely, as a set of shared ideas that are distributed homogeneously among a particular population (see, e.g., Rosaldo 1983). Most scholars have now adopted the view that *multiple* ideologies of language are evident in any social group and that their contestation is of great political significance.

This point brings the discussion back to the question of the social production of privileged discursive arenas. Such spheres are dynamic and contested by virtue of the way they coexist and often compete with other discursive realms. Their dynamism also emerges through the important role in their creation and defense played by processes of authorizing one or more ideologies of language at the same time that others are delegitimated or subordinated. Indeed, when substantial consensus is apparent with regard to the legitimacy of a particular ideology, the analyst must ask how such agreement is constructed, how it gets associated with specific classes, groups, races, and so forth, and what means have been used in subordinating competing ideologies. Brenneis's essay in this volume suggests that the "confidential committee" that structures *pancayat* attempts to preclude the emergence of discourses that do not adhere to its prescriptions. In the United States small-claims courts analyzed by O'Barr and Conley, on the other hand, both rule-oriented and relational orientations are allowed to coexist; the judge's participation nevertheless attempts to pull litigants closer to the former pole, and decisions reflect this discursive hierarchy as well.

Officials operate somewhat differently in the *monikata nome anaka* that take place in Warao communities. While the oratorical discourse referred to as 'counseling speech' is privileged, disputants are required to give voice to the angry words that were spoken in the course of the conflict. Since contestations of language ideologies and discursive practices are often believed to have played a central role in creating the conflict, how can such juxtapositions be managed in the course of events that are socially constructed as a means of 'making them straight'? If 'bad speech' embodies disorder, how can its elicitation serve the interests of individuals who must impose order if they are to retain their positions of authority? How can persons who do not occupy these dominant roles draw on subordinate language ideologies in creating strategic advantage? In taking up these questions, I will turn to the dispute between a woman and her estranged husband.

Monikata Nome Anaka

Warao generally live on tributaries of the Orinoco River. Some Warao live in residential units of one or more houses; others are grouped into communities that may include several hundred persons. Leadership is invested in the *aidamo* 'elders' or 'officials',[1] male medico-religious practitioners and political officials, who are generally 50 to 70 years of age. Larger communities are usually led by a *kobenahoro* 'governor' who is assisted by one or more *kabitana* 'captains' and *bisikari* (from the Spanish *fiscal*). (Although I will use English glosses in designating these officials, the terms should be interpreted as standing for their Warao counterparts.) While these offices are chosen by consensus within communities and generally ratified during *nahanamu* ceremonies, a *komisario* 'commissioner' chosen by government officials has displaced the *kobenahoro* and his subordinates in other communities; *komisario* represent the dictates of the nation-state more directly. The coexistence between these competing models of leadership points to the way that authority and the bases through which it is constructed are highly contested in many Warao communities. Elders oversee projects undertaken by the community as a whole, including maintenance of the *hoisi* 'bridges'; these provide access between houses, an important consideration when houses are built on stilts above the mud and water. They also take charge of small fishing or rice cultivation projects that ideally produce income through sale of the fruits to *hotarao* 'hill dwellers' (i.e., Spanish-speaking non-Warao).

An important component of the role of the elders is maintaining order within the community. If village life is frequently disturbed by intra- or inter-household strife and the elders are unsuccessful in resolving these problems, the residents are likely to complain that *kaidamo ekida diana* 'we no longer have any elders'. The elders have a number of sociolinguistic resources at their disposal for use in preserving order. One is the early morning address delivered by one or two elders. Beginning before the first light of day is visible (between about 4:00 and 5:30 A.M.), an elder begins speaking and often singing from inside his house. Given the absence of walls in most Warao houses, the members of adjacent households can easily listen. These early morning discourses generally include exhortation and discussion of the day's work; curers often report their dreams and sing powerful songs. Exhortations are also delivered in a variety of other contexts. They emerge in the course of such ritual cycles as those of the *nahanamu*, which celebrates the return of the ancestral spirits to the community during the palm starch harvest (cf. Barral 1964). Similarly, couples planning marriage are formally questioned by elders and by relatives, and exhortations regarding proper conduct are delivered.

A process that is particularly crucial to maintaining order within the community is referred to as *monikata nome naka-*. *Monikata* is used in reference to personal problems, interpersonal strife, the guilt of a particular person in creating such a problem, and punishments that are meted out by the elders as a consequence of the establishment of guilt.[2] *Nome* can be glossed as 'straight', 'true', or 'proper'. *Naka-* is a very productive verb that can be glossed as 'to arrive at or be placed in a particular state'. It is used in the phrase both nominatively (*anaka*) and verbally (*naka-*), referring, respectively, to specific proceedings and to the process in general. Taken as a whole, *monikata nome anaka* refers to the process by which elders attempt to resolve interpersonal problems in the setting of a dispute mediation. Many such conflicts involve the members of a single household, and problems between couples, siblings, and siblings-in-law occur frequently. Inter-household disputes, especially as catalyzed by gossip or accusations, are also common. *Monikata nome anaka* are sometimes prompted by claims that a particular curer has killed or is attempting to kill (magically) a member of the community.

The process begins when one or more individuals publicly declare the existence of a dispute in the presence of an elder. Such revelations may come when a woman expresses a grievance as she goes about her work; the message is marked by a combination of great volume and either creaky voice or pharyngeal constriction. Parties to a dispute commonly bring the conflict to light by going to the house of an elder, generally the highest-ranking official in the community, and engaging him in a dialogue; the visitor tells the story of the dispute, while the elder acts as respondent. In some cases, the participants decide that this event constitutes a sufficient means of dealing with the problem, and nothing further will be done. If the dispute involves persons under about 25 years of age, the visit may be made by the father or mother's brother of one of the disputants.

If the elder considers the situation sufficiently serious, he will call together all the officials. Since the governor and/or other officials may be off in Barrancas or Tucupita (administrative and trade centers on the edge of the delta), fishing, collecting palm starch, and so on, for a week or more at a time, exactly which officials are present in the community at any given time fluctuates. If the elders decide that the formal dispute mediation process should be invoked, it will generally be held that evening in the home of an official. The process begins when the elders send an envoy to announce to each involved party: *ihi monikata ha* 'you are involved in a dispute'. The elders each take a hammock, while the house fills with the disputants, witnesses, relatives, and other members of the community.

A Case From Nabasanuka

The *monikata nome anaka* that I will describe is one of seven that I have tape recorded; I have also observed two others. The recorded discourse amounts to about eight hours. Two *monikata nome anaka* took place in Nabaribuhu, a community that is located in a moriche palm forest in the Mariusa area of the central delta, while another occurred in the same region at the mouth of the Mariusa River. Two others were recorded in Murako, a community of several hundred residents located to the south and east of the central delta. The last two were recorded in Nabasanuka. The residents of Nabasanuka have been more heavily influenced by the predominant (criollo) Venezuelan society because of the presence of a mission house and small chapel there. One of the most striking features of speech in this community is the prevalence of Warao-Spanish code switching, and this is quite apparent in the transcripts. Although this *monikata nome anaka* shares a common set of basic elements with those that I observed and recorded elsewhere, variations in details of procedures are evident from situation to situation, elder to elder, and community to community.

The highest-ranking official, the governor or commissioner, may or may not preside; it is his privilege to assign a subordinate to the task. The designated official inaugurates the proceedings with an exhortation regarding the purpose of the meeting or ceremony. The next step involves calling one of the parties to the dispute forward to tell a narrative that expresses his or her view of the conflict and the events that gave rise to it. The Nabasanuka *monikata nome anaka* was held out of doors, and chairs from the local school were provided for both narrators and officials. The official elicits a narrative from each of the disputants by asking a question, often prefaced by an exhortation. If the involved parties are under about 25 years of age, parents, grandparents, and/or other relatives may narrate on their behalf.

The *monikata nome anaka* on which I have chosen to focus was directed by the Commissioner, the most influential official in Nabasanuka; he was assisted by a *burisia* 'policeman'. It deals with a separation between a young woman and an older man who had been married previously; I will refer to them as María and Diego. The two officials sat in two of the three available chairs. Diego and María were called in turn to take the remaining chair and tell their story, and they faced the Commissioner most of the time as they spoke. About 80 members of the community gathered around the officials and disputants, and with the exception of small children, they paid close attention to the proceedings. I will present extensive quotations from the words of the three central participants—husband, Commissioner, and wife—in the order in which they appear in the proceedings.

The Husband's Narrative

The first person to be called in this dispute was the husband. His narrative describes a number of interactions with his wife a short time before the proceedings; he takes particular care in using direct discourse in dramatizing key exchanges. He characterizes his wife as lazy, unwilling to help him cut firewood, and often failing to prepare food for the family. He notes that early on the morning that the fight erupted he sat in his hammock and began to think out loud about how he could provide for his family. He then stood up, left the house, and witnessed the following scene[3]:

(1) *Husband's narrative*

1 *Tai sina, katukane ine kate diana?*
What could it be, how could it also happen to me?

2 *Hebu obonona tai diana,*
It must be the fault of some evil spirit,

3 *tatamo barí takore, ine dibuyaha miae araisama akohoko eku.*
that on turning around I saw [my wife] whispering into her friend's ear.

4 *Tuatane mikore, daisa mikore, hawaneraha mikore, kʷana dibukitane ha.*
On seeing something like this, on seeing someone else, on seeing something terrifying, one must speak out.

5 *Araisama akohoko eku dibuyaha sike ine miae diana.*
Whispering into the ear of another was just what I saw.

6 *Taitane ine denokoae: "Ihi sina miae? Ihi hawaneraha miae, mohoro."*
Afterwards I asked: "What did you see? Perhaps you saw something quite terrifying."

7 *Debué ine yehebuae, "ihi sina miae?*
I then called to her, "What did you see?

8 *Ihi hawaneraha miae, mohoro."*
Perhaps you saw something quite terrifying."

9 *Mawerea hakanae; ine ayamo soronae tanae.*
She ran by me; I looked in the direction from which she had come.

10 *"Ihi sina miae?"*
"What did you see?"

11 *Debué ine diboto ehobonae;*
Afterward, I went outside to see what was going on;

12 *ah! estaba sentao, ahi donde vino ella,*
ah! he was sitting over there in the direction from which she had come,

13 *ahi no tiene nada, ni una muchacha kate ekida tanae.*
there was no one else over there, and there wasn't a girl there either.

Diego reports that he continues to question María; she later replies as follows.

14 *Debué nome dibunae, "no, ine dibunae—a la muchacha Gladys.*
Afterward, she really said to me, "No, I was only talking about—the girl, Gladys.

15 *Yo hablé, Gladys isia dibunae."*
I was talking about, I was talking about Gladys."

16 *Iboma tatuka kate ekida.*
There wasn't any girl over there either.

17 *Tamaha mi, diana yari ahotana.*
Look, this is where I started getting mad.

18 *"Ah, ihi tuatia mohoro.*
"Ah, so I guess that's the way you are.

19 *Bueno, ihi tuatiaha sike obonoya."*
Okay, you want a [young] man just like him."

20 *Tatuka ine yo sabahiae diana.*
That's when I chided her.

21 *Sabahiae, sabahiae, sabahia; tai onae diana.*
   I chided her and I chided her and I chided her; she began to cry.

22 *"Ah! Bueno, ama sike hiabate!"*
   "Ah! Fine, I'm going to leave you right now!"

Diego complains that he has undeservedly gained a reputation as a jealous man. He continues with his narration, noting that María then moved her hammock away from his, saying that she planned to leave him. Feeling miserable and lonely, Diego was unable to get to sleep that night. He reports his attempt to end the fight later in the night.

23 *Desbué, kʷare naruae.*
   Afterward, I went over to her.

24 *"Mira, doña, hiobonona iabanu.*
   Look, doña, don't keep thinking like this.

25 *Ine hisabahiae maribu aisia, ihi wabanaha, dibu isia wabanaha.*
   I only used words in chiding you, you aren't going to die, a person doesn't die from words.

26 *Ama ine hiahine, dau isia, hiahine, hikʷa ahine,*
   Now if I were to hit you, with a stick, to hit you, to hit you on the head,

27 *ama tane hikʷa marose anoko hane, hihotu nakane,*
   now if I were to have wounded you in the head, spilling your blood,

28 *ama sike bahuka sabuka.*
   now then you would be somewhat justified [in leaving me].

29 *Bueno, hiobonona iabanu, dibu isaka dibuya, matida tihi.*
   Okay, don't keep thinking like this, speak a little, because you are my wife.

30 *Sanuka, sanuka, bueno, dios saba obonobu.*
   Just a little, just a little, okay, think about god.

31 *Diana, diana sanuka ihi obonobukitane ha, ihi Warao tihi.*
   You must think just a little now, because you are a Warao.

32 *Bueno, maribu isia nome, maribu isia,*
   Okay, it's true [that I hurt you] with my words, with my words,

33 *bueno, ihi hiamoara abate, cien bolivares hiamoara abate.*
   okay, I'll pay you for them, I'll pay you 100 Bolivares for them.

34 *Bueno, yo así yaotakore, burata nome anaka himoate."*
   Okay, after I've earned the money, I'll just give it to you."

35 *Awere karamunae.*
   I was standing close to her.

36 *"No, maoanaka!*
   "No, don't touch me!

37 *No, ine hiabanae diana, hiabakitanae diana.*
   No, I've already left you, already left you for good.

38 *Diana ine hiobononaha diana.*
   I don't want you anymore.

39 *Ihiwitu nibora ekida; tai nibora era."*
   You're not the only man around; there are lots of men out there."

The next day, Diego leaves to harvest ocumo, a root crop. He returns hungry, not having eaten in more than a day; his wife is still angry, and has not prepared any food. Still hoping that her anger will cool, he goes fishing. He returns to find María asleep. Since she has not prepared any food, Diego's young daughter (by a previous marriage) is attempting to cook *ure,* a root crop: she is inept, and has failed to skin the tubers. He awakens his wife, prompting her to complain. Enraged at his wife's laziness, Diego tells her that if she leaves him, she will have to give back the clothes that he bought for her; he will need to sell them in order to buy food. María refuses, claiming that the clothing is recompense for her work. She rises from her hammock and begins to tear the clothing to shreds. Diego strikes her; afterward, he leaves home. He justifies his departure by claiming that she is likely to kill him in his sleep if he remains. He states that his wife has been telling everyone that he is so jealous that he locks her inside the house. Diego presents a parody of this gossip in María's voice to the effect that she is forced to bathe and even defecate inside the house. He ironically states that her skin is pale due to lack of exposure to the sun and that marks appear on her body where he has tied her up. He cites her words as the point of origin for all the gossip concerning the situation, and he asserts that he himself never gossiped. He argues that he rather related to his wife in the following manner:

40   *Ine tida iabakitane ana.*
       I am not the sort of person who would leave his wife.
41   *MÁ' BIEN, ine deria, matida tihi.*
       I rather counsel her, since she is my wife.
42   *"MIRA, matida, oko sina katukane tate?*
       "Look, wife of mine, what should we do?
43   *Kayaota kasabukaha, oko katukane naute?*
       How should we make our living, and in what way should we go about it?
44   *Yaotakitane, nahorokitane, uruya kanobotomo tane mikore nahorokitane.*
       So that we can work, so that we can eat, so that we can eat once we have children.
45   *Ine obonobuyaha ine."*
       This is what I've been thinking."

Diego characterizes his wife's response to his counseling by once again assuming her voice.

46   *"Ihi idamowitu diana.*
       "You are already a very old man.
47   *Ihi idamo, hiabate diana, daisa nisate."*
       You're an old man, I'm going to leave you now, I'll marry someone else."

He quotes her as heaping on such abuses as the following.

48   *Madariataya,*
       She insults me,

49   *"ihi Warao asida, Warao horohera, Warao kohokoida, Warao horoana,*
     "You're an awful man, a disgusting man, a large-eared man, an ugly man,

50   *Warao* YO NO SÉ QUÉ.*"*
     an I-don't-know-what-kind-of man.''

He then asserts that no one could like this sort of treatment. He opposes her conduct to an ideal of mutual respect in which wife and husband refrain from pointing out each other's defects. Although Warao are bound by this norm, criollos are characterized as having failed to embrace it. Diego underlines this cultural contrast by noting that he used a loincloth as a child. He again asserts that she is lazy and abusive. He repeats more gossip, which he attributes both to María and to community members in general. He suggests that wives are likely to be unfaithful if they are not adequately counseled. When he again claims that María always called him a very old man, she interrupts very briefly to assert that she only said that after he called her a whore. After proclaiming his love and his intention to be reunited with his wife, he ends his narrative in the following manner.

51   BUENO, AQUÍ COMPAI,[4] *tamaha diana kokotuka.*
     Okay, compadre, that's all I have to say.

52   *Tamaha maribu kokotuka.*
     These words of mine are now complete.

Analysis.   The opening episode in Diego's account provides a good example of the way he constructs his discourse. He begins by describing the setting in general, particularly his concern for providing his family with food. He proceeds to paint a vivid picture of a particular morning in which he lay in his hammock, thinking. For Warao, this image embodies traditional authority. Warao generally wake up before dawn, and they remain in their hammocks until it begins to be light. The oldest man in the household gives voice to his thoughts regarding the tasks to be accomplished during the day, long-range plans, recent events, and the like. In some cases, his senior wife (if he has more than one) will respond, *sotto voce.* Fathers-in-law use these monologues as a means of giving instructions to their sons-in-law for the day's work. Such addresses form an intra-household version of the early morning exhortations delivered by political officials and shamans. This type of speech is regarded as a means of counseling social inferiors, and it is associated with the assertion of authority and with the smooth functioning of collective labor.

    In addition to these contextual markers, counseling speech is marked formally by slow and even speech tempo and a predominance of verbs with future tense suffixes and tenseless verbs with infinitive suffixes. Clauses commonly end with *ha;* when preceded by an infinitive verb, it denotes obligation (*nahorokitane ha* '[s/he] must eat'). When *ha* follows a noun or adjective, it denotes existence (*yaota ha* 'there is work').

Diego draws on another metapragmatic device in framing his reported speech, the quotative construction *Ine obonobuyaha, maobonona isia debuyaha* 'I was thinking, I was saying what was on my mind'. One's *obonobu* (or *obonona*) is the locus of personal identity and the nexus of cognition and affect. It is a personal realm, and individuals have the right to reveal only as much as they choose. To be truly Warao, one must think carefully before speaking or acting. Consideration is to be accorded to the counsel that one has received from parents, relatives, and elders and the potential impact of such speech and action on the *obonobu* of others. Such speech is valued as a means of generating harmonious social relations.

The quoted inner speech is followed by an assertion that his words did not reflect 'anger' (*yari*). Speech that is motivated by anger or 'jealousy' (*miahi*) is antithetical to the other two types, counseling discourse and speech that is based on careful reflection and respect for the *obonobu* of other persons; unlike the first two, jealous or enraged words engender conflict. Diego uses a number of metapragmatic resources, including the portrayal of the setting, the formal characteristics of the quoted speech, and the thinking-speaking frame, in contextualizing his speech as conforming to the counseling and *obonobu* modes of speaking rather than the anger/jealousy mode.

Into this scene enters María. We find that she is not sitting next to her husband in her hammock, listening, but is rather whispering into the ear of another woman. Diego sets his next utterance apart from the narrative sequence and frames it as the sort of moral imperative that emerges in counseling speech (line 4). This is marked formally by three clauses ending in *-kore*, which denotes simultaneity, followed by an infinitive plus *ha*, the 'one must' construction. This provides an example of what I will refer to as a *type-based* metapragmatic construction, meaning that the discourse interprets a class of utterances rather than any token in particular. This is followed by a *token-based* metapragmatic construction that associates the previous assertion with a particular event—his wife's secret (line 5).

Diego has attempted to justify in advance his right to ask his wife to repeat the secret. This step is crucial in that it was his repeated questioning and his wife's refusal to reveal her words that gave rise to the initial quarrel. This is one of the weak points in his account. By trying to force his wife to reveal her *obonobu*, he has violated her privacy and personal autonomy. He accordingly must convince his listeners that his questions were not prompted by jealousy but by a legitimate response to a dangerous situation. He embeds his analysis of the severity of the situation in the following phrase, suggesting that '"perhaps you saw something quite terrifying"'. His wife's refusal to answer is succeeded by a token-based construction in which Diego again asserts that his question was not prompted by jealousy.

Diego goes on to quote the conversation that was reportedly sparked by his questioning. He comments on his affective state at the time in line 17, preceding the assertion with a deictic (*tamaha* 'this') that functions temporally. The cohesion (Halliday and Hasan 1976:261) that this creates between the dialogue and the quarrel that followed suggests that the two are linked causally as well. The implicit claim is that his feelings constituted a legitimate response to his wife's secret and subsequent silence. Next comes a description of the effect of the aftermath of the fight. Moving one's hammock is a first step toward dissolving the marriage, and María makes this clear: ' "Now I'm going to leave you" '.

This same combination of metapragmatic elements dominates the remainder of Diego's narrative. He quotes a long utterance in which he counseled María to stay ' "because you are my wife" ' (line 29). Diego claims three additional times that he has counseled (*deri-* and *dibu moa-*) María, and he asserts that she only responds angrily, refusing to think things through in proper Warao fashion.

Diego's account does not consist simply of a host of unconnected quotations and metapragmatic constructions; rather, he draws on several types of features in weaving these elements into a cohesive narrative. One means that Diego uses in creating relations of cohesion is multipart units. In several instances, contiguous quoted utterances are related through the use of an initial *denoko-* 'to ask', followed by *mariboto dibu-* 'my + reply + to speak'. Successive utterances are also related through such devices as topical cohesion and ellipsis.

Temporal deictics play a central role in showing how successive elements of Diego's account are connected. "Pure" temporal deictics, those that bear no relationship to nondeictic methods of temporal reckoning (cf. Levinson 1983:74), include *ama* 'now', *tamaitane* 'when', *tatuka* 'then', *taitane* 'afterward', *diana* 'already', and *mate* 'not yet'. *Ama* can index simultaneity with either the narrating event or the narrated event (cf. Jakobson 1971). *Tamaitane* also suggests simultaneity; Diego connects the end of his early morning ruminations and the beginning of the whispering episode by noting *tamaitane dibune yewará takore* 'when I had finished speaking'. *Tatuka* suggests that two actions were either simultaneous or that one followed closely on the heels of the other (e.g., line 20). The use of *taitane* suggests that a more substantial interval and perhaps a change of scene has intervened. *Taitane* occurs between the description of María's telling the secret and Diego's questioning (line 6), suggesting that she finished the conversation and reentered the house before he began interrogating her. Spanish *después* 'later' (generally rendered *debué* by Warao speakers) is used in several instances to index a similar interval (cf. lines 7, 11, 14, 23, 131, 132, 146). *Diana* and *mate* constitute an opposed set, and they indicate, respectively, that a given state of affairs has or has not come to pass.[5]

As Bauman (1986) and Hopper (1982) have argued, events do not simply exist—they are created in discourse. A basic means of distinguishing actions that count as background from those to be constituted as discrete events is through the use of tense/aspect categories. Although any number of actions that are marked by the imperfective can occur simultaneously, actions that are classed as perfective take place serially. As Wallace (1982) notes, while the imperfective tends to place actions in the background, the perfective foregrounds them. Charged by the Commissioner with giving his interpretation of what has taken place, Diego must make a case for the centrality of particular events in generating the conflict, while at the same time he must suggest why they took place and had a particular effect. He accordingly alternates between, on the one hand, tenseless constructions, durative or iterative suffixes (such as *-yaha* PAST DURATIVE,[6] *-al-ya* PRESENT DURATIVE), *-kore* SIMULTANEOUS, *-ne* GERUNDIVE, and the like and, on the other hand, *-el-nae* PAST PERFECTIVE.

Tense/aspect both contrasts and relates actions, identifying particular moments as key events while at the same time subtly asserting their basis in preceding and/or ongoing actions that count as background. This juxtaposition is beautifully illustrated in the way that Diego portrays the key event that catalyzed the dispute. In lines 3 and 5, he uses the past durative in stating that his wife was whispering. Although this key action could easily have been construed as an event, he frames it instead as background for his own action, that of *seeing* the whispering; this is accorded the perfective. As background, María's action becomes cause and Diego's action (looking) becomes effect. By using subtle deictic relations to provide an ongoing, implicit metapragmatics, the temporal and causal relations between actions come to seem as if they are natural properties of the acts themselves. Diego extends this natural logic by using explicit metapragmatics in asserting that since he saw something terrifying, he was forced to speak out.

Taken as a whole, Diego's account forms a narrative that refracts the temporal and causal connections between a series of interpersonal encounters into a complex set of relations between discourse elements. The story focuses on everyday interaction, and the reported speech is modeled on both conversation and counseling. In the guise of simply recounting who did and said what at which point in the dispute, Diego asserts a self-serving interpretation as to what lies behind these events. Note that this complex mélange of deictics simultaneously maps the relationship between elements of the narrated events and structures the narrating event, constantly shifting the camera angle and focus of the narrative. This implicit interpretive framework is complemented by a running explicit metapragmatic commentary on particular actions and on appropriate modes of talking and acting.

The Commissioner's Exhortation

After he completed his narrative, Diego remained seated. His chair faced those occupied by the Commissioner and Policeman. The floor reverted to the Commissioner, who proceeded to exhort the disputants with respect to the way that married couples should behave. Diego remained seated until the end of the exhortation, thus marking him as the primary addressee for the Commissioner's remarks.

(2) *Commissioner's exhortation*

53   *Oko tamatika, ihi* COMPADRE, *ihi Warao, ine kate Warao.*
You and I here, you, compadre, you are Warao, and I, too, am Warao.

54   *Kokotuka abane, oko Warao, Waraotuma kotai, Warao.*
All of us together, we are Warao, we are the Warao, Warao.

55   *Kaobonobuna tamaha tane hakitane,*
In order to form our thoughts in this way [as true Warao],

56   *oko wahabara obonobukitane ha,*
first we must think,

57   *kaobonona abakitane ha,*
we must place our thoughts,

58   *kaobonona konarukitane ha,*
we must carry along our thoughts,

59   *"katukane sike ine tida nisate?"*
[and ask ourselves] "How must I go about finding a wife?"

60   *Tamaha dibu iabane, ihi aidamokore, ine hitida dibute,* COMPAI: *"tida obonoya."*
Setting aside these words, if you were a leader, and I should speak to you about finding a wife, compadre: "I want a wife."

61   *Tamaha* EJEMPLO *abayaha.*
I give you this example.

62   *Ihi maderite:* "COMPAI, BUE, *tamaha tane, dahe, tamaha tane hau, dibu sabana dibunaka."*
You will counsel me: "Compadre, well, after this, older brother, behave well, don't speak badly."

63   *Ine hiribu nokone, makohoko eku nakakore, are.*
Listening to your words, they would fall into my ears, always.

64   *Atae arakate ine dibu sabana dibunaha takitane ha.*
I must never speak badly again.

65   *Ama tida deria,*
Now the wife is counseled,

66   *tida dibu moate bueno.*
you will then give good advice to the wife.

67   *Kaobonobuna kotai tida ahabara kaobonona abakitane ha,*
Before getting married, one must think things through carefully in our [Warao] way of thinking,

68   *tai tatuka abanewitu yana.*
this is not something to be done in haste.

69   *Dibu emo nakaterone,*
That way things will not happen in keeping with these words of counsel,

70   *tiarone dibu emo nakanaha.*
but [if you think it through], things will happen in keeping with these words of counsel.

71   *Ihi dibu mamoae,*
You counseled me [lit. gave me words],

72 *eku ine abakitane ha.*
now I must behave accordingly.

73 *Ine dibu isaka nokokitane ha.*
I must comply immediately.

The Commissioner then scolds the couple not only for failing to follow through on the advice they were given at marriage but also on the way that the situation has generated gossip. He places the blame on the lack of respect that is evident in the way they speak with one another, particularly in that their angry words, once recast as gossip, have had negative repercussions on others. He contrasts proper and improper modes of conduct in the following terms.

74 *Tamaha tane, ine obonobukore, tamaha tane.*
That's what happened here, when I think about it, that's what happened here.

75 *Nome oko Warao kaobononawitu, kaobononawitu*
Our own way of thinking, our own way of thinking as true Warao

76 *Waraowitu dihibubuya,*
comes out when we speak like true Warao,

77 *ibomamo, anibakamo,*
the young women and the girls,

78 *ebewitu, ebe;*
quite long ago, long ago;

79 *ama hakotai kʷaimotane hotarao diana.*
in recent times, people have begun to think like criollos.

80 *Ebe sike Warao.*
Long ago people were truly Warao.

81 *Tiarone kawaraya Warao,*
Nevertheless, they still call us Warao.

82 *Dawa tane nakaya akotai, dawa;*
He who becomes a son-in-law must act like a son-in-law;

83 *dabai, dabai.*
the mother-in-law, a mother-in-law.

84 *Ine yaha hisaka, hisaka dihibukatabuya.*
Day in and day out, I keep on giving counsel.

85 *Ine hisamika dehe waraya: ebe dawa ha.*
I myself am telling you a story: there used to be true sons-in-law.

86 *Dawa akotai dabai, dabai sabasaba aobonona abaya, dahi sabasaba aobonona abaya.*
A son-in-law like that always thinks about his mother-in-law, always thinks about his father-in-law.

87 *Ama kʷaimo akotai dabai sabasaba abonona abanaha, dahi sabasaba aobonona abanaha.*
Now, in recent times, [a son-in-law] never thinks about his mother-in-law, never thinks about his father-in-law.

88 *Dabai amasaba.*
    The mother-in-law is neglected.
89 *Amawitu akotai, tautuma akotai,*
    Right now, the women of today
90 *nebu obonoya, nebu.*
    want young men, young men.
91 *Idamo obononaha, idamo obono-.*
    They don't want old men, they don't want old—.
92 *Idamo akotai diana, aobonona, obonona nabakayaro.*
    An old man has already become knowledgeable.
93 *Ama neburatu sike diana, obonona abatu mohoro.*
    Since [women] only want young men now, it must be that they are the ones with the
    knowledge.

The Commissioner argues that if everyone gets married without thinking things through, the leaders will be holding *monikata nome anaka* everyday. He asserts that if men do not counsel their wives, conflict is sure to follow. If a couple has problems, the two should not spread news of their fight about the community. He concludes this portion of his counseling with the following exhortation.

94 *Idamotuma: bisikari, kapitán, kobenahoro, komisario.*
    Leaders: fiscal, captain, governor, commissioner.
95 *Ine yatu deria, kokotuka abane,*
    I counsel all of you,
96 *kokotuka, kokotuka abane, ine yatu dibu moaya.*
    all of you, I counsel all of you.
97 *Tautuma yaotakotu, CESTA nonakotu.*
    Work, women, make baskets.
98 *Hanoko eku hakotai,*
    Those of you who stay at home,
99 *CESTA yatu ayaota; ha nonakotu, ure abakotu.*
    your work is making baskets; make hammocks, plant ocumo.
100 *Tai nahoro yatu saba, yatu anobotomo saba.*
    The food that is produced will be for you and for your children.
101 *Yoriminaka, yoridariatanaka,*
    Don't look for trouble with each other, don't deprecate each other,
102 *yari asida, tuatanaka takotu, ine dibuyaha.*
    anger is bad, don't act like that, I am counseling you.

Analysis. The Commissioner's intervention contrasts on a number of grounds with that of the husband. He does not construct an overarching temporal sequence; much of what he says is either not placed at any particular point in time or is located in a distinction between *ebe* 'before' and *ama* 'now'. The Commissioner does not return his audience to the events that gave rise to the conflict, and his account does not focus on daily life or everyday conversation. It does bear a strong resemblance to the segments of Diego's account in which he relates his attempts to counsel María. For the Commissioner, such acts of counseling become the dominant focus. His attempts to shape the discourse are metapragmatically less tied to the sort of rich token-based metapragmatics that was evident in Diego's account. The Commissioner's intervention rather provides a type-based, prescriptive metapragmatics that specifies how Warao ought to talk. Narrativity plays a much less important part here. It emerges in the way the Commissioner explicitly frames his account of how sons-in-law used to behave with *ine hisamika dehe waraya* 'I myself am telling you a story'. Such episodes become material for further counseling rhetoric rather than events in a coherent narrative.

This does not mean, however, that complex metapragmatic constructions are absent from the Commissioner's discourse—both explicit and implicit metapragmatics are used in shaping the counseling process itself, especially the authoritative counseling provided by 'elders' (*aidamo*) to their subordinates. The hypothetical example in which Diego is cast as the elder and the Commissioner plays the young suitor provides an interesting illustration. He begins by creating a situation in which counseling becomes necessary, an impending marriage, and then dramatizing the counseling discourse that it would generate. He then goes on to construct an explicit metapragmatic model as to how such counseling should proceed and what impact it should have. The metapragmatic complexity of this move is increased by the role of the hypothetical counseling event as a means for both constructing a model of counseling and structuring a particular act of counseling—the Commissioner's participation in the *monikata nome anaka*.

In formal terms, the slower tempo that was evident in Diego's reported counseling is particularly pronounced in the Commissioner's speech, his rate is half that of Diego's narrative discourse. Pauses are much more common and much longer. With respect to lexicon and syntax, counseling speech is often characterized by a greater density of parallelism. In line 86, for example, a parallel construction, 'always thinks about his mother-in-law / always thinks about his father-in-law', is evident within a single line. This same pattern is echoed in the succeeding line, but the addition of a negative suffix to the verb foregrounds the contrast between the sons-in-law of past and present. Notice that Diego also uses parallel constructions as he shifts to counseling discourse. Recall his insertion of a moral imperative into the middle of the crucial narrative episode—the whispering scene, line 4. Here the three tokens of *mikore* (*mi-* 'to see' + *-kore* SIMULTANEOUS) mark the line as quasi-counseling discourse, associate seeing someone whispering with seeing 'something terrifying', and add rhetorical weight to the conclusion (*kʷana dibukitane ha* 'one must speak forcefully'). The use of parallelism in this context bears a strong resemblance to the case of Tzotzil dispute mediation described by Haviland elsewhere in this volume.[7] An increase in the density of parallel constructions signals a shift to counseling discourse, adding the authority of 'truly Warao'—and truly hierarchical—social relations to the husband's interpretation of the scene.

With respect to tense/aspect, two major contrasts are evident in Diego's discourse. One distinguishes the tense-marked discourse of narrative action from the primarily tenseless counseling. A second opposition, which lies within the narrative discourse, is durative versus nondurative. The latter contrast plays virtually no role in the Commissioner's discourse. Moreover, the relationship between tenseless and tense-marked verbal constructions is reversed; whereas the latter predominated in Diego's account, only about a third of the Commissioner's verbs are marked for tense.[8] The Commissioner alternates primarily between the use of tenseless verbs in describing hypothetical situations and type-based metapragmatic assertions and, on the other hand, present tense constructions that characterize the time of the mediation event. The tenseless verbs consist primarily of the use of -kore to mark grammatical relations of simultaneity or conditional, infinitives, infinitives + ha ('one must'), and negative constructions. The Commissioner ends his interventions after both the husband's and wife's accounts with a series of second person imperatives (cf. lines 97–102, 154–57). These serve as exhortations aimed at the crowd as a whole.

His statement is also characterized by the use of temporal deictics and metapragmatic markers of discourse structure. These are not modeled on conversational exchanges, as was true of much of Diego's account. In the Commissioner's discourse, they rather model the mechanics of counseling rituals designed for marrying couples and the effects these should have on future behavior. They are also used in contrasting past counseling sessions and traditional relations between sons-in-law and mothers-in-law with the purported growing the reflection of criollo values in the present. The Commissioner uses these deictics and discourse markers in imposing a metapragmatic model of discourse structure and social relations on both the *monikata nome anaka* and the hypothetical and past counseling sessions.

The three modes of speaking that emerged in Diego's account underlie the Commissioner's perception of the nature of this *monikata nome anaka*. In responding to the husband, the Commissioner used the hypothetical role reversal to model appropriate modes of speaking and acting. Successful counseling should imbue individuals with what we might refer to, following Vološinov (1973 [1930]), as a body of inner speech that generates discourse and behavior in keeping with the teachings of *kaidamotuma* 'our ancestors'.

By 'setting aside these words' (line 60), the couple has turned against patterns that embody social and spiritual authority. Since contemporary elders stand in for the ancestors in such events, the Commissioner notes the gravity of the infraction, describing it as 'shameful'. After reminding Diego that María is about to publicly declare that she is leaving him, the Commissioner provides his assessment of the origin of his dispute: 'That's what happened here, when I think about it, that's what happened here' (line 74). Exegesis confirms that the statement anaphorically refers to the couple's rejection of speech based on counseling and thinking-speaking in favor of 'bad words' (line 64); the seriousness of the offense was compounded by the gossip that spread its disruptive effects into the community at large.

The Wife's Rebuttal

The Commissioner then turns to María, who had just taken the disputant's chair. He invites María to tell her side of the story in the following exchange:

(3) *The wife's narrative*

Commissioner:

103   *Dibanu mikí,* COMADRE.

     Speak up now, comadre, and let us know.

104   *Nomewitu iabaya diana?*

     Are you truly leaving him?

105   *Nome, nome?*

     Truly, truly?

Wife:

106   *Masabahibuaha monida manisanae tatukamo,*

     He has chided me all the time ever since he married me.

107   *Masabahiae, atae masabahiae, atae masabahiae diana.*

     He chided me, again he chided me, and he chided me again now.

108   *Ine dibu ebe onanewitu ha diana.*

     Having listened to so many words, it's become impossible.

109   *Tuatane ine kate obononaha.*

     So I don't want to keep on like this either.

110   *Ine amaha Sermira akohoko eku dibunaha arakate,*

     Also, what I said to Sermira in her ear

111   *tai arakate mamaha* EL HOMBRE *isia dibunaha tanae,*

     had nothing to do with any man,

112   UN MUCHACHO *isia arakate dibuna tanae.*

     had nothing to do with any boy.

113   *Ine yakeraha Sermira akohoko eku dibuna tanae.*

     I wasn't whispering into Sermira's ear.

114.   *Sermira karamunae,*

     Sermira was standing [outside our house],

115   *ine bohí takore akai Gladys hai,*

     when I went outside I saw Gladys all dressed up,

116   *akai Gladys hai,* MEDIA *abanae, harau tia mi.*

     Gladys was all dressed up, she had put on her socks, you could see that she was neatly dressed.

117   *Tanewitu ine dibunae diana.*

     That's all I said.

118   *Ine barí tanae, ine tamatika Diego kotai mariboto bohí.*

     I turned to go back inside, and Diego came outside and faced me.

119 *Dibuya diana, "maidamo* MANTECA *sanuka obonoya yama.*
   He says, "I've been told that my protector[9] wants a little cooking oil.

120 *Yo* NO SÉ, *moau,* BUE.*"*
   I don't know, give him some."

121 *Tane madenokokore, tai akotai madenokoae diana,*
   Having asked me that, he then asked me,

122 *"Katukane dibunae hiraisama akohoko eku?"*
   "What did you tell your friend when you whispered in her ear?"

123 *Ine diboto dibunae, "*NO, *ine asidaha dibuna tanae."*
   I responded, "No, I didn't say anything bad."

124 *Ine kotai nome ine Gladys isia dibunae,*
   I truly was only talking about Gladys,

125 *"akai, Gladys* MEDIA *abanaha arau tiané!"*
   "Gladys' socks sure look nice!"

126 *Tanewitu inewitu dibunae diana.*
   That's all I said.

127 *Ama kotai kʷarika madenokoya diana.*
   Now he keeps asking me again and again.

128 *"Nome waranu, nome waranu," tia diana.*
   "Tell the truth, tell the truth," he says.

129 *Katukane ine "nome warate"? Ine dibu asidaha dibunaha.*
   How can I "tell the truth"? I didn't say anything bad.

130 *Kʷarika masabahia, masabahí, masabahí;*
   He chides me more, he chided me and chided me;

131 DEBUÉ *manabanae.*
   later he hit me.

132 DEBUÉ *ine kate oriasiae diana.*
   Later I, too, got angry.

133 *Tai hese dibunae diana: "Hihá hahenu; naru, ehobonu.*
   He himself said: "Untie your hammock; go away, get out of here.

134 *Hionukamo kokotuka* RECOGER *tane, naru diana.*
   Gather up all your belongings and go away.

135 *Ine kate hiobononaha.*
   I don't want you anymore either.

136 *Ihiwitu tida ekida; masaba tida era, ine Warao taera kʷare."*
   You're not the only woman around; there are lots of women for me, because I am a strong man."

137 *Ihi dibuya "wakera."*
   You call me "lazy."

138 *Ine, ine dibunaka tanae diana.*
   I, I still didn't say anything.

139 *Ine kau tanae, "ine mahá hahite.*
   I stood up, [I said] "I will untie my hammock.

140 *Ine kate hiwere nakanaha diana."*
   I won't get near you either."

141   *Ihi ebe atamo masabahikore, ihi tuatane hese dibuya.*
      Since long ago when you chide me, you talk to me just like that.

142   *"Ine kate yakeraha hiobononaha, ihi kate matida arau yana,"*
      "I don't like you very much either, you aren't the kind of woman that pleases me,"

143   *tane ihi maisia dibuya.*
      that's the way you talk to me.

144   *Ama ine kate hiriboto dibukore, hiobonona emo ehoboya.*
      When I respond to you now, you never like the way it comes out.

145   *Tane oko orisabahiabuae diana.*
      That's the way we kept chiding each other.

146   DEBUÉ *diana maha hahine diana.*
      Afterward, I untied my hammock.

147   *Mainataba yame ine maha haine, emo koyane diana.*
      Since you ordered me to do so, I untied my hammock and tied it again elsewhere.

148   *Tiarone k^warika mayaokabaya.*
      Nevertheless, you keep on bothering me.

149   *Ine arakate oriasiae diana, "hiobononaha diana, ihi mamandatae k^ware."*
      I, too, got angry, "I don't want you anymore, and it's because you ordered me [to leave]."

María then repeats other insults that her husband leveled against her. She goes on to repeat the accusation that she interjected during Diego's narrative.

150   *Ama kotai dibuya diana, "idamo," tai dibunaha kotai,*
      Now he says that I called him an "old man," and I did say this,

151   *ama dibunae.*
      I said it today.

152   *¿POR QUÉ? Ma "PUTA" waranae k^ware.*
      Why? Because he called me a "whore."

María proceeds to disclaim any responsibility for spreading gossip. After she suggests that she did not use her grandmother as a conduit for spreading gossip, the grandmother speaks briefly (without moving to the narrator's chair). She repeated some of the gossip that had been attributed to her, noting that she had not started it. María then asserts that the origin of the conflict lies in the constant chiding that she received at the hands of her husband and in that he ordered her to untie her hammock and leave. She claims that he always uses 'very bad words' (*dibu asidahawitu*) in chiding her, and she repeats a number of these expressions. María notes that Diego has threatened violence against her on a number of occasions. She claims that Diego is so jealous that he is constantly accusing her of flirting with young men even though she seldom leaves the house.

Analysis.   Diego presented a detailed account of the critical events, one in which his own interpretation of what went wrong has been woven into the fabric of the action both explicitly and implicitly. The Commissioner mustered an authoritative mode of discourse—counseling talk—in suggesting that 'bad words' generate conflict. A central theme in Diego's narrative is that his wife speaks badly and is continually enraged. In view of all that has been said thus far, what rhetorical resources are available to María in mounting an effective counterstrategy?

Counseling discourse provided a key element in Diego's account, and it formed the backbone of the Commissioner's. This option is entirely closed to María, because gender and status relations prevent her from counseling persons occupying the roles of husband and Commissioner. Her access to type-based metapragmatic constructions is also severely limited. She does characterize the way that Diego spoke to her in general, but she does not present any prescriptive formulas designed to regulate language use outside of the relationship.

Diego's narrative placed the 'bad words' in his wife's mouth; he characterized his own conduct as a natural response to his wife's unreasonable behavior. Whereas his speech purportedly emerged from careful reflection on the needs of his family, hers reflected a displacement of reflection by anger. One weakness in this type of defense is the potential for reappropriating the same actions in constructing an alternative narrative; the same type of deictics can be used in attaching a different interpretation to the same reported speech. This process adds another level of linguistic complexity to the discourse, since the new narrative builds reflexively not only on the narrated events but on the husband's narrative. This is precisely what María accomplishes in her account.

After noting that she indeed plans to leave her husband, María metapragmatically reframes his quarrelsome speech. Whereas Diego suggested that he only fought with her recently and in response to her 'bad words', María begins her account by noting that Diego quarrels with her all the time and that he has been doing so ever since they married (line 106).

After attempting to characterize the way Diego speaks to her in general, María turns to the task of reinterpreting the crucial whispering episode. Even though she tells her husband that the secret had nothing to do with a man, he continually questions her about it: she quotes Diego as ordering her to 'tell the truth' (line 128). By using the present durative in framing her husband's words, she emphasizes the fact that he asked her over and over; she also places her audience at the scene of the questioning as it unfolds. María goes on to reveal the presupposition that lies in Diego's question: how can she stop lying and tell the truth now if she did not lie in the first place?

At this point, she shifts her metapragmatic strategy from temporal deixis to person deixis. She uses the third person singular pronoun (*tai*) in suggesting that it was *he* who first got angry and *he* who told her to move her hammock away from his and to leave the house (line 133). She follows the pronoun with *hese*, which can be translated as 'exactly' or 'only'; it serves as an emphatic element that focuses the narrative spotlight on 'he himself'. Presupposing that the anger and the impetus for moving the hammock were attributed to María in Diego's account, *hese* stresses the deictic shift.

María proceeds to drastically change the deixis that emerged from a key element of her husband's account. Diego claimed that he tried to make amends after the first fight, but that she responded by telling him to leave her alone, that she no longer wanted him. He quoted her as saying ' "You're not the only man around; there are lots of men out there" '. María now turns this around completely. Utterances referring to such acts as leaving and untying hammocks become directives in which Diego is ordering her to leave. Similarly, she attributes this boast to Diego: ' "there are lots of women here" '. María goes on to transform Diego's model of their conversational exchanges: it is not true that she fails to respond to him; rather he never likes her responses.

Having restructured crucial deictic relations in her account of the key events in the dispute, María returns to the task of recontextualizing her husband's discourse in general. She notes that he began threatening to leave long before this quarrel. She quotes him, using the present durative, as telling her that she does not please him. She asks rhetorically why he married her if he has never been happy with her. She proceeds to charge that he quotes her on statements that she has never uttered. She admits to having called him an old man, but claims that she said this for the first time on the day of the *monikata nome anaka* and only in response to his calling her a whore. She proceeds to deny having gossiped about her husband and claims that she did not have any lovers. The truth, she claims, is that whenever he leaves the house he returns enraged, jealously accusing her of flirting with other men. She further asserts that 'Whenever we chide each other, he says, "I'm going to kill you, I'm going to kill you, I'm not going to stop until I kill you, I'm going to kill you, I'll end up in the penitentiary" '.

María concludes by reiterating her case. She argues that whenever Diego quarrels with her, he always uses the same 'bad words' (*dibu sabana*): ' "I'm going to leave you, there are many women for me" '. She notes that it is because she is so tired of constant verbal abuse and 'very bad words' (*dibu asidaha*) that she is leaving him.

María makes clever use of both person deixis and temporal deixis in standing Diego's account on its head. She returns to the stage that has been set up in his narrative, and she replays the same crucial lines. Her version recontextualizes the quoted utterances by attributing the 'bad words' to a different speaker, Diego, and by placing the 'bad words' at contrastive points in the narrative. This reverses the causal relations that are signaled by temporal deixis and person deixis, thus producing a contrastive sense as to who is to blame. María shifts the temporal deixis associated with a number of the quotes used by her husband in a more radical way. She not only attributes the threats of abandonment to her husband, but she places them outside these particular events—he has said things like this all along. She then takes the words and actions that she was accused of saying and doing throughout the marriage and localizes them at particular points in the conflict. In each case, these actions are reinterpreted as effects, not causes.

In my discussions with elders after the *monikata nome anaka*, the collective view of what transpired was much closer to the wife's account. They argued that it was the husband's jealously that prompted him to ask repeatedly about the whisper. His questioning was judged to constitute 'bad words' both because of his angry tone and annoying persistence and because he had no right to invade her privacy by asking the question in the first place. María did not escape criticism; the consensus was that Diego was within his rights in finding fault with his wife for failing to prepare food, particularly in view of his status as a good provider. Nevertheless, María's assertion that jealousy had prompted Diego to criticize her throughout their marriage was cited as the cause of its demise.

The Commissioner Brings the Monikata Nome Anaka to a Close

The Commissioner asks María if she is truly leaving her husband; once she replies in the affirmative, he tries to cut her off. The Commissioner regains the floor again and attempts to bring the proceedings to a close:

(4) *Commissioner cuts off María and attempts to end* monikata nome anaka

153   *Yakera, monika oko nome nakae,*
      Okay, we have settled things properly,

154   *ama tane yatu oremo nakaya, yatu aobonona isia, pues.*
      now you have both accepted the way we settled things of your own accord, right?

155   *Así QUE tamatikamo dibu inaré;*
      From here on, remain silent;

156   *amasaba arakate dibu, dibu tanaka;*
      don't start talking again;

157   *NO SÉ QUE daisa sabasaba dibu nakanaka, inaré.*
      don't throw who knows what words at one another, remain silent.

After silencing another man's attempt to raise an issue that had been dealt with in a previous *monikata nome anaka*, the Commissioner turns to the second and final proceeding of the night.

The Commissioner was successful in achieving consensus. Whereas María and Diego had separated and reunited several times in the past, their separation became final after the proceedings. About a year later, Diego married a woman from a nearby community and established residence there. The gossip and antagonism that had emerged from the conflict subsided shortly after the *monikata nome anaka*.

Metapragmatics and the Constitution of Social Relations

I have argued thus far that both explicit and implicit metapragmatics play a key role in shaping the form and meaning of discourse in this *monikata nome anaka*. I have suggested that the explicit metapragmatic commentary follows two courses. One, which I termed token-based metapragmatics, consists of a blow-by-blow interpretation of key conflictual events. In the case of the wife's account, token-based metapragmatic commentary simultaneously structures these conflictual events, restructures Diego's narrative, and shapes her narrative. The husband and Commissioner also present a type-based metapragmatic interpretation of broad patterns of language use, particularly with respect to what sorts of speech engender harmonious social relations. Although María is not accorded the right to present a full-fledged type-based metapragmatics, she does comment on the conversational exchanges that have characterized her marriage as a whole. I argued that both type- and token-based metapragmatic commentaries draw on three explicit metapragmatic models of discourse production: counseling, thinking-speaking, and anger/envy.

There is a long-standing tendency in linguistic analysis to reject such explicit metapragmatics as "native models" or "native theories" that bear little or no relation to the "real" systematic patterning of language, that is, the linguist's model of how language works. Recall Boas's (1911:63) statement in his Introduction to the *Handbook of American Indian Languages* that "the laws of language remain entirely unknown to the speakers, . . . linguistic phenomena never rise into the consciousness of primitive man," a view that has hardly disappeared from scholarly writings.

The explicit metapragmatics that I have described, including the three models of language production, hardly provide an exhaustive analysis of what takes place in *monikata nome anaka*. I have also called the reader's attention to implicit metapragmatic constructions based on parallelism, temporal and person deixis, tense/aspect forms, and features of speech events (turn-taking, participant roles, etc.) that embed the speaker's interpretation of key speech events in the manner in which he or she represents them. Nevertheless, the role of the explicit metapragmatics cannot be relegated to the status of an intellectual curiosity that may tell us how Warao conceptualize language production but bears little relation to "real" discourse processes. Not only do linguistic ideologies help shape formal-functional patterning in this case, but they provide us with a key for understanding how *monikata nome anaka* discourse gains the power to regulate social relations. I would argue that these explicit metapragmatic modes structure the discourse in several ways.

1. The three modes are used referentially in negotiating how the narrated events are to be interpreted. For the Commissioner and husband, counseling speech forms an important means of constructing the narrated events. Diego also draws substantially on the thinking-speaking mode in attempting to interpret his own actions. María is primarily restricted to implicitly denying the applicability of both counseling and thinking-speaking modes to Diego's speech by explicitly substituting the mode of speech production based on anger and rage. Diego and the Commissioner also use the anger/envy mode in characterizing reported speech in narrated events.

2. Speech that embodies the three modes is not simply referred to as forming part of the narrated events—it also is produced within the narrating event itself. Just

as the Commissioner speaks mainly *about* counseling, his contributions form a token of this type of discourse. The slower tempo, preponderance of tenseless verbs, modality, and emergence of parallelism mark his words formally as counseling. A link between ideologies of language and conflict shapes *monikata nome anaka*. The basic concept that lies behind the structure of this type of speech event is that only by enabling each person whose *obonobu* has been affected by the dispute to articulate every thread of their involvement in it can the true or proper *obonobu* reemerge. Elders thus urge disputants to tell all, and the narratives offered by disputants generally end with statements such as that provided by Diego in line 52: 'These words of mine are now complete'. *Monikata nome anaka* conclude with the elders' injunction to never speak of the dispute again (cf. lines 155–57).

The Commissioner only reports indirectly the 'bad words' that emerge from rage and jealousy. The disputants' narratives, on the other hand, are punctuated with direct quotations of angry and jealous speech. Expressing the emotions that have been generated by a conflict is deemed essential for achieving successful closure. My analysis of deictic elements in the narratives suggests that replaying the dialogues that catalyzed these emotions provides the couple with a means of trying to demonstrate that their outbursts only emerged as inevitable responses to the unreasonable and unwarranted 'bad words' of their spouse. By replaying the 'bad words' as direct discourse rather than conveying their semantic content indirectly, each narrator naturalizes his or her interpretation by embedding it in the way the utterances are quoted. Producing both thinking-speaking and 'bad words' discourse is thus requisite to the realization of the goals pursued by all of the participants—but in different ways, by different means, and with contrastive effects.

3. Finally, these three metapragmatic modes are tied to opposing types of social relations. As Wilbert (1980:7–8) has noted, "Warao society is sharply segregated into an elite of elders, patriarchs or chiefs, and a class of workers." Counseling discourse iconically represents these hierarchical social relations. Contextually, this type of speech can only emerge when social superiors stand in the role of speakers and their inferiors constitute the audience. Such officials as the *kobenahoro* 'governor', *kabitana* 'captain', and *komisario* 'commissioner' can counsel all members of their community, husbands can counsel wives, and parents can counsel children. Counseling speech is contextually associated with settings in which these hierarchical relations are foregrounded, including early morning discourses, meetings in the house of an official, *monikata nome anaka,* and other events.

This iconicity is evident in formal features as well. The slow and even tempo punctuated by frequent pauses suggests thoughtfulness and composure. The greater density of parallel constructions marks the speech as a token of "truly Warao" speech, discourse that is inherently authoritative. The deictic features do not transport the audience imaginatively to events that give rise to conflicts. Events rather tend to be hypothetical, as in the case of the fictional marriage portrayed by the Commissioner's narrative. Even when specific events are recalled, they are presented in outline form as tokens of the type that is being illustrated. Temporal deictics and markers of discourse structure locate utterances within these events of counseling, but the events themselves are seldom firmly rooted in temporal sequences. Verbs are often tenseless, couched as infinitives or directives.

These formal features place counseling discourse as timeless speech that is rooted in hierarchical social relations and conceptions of what is proper Warao behavior. The formal patterning, referential content, and contextualization of counseling discourse are used in traditionalizing it (cf. Bauman 1990; Hymes 1975), connecting this speech with the words of the powerful *kaidamotuma* 'our ancestors'. Counseling is thus monologic in a Bakhtinian sense; like authoritative discourse in general (cf. Bakhtin 1981:342–43), it is relatively insulated, semantically and stylistically, from the particular settings in which it emerges. Counseling speech is also monologic in terms of turn taking; social inferiors generally only respond when a question is directed to them, and back talk is proscribed. Formally, contextually, and semantically, counseling embodies hierarchical social relations and the authority that is attached to them.

Nevertheless, as Heinen (1987:659) argues, an ideology of social equilibrium also plays a central role in Warao society. He suggests that Warao contrast power with authority. Although an individual may achieve a relatively high amount of economic power by serving as an intermediary with criollos or supernatural power by becoming competent as a curer, authority is accorded those individuals who can keep the members of the community feeling content (*oriwakaya*). To do so, it is deemed necessary to achieve the sort of consensus that is predicated on each individual's sense that they have been accorded opportunities to express themselves and that their words have been taken into account. Thinking-speaking speech models this type of social relations in two respects. First, the act of performing a narrative in a *monikata nome anaka* demonstrates personal autonomy, declaring the right to make one's voice heard. Second, in the act of telling everything that is on their mind with respect to a particular situation, disputants are forced to lay all of their cards on the table. No suppressed emotion or withheld fact can give rise to a renewal of the conflict.

This metapragmatic mode models egalitarian and consensual social relations formally as well. Turn taking is largely absent in the course of disputant narratives. The presiding official or another elder will occasionally ask a question, but the narrative is told by one person. Nevertheless, the core of this type of discourse is the replaying of dialogues. Deictic elements emphasize ideological and stylistic dimensions of the dynamic interplay of different voices. Temporal and person deixis and tense / aspect forms also locate the discourse in time, contextualizing each utterance in terms of unique configurations of actors and events that constitute the social history of the community. This mode thus roots speech in types of interactions in which egalitarian relations are foregrounded and hierarchy is less evident.

Warao social relations are not dominated exclusively by social relations based on a combination of orderly hierarchical patterns and egalitarian relations of mutual respect. People are also preoccupied with relations based on the unpredictable and potentially destructive behavior that emerges from a lack of self-control, unrestrained anger and jealousy, and failure to consider the *obonona* of others. The sine qua non of such relations is the behavior of malevolent curers. All curers possess the ability to heal and to kill. Some use their powers in curing the members of their community; they utilize their ability to cause sickness only in response to potentially destructive provocations. The epitome of 'bad words' lies in the actions of 'bad curers' (*hoarao sabana*), those who purportedly react angrily to a perceived slight or simply out of jealousy for another's success by purportedly killing an innocent victim. Such social relations are also believed to be evident in the behavior of many criollos; whereas 'true Warao' respect the *obonona* of others, criollos are capricious, insensitive, and unpredictable, and their speech is quick to reflect anger and jealousy.

The distinction between the thinking-speaking 'good words' and angry or jealous 'bad words' modes as they emerge in disputants' narratives is subtle. Although the rate of speaking in participant narratives is quite rapid in general, it tends to increase as 'bad words' are quoted. Such utterances are also characterized by sharp fluctuations in pitch. These changes in voice quality reflect the emotional character that is attributed to the speech; the narrator often seems to be angry while quoting a character who is enraged. Both metapragmatic modes are embodied in dialogic accounts of conversational interactions. Speech that emerges from thinking-speaking is properly contextualized, suitably reflecting the words and actions that surround it. In the case of angry / jealous speech, deictic forms are used in pointing to a *lack* of fit between 'bad words' and the circumstances that surround it. María thus notes that even though she told Diego that her whispered message was in reference to Gladys, not a man, *ama kotai kʷarika madenokoya diana* 'now he keeps asking me again and again'. Since she stated clearly that the whisper provided no grounds for jealousy, his repeated questions were unreasonable. The suffix -*rone* 'in spite of' or 'although' is often placed at the end of a verb or verb phrase that refers to the preceding speech, pointing dramatically to the lack of fit evident.

'Bad words' are sometimes deictically "de-centered" (Silverstein and Urban 1996) in a more global sense, that is, taken out of a particular communicative setting and framed as relevant to a broader range of settings. María tries to show that her own speech follows directly from its immediate context; contrastively, she de-centers her husband's 'bad words', suggesting that he always uses 'bad words' in quarreling with her. 'Bad words' thus form the contextual opposite of counseling speech. The latter can emerge appropriately in nearly any setting (and is obligatory in certain situations)—it is inherently de-centered. 'Bad words', on the other hand, are rarely adequately situated.[10] Similarly, hostile social relations that reflect anger and jealousy are never warranted.

The dynamism that is inherent in the relationship between the three modes of speech and social relations affects the conduct of *monikata nome anaka* quite directly. Since these three ways of organizing discourse compete for predominance, the proportion of each type that is evident in a given mediation event varies greatly. In the Nabasanuka case, none of the modes predominates. In one of the *monikata nome anaka* that I recorded in Murako, nearly all of the discourse was devoted to counseling. A Mariusa example is particularly interesting in that thinking-speaking and 'bad words' modes largely displace counseling speech. 'Bad words' became so prevalent that the event turned, for a time, into a shouting match, and a principal disputant struck a witness.

Discursive Disorder, Authority, and Patriarchal Violence

My analysis suggests that *monikata nome anaka* constitute a privileged discursive realm that is constructed by *aidamo* with the active participation of a number of individuals who have been involved in a dispute. As I noted, these meetings are called by leaders, and they determine who can—and must—participate and who cannot. Receiving the message that *ihi monikata ha* 'you are involved in a dispute', in other words, that your participation in a *monikata nome anaka* is required, is often greeted with less than enthusiasm. Individuals who have been involved in a dispute sometimes leave suddenly for the forest or coastal fishing waters when they suspect that such an invitation may be imminent; when this occurs, the meeting may be postponed until they return, by which time officials and other disputants may no longer feel the need to hold a meeting. Some persons actively seek the opportunity to air their greivances in a *monikata nome anaka* by visiting a 'leader' and narrating an account of a conflict; they do not know in advance, however, whether the elder will just listen, counsel them on the spot, or hold a meeting. If, after consultation, the leaders agree that a *monikata nome anaka* should be held, they determine who speaks, in what order, and at what length; they also have the right to interrupt narrators with questions and / or counseling speech at any point. Finally, the official who is in charge of the *monikata nome anaka* enjoys the nearly exclusive right to deploy a highly authoritative metapragmatic mode, counseling speech.

Nevertheless, it is not simply the case that officials rigidly control everything that is said in these events, prohibiting any speech that they deem to be improper. Rather, their very success in 'straightening out' the dispute is contingent on the emergence of the speech that they deem responsible for having starting the fight. As the dispute is represented in competing narratives, it is always possible that its discursive disorderliness may spill over into the *monikata nome anaka* itself and/or its aftermath, thereby sparking more conflict. Imposing authority thus entails a complex and somewhat unpredictable process of regulating speech that is produced in keeping with opposing ideological and metapragmatic parameters. Unlike the descriptions of authoritative speech presented by Bloch (1975) and Bakhtin (1981), building discursive hegemony in *monikata nome anaka* is less concerned with the imposition of homogeneity and order than with the regulation of heterogeneity and disorder.

Officials require disputants to tell narratives that foreground both good and bad speech; since both of these modes are less prestigious than counseling speech, their use indexes the social subordination of their users. Even though he was unable to counsel anyone in the *monikata nome anaka,* the husband managed to partially circumvent this position of inferiority and identify himself with the authority of the Commissioner by reporting his own counseling speech in his narrative. In addition to placing other ideologies of language and metapragmatic modes in the voices of others, officials are able to create hierarchical orderings of the three modes by representing 'good speech' and 'bad speech' (directly and indirectly, respectively) in the exhortations that follow the disputants' interventions. In modeling the relationship between discursive ideologies and practices, leaders also model persons, interpersonal relations, social structures, and intergroup relations. *Ebewitu* 'quite long ago', *aidamo* purportedly used counseling speech and subordinates uttered only good speech, while people *kʷaimotane* 'in recent times' commonly deploy bad words. By using this same discursive opposition to model what it means to be 'truly Warao' versus 'like criollos', elders can map cultural differences and impose notions of proper conduct. As they seek to mediate the very conflicts that test their authority, leaders also impose interpretations of the nature of the dispute and its causes, assign blame, impose outcomes, and project visions as to how conflict should be avoided in the future.

Rather than simply assuming that this discourse reflects stable relations of power, I believe it is crucial to see how such authority gets constructed in the course of *monikata nome anaka.* Other men are always ready to challenge established leaders; a rash of illnesses or deaths, changing demographics, and shortages of economic resources, along with recurrent social conflicts, provide excellent opportunities for pressing these challenges. The institutions of the Venezuelan state, missionaries, and entrepreneurs have significantly shaped the bases for establishing authority in Warao communities for at least two centuries; as the penetration of these forces shifts, leadership is contested in new ways. In the preceding example, the presiding official, the Commissioner, is a leader who was chosen by and answerable to representatives of the nation-state; he was assisted in the *monikata nome anaka* by the leading official of the Christian Democratic Party for the entire delta. Moreover, the meeting was held in front of the Catholic mission; if the priest had been in Nabasanuka that day, he might well have attended. Individuals who do not derive their authority from the nation-state—such as curers—or men associated with institutions such as opposing political parties constantly challenge the leadership of the Commissioner and other officials. While the Commissioner's position was based, in large measure, on his contacts with the regional government in Tucupita (as mediated by the local representative of the political party in power), he was also dependent on gaining a substantial measure of authority in the eyes of the residents of

Nabasanuka. Performing counseling speech, promoting good speech, and denigrating bad words in *monikata nome anaka* provided him with a highly visible opportunity to construct himself not as a pawn of criollo politicians but as a man who embodies the 'truly Warao' leader.

In short, the official must make sure that good and bad words about the conflict emerge in the meeting in ways that enable him to control their production and contain their effects. His success or failure will ultimately depend upon his ability to regulate conflictual discourse that is produced and received beyond the confines of the *monikata nome anaka*. As I noted earlier, the reason that officials gave for staging this recounting of the breakup of a relationship as a community-wide event was that gossip about the conflict was creating tension rather broadly in the community. This gossip consists of the circulation of representations of a dispute in ways that cannot be controlled by officials. After soundly condemning these unauthorized narratives, the Commissioner attempts to convert his ability to oblige the participants to repeat good and bad words about the dispute in the course of its mediation into an interdiction—'don't start talking again; don't throw words at one another, remain silent' (lines 156–57).

The wife's depiction of the way that gender-based inequality structures the social relations in which her life is embedded is compelling. She argues that Diego rationalized pervasive attempts to control her actions and constant verbal abuse on the basis of sexual jealousy—even though she had not sought other partners. This presentation extends beyond the parameters of the specific case; whereas men are free to imagine women's words and actions in such a way as to legitimate abusive forms of control, what women actually do and say has no role in occasioning them. Her narrative locates ideologies of language and structures of discursive control in relation to ideologies of gender, authority, sexuality, and labor, as well as to patriarchal institutions. María thus not only challenges Diego's representation of who said what and when and the effects of these words but also questions a basic premise that underlies both men's discursive strategies by suggesting that discursive order involves a great deal more than just thinking clearly and speaking properly. This message is painfully clear in her account of the way discursive control within the family is closely connected with domestic violence; whereas she admits that both parties used bad words, the outcome was quite different for each: he beat her. These discursive struggles took place against the constant backdrop of a threat against María's life: "Whenever we chide each other, he says, 'I'm going to kill you, I'm going to kill you, I'm not going to stop until I kill you, I'm going to kill you, I'll end up in the penitentiary.'"

By rooting discussions of conflict so intimately with representations of contrastive linguistic ideologies, the husband and Commissioner deflect attention away from this systematic relationship between discursive control and physical violence. Whereas the husband's admission that he hit María seems to characterize his actions as an isolated incident that reflected a temporary loss of self-control, she links the two as a systematic assertion of interpersonal control. Interestingly, the husband's own words can be read back at him through María's interpretation of the threat of physical violence as being all-pervasive in their relationship. When he attempts to make up with her the night of the fight, he quotes himself as saying "I only used words in chiding you, you aren't going to die, a person doesn't die from words. Now if I were to hit you, with a stick, to hit you, to hit you on the head, now if I were to have wounded you in the head, spilling your blood, now then you would be somewhat justified [in leaving me]" (lines 25–28). It would not be hard to read these words spoken by a man who has been abusive repeatedly as rather more threatening than consoling and conciliatory. Recall how Diego attempts to turn the question of domestic violence on its head, arguing that he only left home on the night he struck her because he was afraid that she would kill him in his sleep.

Even after María speaks, the Commissioner continues to characterize the dispute as revolving around the utterance of abuse words, the lack of careful reflection, and the failure to heed counseling speech. Physical violence never figures in his account. The women in the community, on the other hand, certainly picked up on María's message; I heard a number of women comment that no one in Nabasanuka would marry Diego now that his propensity for verbal abuse and physical violence had become so clearly evident. Indeed, he left the community shortly thereafter.

Disorder, Discursive Authority, and the Construction of Social Order

I would like to return to some of the general issues I raised at the beginning of this essay. Maurice Bloch (1975) argues that in events that are saturated with "formal" discourse, such as political oratory, privileged discursive forms are closely tied to authority. He suggests that speech and social structure are so closely woven together in such settings that audience members have little choice but to accept a speaker's position if he or she is allowed to deploy an authoritative voice. Bloch argues that discursive forms as well as social structures get reified in such events, so that acceptance of "traditional authority" goes hand in hand with the imposition of severe constraints on creativity, referential content, and the range of interpretive options open to audiences. A number of scholars attacked Bloch with respect to the assumptions regarding formality, creativity, context, and reference that underlie his work and the way he relates them (see Irvine 1979; Myers and Brenneis 1984; Paine 1981a, 1981b; Parkin 1984).

While his formulation may well be flawed in important ways, Bloch was onto something when he stressed the tremendous social significance of the way that privileged discursive forms get linked to questions of social structure and authority. Greg Urban (1986, 1988, 1991) subsequently presented a more fine-grained analysis of the way that formal features evident in culturally salient performance genres are linked indexically to dominant social structural models. He argues that form stands to social action as a "meta-signal" in an iconic relation that both reflects predominant forms of social solidarity and uses them in regulating conduct. Urban characterizes the ceremonial dialogues performed by indigenous groups in South America as "core ritualized communicative, and especially linguistic events"; used particularly in settings of potential conflict, they form "the generative core of regulation" (1986:384–85). With particular reference to ritual wailing, Urban argues that these meta-signals are effective because the messages they convey are not stated referentially and "do not require that the beacon of consciousness be cast upon the underlying signaling phenomenon" (1988:398).

The essays included in this volume can greatly deepen our understanding of this question in that all describe discourses that are closely connected with fundamental patterns of social order, disorder, and authority. I believe that they confirm the importance of investigating the nature of these connections. I would suggest, however, that these phenomena can best be explained by a rather different model of the relationship between discourse and social authority; I will extend some of the implication of my analysis of Warao *monikata nome anaka* in proposing this interpretation.

Bloch and Urban characterize these relationships as correlations between conventionally used and valued discursive forms and preexisting and stable dominant forms of social solidarity, social relations, or authority. I would characterize them as involving the social construction of links between forms, linguistic ideologies, and discursive practices, on the one hand, and forms of authority, on the other. I believe that all of these cases suggest that even when the most privileged discourses are invoked by persons occupying dominant roles (fathers, mediators, culture heroes, confidential committees, judges, Supreme Court justices, and crafty livestock owners), competing discourses, linguistic ideologies, and discursive practices are used in launching challenges from the centers or peripheries of these events. Just as the relationship between dominant and subordinate discourses is contested and dynamic, social authority emerges through a fluid process of controlling competing claims to power and alternative bases for establishing it.

The image of one type of discourse linked to one type of authority seems to be better characterized as an interested, ideologically based social construction than a statement of linguistic or social fact. The idea that the dominance accorded to particular discursive forms and models of social relations springs from a shared cultural or cognitive substratum that is relatively inaccessible to conscious assessment would seem to be an equally powerful means of legitimating them. If researchers ratify these notions without viewing how they are constructed and contested, they would seem to run the risk of reifying dominant ideologies. Just as the relationships that are constructed are not entirely monolithic or static, the displacement of competing discourses and claims to authority is seldom *entirely* successful. As Susan Gal (1991), Ann Rosalind Jones (1986), Joan Radner and Susan Lanser (1993), and others have argued with respect to women's responses to partriarchal discourses, neither silence nor the imitation of dominant forms can be automatically assumed to signal acquiescence. Even when it appears that competing voices have been subordinated as authority is being performed, analysts must carefully explore the possibility that discursive dominance is questioned, subverted, or rendered irrelevant in subsequent recontextualizations. As nation-states and global capitalism develop new modes of penetrating daily practices, it becomes harder to conceive of stable and monolithic forms of authority and social relations as existing anywhere.

I do not wish to suggest that the search for connections between discourse and dominant forms of social relations is misguided. Over two decades ago Bloch pointed to the importance of attending to the discourses and settings in which power is enacted. Recent interest in public spheres and public cultures has renewed our sense of the importance of this desideratum at the same time that it has widened the ethnographic scope of such investigations. Political anthropologists have long argued that conflicts generate contexts in which social structures and symbolic systems become more accessible to both scrutiny and change. The essays included in this volume suggest that it is more the moments in which conflicts are *represented* than the times in which they erupt that crucial contestations shape discursive and social relations and inequalities. I hope that the foregoing careful documentations of the creation and legitimation of privileged discursive regimes in which authority is constructed and enacted in a wide ranges of societies and settings will spark additional research and new insights into these crucial dimensions of social life.

Notes

I would like to thank the residents of Nabasanuka, particularly the Commissioner, for permitting me to tape record this *monikata nome anaka* dispute mediation. Conrado Moraleda helped me make sense of what had taken place, while his brother, Librado Moraleda, kindly assisted me in transcribing the recording. H. Dieter Heinen, Julio Lavandero, and Johannes Wilbert also shared their insights into *monikata nome anaka* with me, while Ellen Basso, Aaron Cicourel, and H. Dieter Heinen provided critical readings of a previous draft. I also appreciate the role of the Universidad de Oriente, Cumaná, and the Instituto Venezolano de Investigaciones Científicas in sponsoring my research and the assistance of Andrés Romero-Figueroa and H. Dieter Heinen of these institutions. Financial support was provided by a sabbatical leave and Mellon Grant from Vassar College and a research grant from the Linguistics Program, National Science Foundation. A return to the delta in 1989, kindly funded by a grant-in-aid from the Wenner-Gren Foundation for Anthropological Research, Inc., enabled me to recheck the transcription and conduct additional research on Warao counseling discourse. The time needed to prepare a final draft was provided by a fellowship from the National Endowment for the Humanities.

1. *Aidamo* is unmarked for singular versus plural, while *aidamotuma* is marked for plural. Warao generally use the term *aidamo* as the plural for contemporary leaders, while *aidamotuma* is used more frequently in reference to 'the ancestors'.

2. Johannes Wilbert (personal communication, 1988) reports seeing several *monikata nome anaka* in which corporal punishment was used. H. Dieter Heinen (personal communication, 1988) has suggested that such outcomes are only likely to occur when the presiding official has achieved an unusually high degree of authority. See Heinen (1987:661–63) for a brief description of *monikata nome anaka*.

3. In the transcription, all Spanish lexical items have been typed using SMALL CAPITALS, thus differentiating them from Warao words and phrases. The discourse has been segmented into narrative and rhetorical lines on the basis of prosody, syntax, and referential content.

4. The Commissioner is the godfather of a child born to the husband prior to the present marriage. The husband thus addresses the Commissioner as *compai* (from Spanish *compadre*), while the Commissioner addresses the wife as *comai* (from Spanish *comadre*).

5. *Diana* also serves other communicative functions, including signaling the speaker's commitment to a particular statement and demarcating textual patterning.

6. Drawing on data collected in the Caño Bagre on the eastern edge of the delta, Osborn (1967) suggests that *-ha* is perfective, whereas *-hi* signals past durative. Since the recordings used in this paper were made in Nabasanuka I in the Central Delta, dialect differences may account for the discrepancies between his data and mine.

7. This is not to say, however, that parallelism is accorded the same weight as in Tzotzil mediation. Not all Warao counseling discourse is marked by parallelism, and parallel constructions are evident in noncounseling speech in *monikata nome anaka*, such as in María's narrative. In the Warao case, parallelism is one of many types of formal patterning that can be used in shaping counseling discourse.

8. This calculation is based on the portion of the Commissioner's speech that comes between the accounts given by the husband and wife.

9. *Ma + aidamo* is often used to refer to a healer who has cured the speaker of a serious illness. A continuing relationship is established, such that the healer must help the former patient in times of need and the latter can be called on by the healer for assistance in building a new house or other projects and for such favors as the gift of some cooking oil.

10. This statement does not apply to the quotation of 'bad words' in *monikata nome anaka*, where they are necessary. 'Bad words' can also appropriately emerge in *sana*, women's funerary laments, where they are similarly seen as crucial means of expressing emotions and revealing heretofore concealed truths (see Briggs 1992).

Works Cited

Anderson, Benedict. 1991 [1983]. *Imagined communities: Reflections on the origin and spread of nationalism.* London: Verso.

Austin, J. L. 1962. *How to do things with words.* Oxford: Clarendon Press.

Bakhtin, M. M. 1981. *The dialogic imagination: Four essays,* ed. Michael Holquist, translated by Caryl Emerson and Michael Holquist. Austin: University of Texas Press.

Barral, P. Basilio María de. 1964. *Los indios guaraunos y su cancionero: Historia, religión y alma lírica.* Madrid: Departamento de Misionología Española, Consejo Superior de Investigaciones Científicas.

Bauman, Richard. 1986. *Story, performance, and event: Contextual studies of oral narrative.* Cambridge: Cambridge University Press.

———. 1987. The de-centering of discourse. Paper presented at the annual meeting of the American Anthropological Association, Chicago, 1987.

———. 1990. Contextualization, tradition, and the dialogue of genres: Icelandic legends of the *kraftaskáld.* In *Rethinking context,* ed. Alessandro Duranti and Charles Goodwin. Cambridge: Cambridge University Press.

Bauman, Richard, and Charles L. Briggs. 1990. Poetics and performance as critical perspectives on language and social life. *Annual Review of Anthropology* 19:59–88.

Bloch, Maurice. 1975. Introduction. In *Political language and oratory in traditional society,* ed. Maurice Bloch, pp. 1–28. New York: Academic Press.

Boas, Franz. 1911. Introduction. In *Handbook of American Indian languages,* ed. Franz Boas, pp. 1–83. Bureau of American Ethnology, Smithsonian Institution, Bulletin 40. Washington, DC: Government Printing Office.

Bourdieu, Pierre. 1977. The economics of linguistic exchanges. *Social Science Information* 16:645–68.

———. 1991. *Language and symbolic power.* Translated by Gino Raymond and Matthew Adamson. Cambridge, MA: Harvard University Press.

Brenneis, Donald Lawrence. 1984a. Grog and gossip in Bhatgaon: Style and substance in Fiji Indian conversation. *American Ethnologist* 11:487–506.

———. 1984b. Straight talk and sweet talk: Political discourse in an occasionally egalitarian community. In *Dangerous words: Language and politics in the Pacific,* ed. Donald Lawrence Brenneis and Fred R. Myers, pp. 69–84. New York: New York University Press.

———. 1987. Performing passions: Aesthetics and politics in an occasionally egalitarian community. *American Ethnologist* 14:236–50.

———. 1988. Language and disputing. *Annual Review of Anthropology* 17:221–37.

Brenneis, Donald Lawrence and Fred R. Myers, eds. 1984. *Dangerous words: Language and politics in the Pacific.* New York: New York University Press.

Briggs, Charles L. 1992. 'Since I am a woman, I will chastise my relatives': Gender, reported speech, and the (re)production of social relations in Warao ritual wailing. *American Ethnologist* 19:337–61.

Calhoun, Craig, ed. 1992. *Habermas and the public sphere.* Cambridge, MA: MIT Press.

Comaroff, John L., and Simon Roberts. 1981. *Rules and processes: The cultural logic of dispute in an African context.* Chicago: University of Chicago Press.

Conley, John M., and William M. O'Barr. 1990. Rules versus relationships in small claims disputes. In *Conflict talk: Sociolinguistic investigations of arguments in conversations,* ed. Allen D. Grimshaw. Cambridge: Cambridge University Press.

Danet, Brenda. 1980. Language in the legal process. *Law and Society Review* 14:445–564.

———. 1985. Legal discourse. In *Handbook of discourse analysis,* vol. 1: *Disciplines of discourse,* ed. Teun A. van Dijk, pp. 273–91. London: Academic Press.

Duranti, Alessandro. 1988. Intentions, language, and social action in a Samoan context. *Journal of Pragmatics* 12:13–33.

Duranti, Alessandro, and Donald Brenneis, eds. 1986. The audience as co-author. *Text* 6(3):239–347.

Gal, Susan. 1989. Language and political economy. *Annual Review of Anthropology* 18:345–67.

———. 1991. Between speech and silence: The problematics of research on language and gender. In *Gender at the crossroads of knowledge: Feminist anthropology in the postmodern era*, ed. Michaela DiLeonardo, pp. 175–203. Berkeley: University of California Press.

Gal, Susan, and Kathryn Woolard. 1995. Constructing languages and publics. *Pragmatics* 5(2):129–282.

Gramsci, Antonio. 1971. *Selections from the prison notebooks of Antonio Gramsci*. Translated by Quintin Hoare and Geoffrey Nowell Smith. New York: International Publishers.

Grimshaw, Allen D., ed. 1990a. *Conflict talk: Sociolinguistic investigations of arguments in conversations*. Cambridge: Cambridge University Press.

———. 1990b. Introduction. In *Conflict talk: Sociolinguistic investigations of arguments in conversations*, ed. Allen D. Grimshaw, pp. 1–20. Cambridge: Cambridge University Press.

———. 1990c. Research on conflict talk: Antecedents, resources, findings, directions. In *Conflict talk: Sociolinguistic investigations of arguments in conversations*, ed. Allen D. Grimshaw, pp. 280–324. Cambridge: Cambridge University Press.

Gumperz, John J. 1982. *Discourse strategies*. Cambridge: Cambridge University Press.

Habermas, Jürgen. 1989 [1962]. *The structural transformation of the public sphere: An inquiry into a category of bourgeois society*. Translated by Thomas Burger. Cambridge, MA: MIT Press.

Halliday, M. A. K., and Ruqaiya Hasan. 1976. *Cohesion in English*. London: Longman.

Heinen, H. Dieter. 1972. *Adaptive changes in a tribal economy: A case study of the Winikina-Warao*. Doctoral dissertation, University of California, Los Angeles.

———. 1987. Los Warao. In *Los aborigenes de Venezuela*, vol. 3: *Etnología contemporánea*, eds. Walter Coppens, Bernarda Escalante, and Jacques Lizot, pp. 585–689. Fundación La Salle de Ciencia Naturales, Instituto Caribe de Antropología y Sociología. Caracas: Instituto Caribe de Antropología y Sociología.

Hopper, Paul. 1982. Aspect between discourse and grammar: An introductory essay for the volume. In *Tense-aspect: Between semantics and pragmatics*, ed. Paul J. Hopper, pp. 3–18. Amsterdam: John Benjamins.

Hymes, Dell. 1975. Folklore's nature and the sun's myth. *Journal of American Folklore* 88:345–69.

Irvine, Judith T. 1979. Formality and informality in communicative events. *American Anthropologist* 81:773–90.

———. 1989. When talk isn't cheap: Language and political economy. *American Ethnologist* 16:248–67.

Jakobson, Roman. 1971. Shifters, verbal categories, and the Russian verb. In *Roman Jakobson: Selected writings*, vol. 2, pp. 130–47. The Hague: Mouton.

Jones, Ann Rosalind. 1986. Surprising fame: Renaissance gender ideologies and women's lyric. In *The poetics of gender*, ed. Nancy K. Miller, pp. 96–116. New York: Columbia University Press.

Keenan, Elinor O. 1973. A sliding sense of obligatoriness: The poly-structure of Malagasy oratory. *Language in Society* 2:225–43.

Landes, Joan. 1933. *Women and the public sphere in the age of the French revolution*. Ithaca, NY: Cornell University Press.

Lee, Benjamin, ed. 1993. Special issue of *Public Culture* 5(2):165–313.

Levinson, Stephen C. 1983. *Pragmatics*. Cambridge: Cambridge University Press.

Lutz, Catherine. 1987. Emotion, thought, and estrangement: emotion as a cultural category. *Cultural Anthropology* 1:287–309.

———. 1988. *Unnatural emotions: Everyday sentiments on a Micronesian atoll and their challenge to Western theory*. Chicago: University of Chicago Press.

Myers, Fred R. 1986. Reflections on a meeting: Structure, language, and the polity in a small-scale society. *American Ethnologist* 13:430–47.

Myers, Fred R., and Donald Lawrence Brennis. 1984. Introduction: Language and politics in the Pacific. In *Dangerous words: Language and politics in the Pacific*, eds. Donald Lawrence Brenneis and Fred R. Myers, pp. 1–29. New York: New York University Press.

Negt, Oskar, and Alexander Kluge. 1993. *The public sphere and experience*. Translated by Peter Laganyi, Jamie Daniel, and Assenka Oksiloff. Minneapolis: University of Minnesota Press.

O'Barr, William M. and John M. Conley. 1985. Litigant satisfaction versus legal adequacy in small claims court narratives. *Law and Society Review* 19:661–702.

Osborn, Henry A. 1967. Warao III: Verbs and suffixes. *International Journal of American Linguistics* 33:46–64.

Paine, Robert, ed. 1981a. *Politically speaking: Cross-cultural studies of rhetoric*. Philadelphia: Institute for the Study of Human Issues.

———. 1981b. Introduction. In *Politically speaking: Cross-cultural studies of rhetoric*, ed. Robert Paine, pp. 1–6. Philadelphia: Institute for the Study of Human Issues.

———. 1981c. When saying is doing. In *Politically speaking: Cross-cultural studies of rhetoric*, ed. Robert Paine, pp. 9–23. Philadelphia: Institute for the Study of Human Issues.

Parkin, David. 1984. Political language. *Annual Review of Anthropology* 13:345–65.

Philips, Susan U. 1986. Reported speech as evidence in an American trial. In *Languages and linguistics: The interdependency of theory, data, and application*, eds. Deborah Tannen and James E. Alatis. Georgetown University Round Table on Languages and Linguistics, 1985. Washington, DC: Georgetown University Press.

Radner, Joan N., and Susan S. Lanser. 1993. Strategies of coding in women's culture. In *Feminist messages: Coding in women's folk culture*, ed. Joan Newlon Radner, pp. 1–29. Urbana: University of Illinois Press.

Rosaldo, Michelle Z. 1973. I have nothing to hide: The language of Ilongot oratory. *Language in Society* 2:193–223.

———. 1982. The things we do with words: Ilongot speech acts and speech act theory in philosophy. *Language in Society* 11:203–35.

Silverstein, Michael. 1976. Shifters, linguistic categories, and cultural description. In *Meaning in anthropology*, eds. Keith H. Basso and Henry A. Selby, pp. 11–55. Albuquerque: University of New Mexico Press.

———. 1979. Language structure and linguistic ideology. In *The elements: A parasession on* linguistic units and levels, eds. Paul R. Clyne, William Hanks, and Carol L. Hofbauer, 193–247. Chicago: Chicago Linguistic Society.

———. 1981. *The limits of awareness. Sociolinguistic working paper 84*. Austin, Texas: Southwest Educational Development Laboratory.

———. 1985. Language and the culture of gender: At the intersection of structure, usage, and ideology. In *Semiotic mediation: Sociocultural and psychological perspectives*, ed. Elizabeth Mertz and Richard J. Parmentier, pp. 219–59. Orlando, FL: Academic Press.

———. 1992. The indeterminacy of contextualization: When is enough enough? The contextualization of language, ed. Peter Auer and Aldo Di Luzio, pp. 55–76. Amsterdam: John Benjamins.

———. 1993. Metapragmatic discourse and metapragmatic function. In *Reflexive language: Reported speech and metapragmatics*, ed. John A. Lucy, pp. 33–58. Cambridge: Cambridge University Press.

Urban, Greg. 1986. Ceremonial dialogues in South America. *American Anthropologist* 88:371–86.

———. 1988. Ritual wailing in Amerindian Brazil. *American Anthropologist* 90:385–400.

———. 1991. *A discourse-centered approach to culture: Native South American myths and rituals*. Austin: University of Texas Press.

Vološinov, V. N. 1973 [1930]. *Marxism and the philosophy of language*, translated by Ladislav Matejka and I. R. Titunik. New York: Seminar Press.

Wallace, Stephen. 1982. Figure and ground: The interrelations of linguistic categories. In *Tense-aspect: Between semantics and pragmatics*, ed. Paul J. Hopper, pp. 201–23. Amsterdam: John Benjamins.

Watson-Gegeo, Karen A., and Geoffrey White, eds. 1990. *Disentangling: Conflict discourse in Pacific societies*. Stanford, CA: Stanford University Press.

Wilbert, Johannes, 1980. The Warao Indians of the Orinoco Delta. In *Demographic and biological studies of the Warao Indians*, eds. Johannes Wilbert and Miguel Layrisse, pp. 3–9. Los Angeles: UCLA Latin American Center Publications.

Woolard, Kathryn A. 1985. Language variation and cultural hegemony: Toward an integration of sociolinguistic and social theory. *American Ethnologist* 12:738–48.

Index

abortion law, 138–39
Abu-Lughod, Lila. 49, 92n. 1
accountability. *See* excuses, justification, responsibility
accounts, 45, 46, 47, 48
    litigants', 116
    co-production of, 12
    in-court, 116, 129
    out-of-court, 116
activity system, 95, 96, 110
addressivity, 196
African-Americans, 14, 15, 24, 142, 144, 145
age, 76–77, 92n. 7, 205, 208, 209
agency
    cultural, 64–66, 67, 69, 118
    syntactic, 26, 27, 142, 144–48, 151
anarchism, 72, 78
Anderson, Benedict, 6, 15, 205
anger, 206, 214, 228, 231
Appadurai, Arjun, 6
Ardener, Edwin W., 80
argument, 20, 49
Atkinson, J. M., 164
audience, 136, 153
    focus on, 15, 23
    involvement in narration, 12, 31n. 9, 43, 46, 48, 98, 136, 140, 153
    secondary, 46
Austin, J. L., 73, 85–86, 91, 92n. 6
authority, 9, 11, 13, 18, 25, 42, 43, 44, 47, 135–36, 138, 144, 152–53, 155, 166, 190, 194, 230
    discursive construction of, 205, 213, 225, 232–33
    and the distribution of discursive practices, 205, 232
    and formal patterning, 17, 24, 27, 28, 144, 229–30
    of legal texts, 136
    moral, 180
    in narrative, 99
authorship, 42, 43, 46, 48, 49, 136
avoidance, 44

backgrounding, 73, 215–16
Bakhtin, M. M., 22, 27, 28, 143–44, 154–55, 158, 191, 196, 230, 232
Banfield, Ann, 178
Barkun, Michael, 197
Basso, Ellen B., 8–9, 10, 16, 18, 21, 26, 27, 50, 53–71
Bauman, Richard, 14, 15, 22–23, 42, 47, 49, 51n. 1, 142, 158, 192, 215, 230
Bennett, W. Lance, 14, 48
Benveniste, Emile, 158
Bersani, Leo, 55
betrayal, 73, 80, 83, 89, 91
Bloch, Maurice, 17, 232, 235, 236, 237
Boas, Franz, 53, 228
Borges, Jorge Luis, 159, 160
Bourdieu, Pierre, 5, 6, 18, 74, 77, 159, 197, 205
13.6Brenneis, Donald, 5, 8, 10, 17, 19, 20, 21, 24–25, 27, 41–52, 140, 200n. 9, 206
Bricker, Victoria, 161, 200n. 11
bride-theft, 75
Briggs, Charles L., 9, 12, 15, 20, 21, 22, 23, 24, 29, 80, 142, 159, 160, 199, 204–42
Brown v. Board of Education, 135, 141–42, 146–47, 149–53
Brown, Justice Henry B., 142, 147, 148
bureaucracy, 84, 85, 89

Campbell, J. K., 84, 92n. 8
Cancian, Frank, 190, 200n. 12
capital, symbolic, 18, 197
categories, native, 160
censorship, 197
Chamula (Mexico), 9, 183
Chatman, Seymour, 41
Chiapas (Mexico), 9, 158
children
    and control, 97
    and disputing, 4, 7, 12, 21
    and narrative socialization, 110
Cicourel, Aaron, 6, 18
class, social. *See* social class
Clifford, James, 14

243

LaVergne, TN USA
21 December 2010
209633LV00002B/41/A